THE
VATICAN
HERESY

"With his usual care and attention to detail, Robert Bauval spins out the thread that joins the solar religion of pharaonic Egypt to the utopian hopes of the fading Renaissance. His theory climaxes with the dramatic and dangerous project of a pope (Urban VIII), a polymath (Kircher), an architect (Bernini), and an exiled queen (Christina). Their dream was of a united Christendom orbiting around Rome; their method, the marriage of Hermetic philosophy with the new astronomy, through symbolic architecture. Like Bauval's other books about times and places when science and magic were one, *The Vatican Heresy* arouses curiosity, disbelief, nostalgia, and finally hope."

JOSCELYN GODWIN, PH.D., AUTHOR OF
THE PAGAN DREAM OF THE RENAISSANCE AND
ATHANASIUS KIRCHER'S THEATRE OF THE WORLD

"In this enchanting book, Robert Bauval and Chiara Hohenzollern reveal an astonishing fact hiding in plain sight. Surely thousands of visitors to the Vatican's Saint Peter's Square over the past three centuries have been puzzled by the gigantic ancient Egyptian obelisk featured in its center. Through meticulous research, *The Vatican Heresy* illuminates the profoundly evolutionary adventurers who employed deep symbolic insights and astute political maneuvering to construct a talismanic Hermetic City of the Sun in the heart of the citadel of Christendom. Read *The Vatican Heresy*. . . . I couldn't put it down."

"It looks like Robert Bauval (now with coauthor Chiara Hohenzollern) has done it again, revealing that not just the pyramids but the Vatican itself is a celebration of sacred architecture. A fascinating theory and very timely."

"Robert Bauval is a brilliant investigator of the hidden corners of history, and he has surpassed himself with *The Vatican Heresy*. It is a true time bomb of a book revealing stunning intrigues that have shaped the modern world and that call into question our most fundamental perceptions of the role of the Church of Rome."

THE
VATICAN
HERESY

Bernini and the Building of the Hermetic Temple of the Sun

ROBERT BAUVAL
AND
CHIARA HOHENZOLLERN

Bear & Company
Rochester, Vermont • Toronto, Canada

Bear & Company
One Park Street
Rochester, Vermont 05767
www.BearandCompanyBooks.com

Bear & Company is a division of Inner Traditions International

Library of Congress Cataloging-in-Publication Data

Bauval, Robert, 1948– author.
 The Vatican Heresy : Bernini and the Building of the Hermetic Temple of the
Sun / Robert Bauval and Chiara Hohenzollern.
    pages cm
 Summary: "Reveals how the largest Sun Temple in the world, built according to
Hermetic principles, is located at one of Christianity's holiest sites: the Vatican"—
Provided by publisher.
 Includes bibliographical references and index.
 ISBN 978-1-59143-178-7 (pbk.) — ISBN 978-1-59143-756-7 (e-book)
 1. Piazza San Pietro (Vatican City) 2. Bernini, Gian Lorenzo, 1598–1680—
Criticism and interpretation. 3. Symbolism in architecture—Vatican City. 4.
Temples, Egyptian—Vatican City. 5. Vatican City—Buildings, structures, etc. I.
Hohenzollern, Chiara, 1976– author. II. Title.
 NA9072.R65S2525 2014
 711'.560945364—dc23
                                                          2013034235

Printed and bound in the United States by McNaughton & Gunn

10 9 8 7 6 5 4 3 2 1

Text design by Virginia Scott Bowman and layout by Brian Boynton
This book was typeset in Garamond Premier Pro with Swiss and Gill Sans as
display typefaces

To send correspondence to the author of this book, mail a first-class letter to the
author c/o Inner Traditions • Bear & Company, One Park Street, Rochester, VT
05767, and we will forward the communication, or contact the author directly at
www.robertbauval.co.uk.

To Alexandria, my city of memories . . .
ROBERT BAUVAL

To my mother . . .
CHIARA HOHENZOLLERN

Ninety percent, perhaps even more, of history is not documented. And as for the little that is documented or recorded, much of it may not be history at all but the warped perception, dissimulation, cover-ups, and bias of those documenting or recording it. The task of the true historian is to detect the history that is not told, much like a cosmologist detects the structure of the universe that is not seen. To read between the lines or see between the empty spaces, that is the exciting challenge . . .

CONTENTS

ACKNOWLEDGMENTS

I first would like to thank Dr. Sandro Zicari of Sapienza University of Rome for his collaboration and helpful advice on this project. Also and as always, I am eternally grateful to my wife, Michele. This is my tenth book, and she has endured yet again with true grit and patience the long, solitary hours and the ups and downs of a temperamental author. Michele is the real, unnamed, and unspoken heroine of my intellectual journeys into the mysteries of the past. I also thank my pleonastic but very lovable "big" brother, Jean-Paul. His never-ending support, even though disguised in typical "Alexandrian" cynical humor, is always appreciated. My warm gratitude also is extended to my many friends, old and new: Vicky Metafora from Naples, Laura Salvucci from Le Marche, Dr. Maria Pia Tocco from Rome, Pino Morelli from Pescara, Richard Fusniak from Cambridge, Father Nicola Mapelli and Katherine Aigner of the Vatican Museum's Ethnological Collection, Graham and Satha Hancock from Bath, and Adriana Dainelli from Rome. Thanks to Ed and Barbara Mattis for sharing their Sunday Special pizza with me! Thank you dear Mindy Branstetter, my very professional, very efficient, and very gentle editor at Inner Traditions. Special thanks also to Jon Graham and John Hays, who quickly saw the importance of this project. Thank you dear Manzanita Carpenter, Kelly Bowen, and superhero-operator Cindy Marcotte, also at Inner Traditions. Last but not least, and from the bottom of my heart, I send genuine thanks to all my readers around the world for your support and affection. It is you, after all, who make all the effort from authors and publishers worthwhile.

ROBERT BAUVAL,
TORREMOLINOS, SOUTHERN SPAIN

I wish to thank Massimo, a dear friend who, in recent years, has always prompted me to believe in myself and my work and never give up even in the hardest and most difficult moments.

CHIARA HOHENZOLLERN

HIDING THE TRUTH IN PLAIN SIGHT

It is not the critic who counts; not the man who points out how the strong man stumbles, or where the doer of deeds could have done them better. The credit belongs to the man who is actually in the arena.

THEODORE ROOSEVELT

This book was a very ambitious project, and I readily admit that researching and writing it was not only a thrilling experience but also a very daunting one, as well. The complexity of the topic and the sheer volume of research material made it feel like I was recklessly challenging a bookish Goliath with only a reed twig in my hand to bring him down! Yet the temptation to quest and sleuth a historical mystery of this scale was too tantalizing to pass over. There was, certainly, the initial apprehension that all authors have when taking on such a task. A long, dark tunnel must be crossed solo, and then at the other end await the inevitable lashes by experts whose feathers you are bound to have ruffled. But such qualms are then quickly dismissed by a weird—almost perverse—gladiatorial thrill of marching into the arena to do battle again with that old foe: academic consensus.

1

A decade ago I wrote with Graham Hancock *Talisman: Sacred Cities, Secret Faith.* In this book we explored the Hermetic tradition and tracked its journey out of Egypt and its influence on the design of major capital cities of the Western world. Academics, needless to say, ignored it. And the only academic who didn't ignore it ended up repaying us by blatantly plagiarizing a discovery we made regarding the layout of ancient Alexandria. I bring this up because there was also a tiny—although immensely important—"city" that Graham and I barely touched in our book: the *Vatican City* in Rome. With hindsight I can say that we had thus overlooked the most important piece of that huge historical puzzle we had set about to solve. After much deliberation I finally decided to reopen the case for the Vatican City in late 2011. It was at this point that I invited the Italian author Chiara Hohenzollern and also Dr. Sandro Zicari to join me.

Let me quickly get to the point: it is often stated by historians of art and architecture that the Piazza St. Peter's at the Vatican was designed to represent *"the open arms of Mother Church."* This, in fact, is indeed claimed by Gian Lorenzo Bernini himself, the architect responsible for the design. We believe it to be a truth, but not the *whole* truth. Truth often comes in many layers. Revealing only one layer yet dissimulating another will make this partial truth seem to be something very different indeed. This is why today a person on the stand in a court of law will be sworn in to tell not only the truth, but rather the *whole truth.* We believe that there is another, far more important layer in which rests the *whole truth* behind Bernini's grandiose design. This whole truth he, nonetheless, took to his grave, for it was such an unspeakable truth, such a taboo, such a forbidden fruit in his time that the mere mention of it might have brought down the whole edifice of Mother Church— that is to say, the Vatican itself. Yet the amazing daringness of Bernini's ploy was to hide the truth in plain sight for all to see. Indeed, so well did he do this that everyone who looked—and there have been millions since—did not *see* it all. And when finally some did see it, so outrageous, so fantastic was its implication that they simply preferred to dismiss it as mere coincidence. Bernini clearly intended it to be a sort of intellectual time bomb meant to be detonated not in his time but when the time was right, when its revelation would not bring down the Vatican, but do, instead, the opposite. To fully appreciate the magnitude of this revelation, and to make our case worthy of the most serious consideration, we had to undertake a chase across nearly two millennia of history, from Greco-Roman Alexandria to Renaissance Rome, sometimes moving at breakneck speed, making Dan Brown's *Angels & Demons* seem like a Sunday stroll in the park. It was a thrilling undertaking and, most of all, an amazing eye-opener. No matter what one may think of it, one thing is certain: Christianity and Western culture will never seem the same again.

But enough said. The die is cast. You have the evidence in your hands. No need to tarry.

We are ready to present our case . . .

1

THE TRUE RELIGION OF THE WORLD

Because of this, Asclepius, a human being is a great wonder, a living thing to be worshipped and honored: for he changes his nature into a god's, as if he were a god.

BRIAN P. COPENHAVER, *HERMETICA*

I would have you then, Holy Father, and all future popes, give orders that some of the books which I have named [books on the Hermetica] shall be continually taught everywhere as I have taught them in the last fourteen years at Ferrara. You will thus make all able men in Italy, Spain, and France friendly to the Church, and perhaps even the German Protestants.

DEDICATION TO POPE GREGORY XIV,
NOVA DE UNIVERSIS PHILOSOPHICA,
BY FRANCESCO PATRIZZI, 1591;
QUOTED FROM FRANCES A. YATES,
GIORDANO BRUNO AND THE HERMETIC TRADITION

REBIRTH

The story we are about to tell is as strange as it is controversial. If we are right, then Roman Christianity, indeed perhaps all of Christianity, is about to be turned on its head. Most Christians today are unaware that not so long ago a handful of very wise and very brave philosophers kickstarted an intellectual and spiritual revolution in a seemingly impossible bid to reform the church into a very different thing indeed. Their mission, no less, was to liberate Christianity from the stranglehold of an oppressive clergy and their dogmas, and turn it into a *magical religion* of nature, the "true religion of the world," governed by wise and benevolent philosopher-priests from a "city of the sun" set in the heart of Christendom: Rome. The task we have set for ourselves is to chronicle the mission of these most extraordinary men and women and to seek this legendary and magical city of the sun. The historical period we shall explore is known as the *Renaissance*—literally the "Rebirth"—when Europe was

> seeking intensively for knowledge of reality, for an answer to its problems, which normal education failed to give. . . . It turned to other ways of seeking an answer: intuitive, mystical, magical . . . it sought to cultivate the . . . intuitive faculty of man.[1]

Spanning two centuries from 1460 to 1675,* the cultural rebirth that we will cover was kick-started in the city of Florence. There, in a Europe slowly emerging from the throes of the Dark and Middle Ages, wearied by the oppression of the church,† sickened by the centuries of

---

*Historians bracket the Italian Renaissance from ca. 1405 to ca. 1580, but we see it sliding forward a century or so. True, it technically slowed down to almost a halt around 1580, yet its strong momentum propelled it for another century or so before the Enlightenment fully kicked in.

†Although the Roman Inquisition was not officially established by the Vatican until 1542, the persecution of suspected "heretics" by the church had been going on since the early Middle Ages.

crusading wars, and spiritually depleted by the rampant religious bigotry, intrigue, and hypocrisy, a few enlightened men displayed amazing grit by questioning and even challenging the ecclesiastical establishment, and boldly stood out to express their new vision for healing the world. Often working singlehandedly, their common mission was to peacefully bring about a great reformation of the Vatican and, by extension, of Christendom as a whole. They were the Renaissance philosophers, or as some historians sometimes call them, the "Hermetic magicians." They were highly learned, highly eloquent, and highly motivated, and their powerful weaponry was not the sword but the pen and the word. Working in dimly lit rooms and often by candlelight, they poured their intellectual epiphanies into books, tracts, and theses that promoted a theology and philosophy of a lost golden age that was compatible with the new scientific discoveries and, more importantly, human dignity and intellectual freedom.

We shall propose to focus our investigation on three major movements whose influence, we believe, led to the actual construction of the elusive "Hermetic City of the Sun." These movements were Hermetism, heliocentrism, and utopianism. Although caught up in a parallel crisis that befell Christendom, namely the Protestant Reformation and the Catholic Counter-Reformation, the strong mental brew these movements created when merged together provided the cerebral fuel for the Renaissance and, as some historians are also inclined to believe, the subsequent age of discovery and the Enlightenment. But on a deeper, more occult level—the level that we are going to explore in this book—these movements, especially Hermetism, also created a sort of spiritual-*cum*-intellectual time bomb that was to explode at the very threshold of the Vatican. We shall examine these movements in detail in the following chapters, but briefly for now:

The Hermetic Movement

This was a concerted attempt to restore the "magical religion of ancient Egypt," as rediscovered in the Corpus Hermeticum or the Hermetica, a body of books believed to be the work of an all-wise, all-knowing Egyptian sage called Hermes Trismegistus. The Renaissance philosophers saw in the Hermetica a powerful perennial theology that elevated man to divine status through the pursuit of knowledge (gnosis). Most, but not all, Renaissance philosophers desperately tried to have it embraced, even canonized by the Vatican, sometimes at the cost of their lives.

The Heliocentric Movement

This was the new scientific discoveries of Nicolas Copernicus, Johannes Kepler, and Galileo: essentially that *not* the Earth but the sun was the center of the visible universe. Unfortunately the Vatican upheld that such discoveries were against the Holy Scriptures and, as a consequence, forcefully repudiated them and declared them a vile heresy. In spite of this, some Renaissance philosophers audaciously tried to convince the Vatican to recognize and embrace these discoveries, again at the risk of their own lives.

Geocentrism versus Heliocentrism

Geocentrism, or Earth-centrism, is the (erroneous) astronomical model in which the sun and all other celestial bodies orbit or revolve around the Earth. The theory had already been advanced by Aristotle ca. 340 BCE, but was fully developed by Claudius Ptolemy of Alexandria in the second century CE in his book *The Almagest*. The Ptolemaic system was favored, indeed voraciously supported by the Catholic Church because it was deemed to conform to various statements in the Holy Scriptures, implying that the Earth was stationary and immovable and that all celestial bodies revolved around it. For example, (from the King James Bible): First Chronicles 16:30 states, "The world also shall be stable, that it be not moved"; Psalms 104:5 states, "[God] who laid the foundations of the earth, that it should not be removed forever"; and Ecclesiastes 1:5 states, "The sun also arises, and the sun goes down, and hastens to his place where he arose."

Heliocentrism, or sun-centrism, is the (correct) astronomical model in which the Earth and planets orbit or revolve around the sun. Although it was discussed in antiquity, especially by Aristachus of Samos in the third century BCE, it was largely ignored. It was not until the mid-sixteenth century when the Polish astronomer Nicolas Copernicus developed a mathematical model (described in *De revolutionibus orbium coelestium* [On the Revolutions of the Heavenly Spheres], published in 1543) that Renaissance scientists and philosophers began to really pay attention. At first the church did not see it as a serious threat since it was, after all, just another theory. But when half a century later the astronomer Johannes Kepler developed it with his elliptical model and presented his three laws of planetary motion and especially after Galileo, using his telescope, provided visual supportive evidence, the Vatican did everything to suppress it.

The Utopian Movement

This movement promoted the founding of idealistic republics or city-states where people could live and prosper in relative harmony and peace. The utopian city-state that we are primarily interested in is the so-called City of the Sun, a sort of hybrid of theocracy-democracy headed by an enlightened philosopher-scientist-priest. With the split of Western Christendom into Protestantism and Catholicism, and the bloody genocidal Reformation and Counter-Reformation that ensued, the Renaissance philosophers desperately tried to reunite Christendom under a reborn perennial theology administered from a centralized City of the Sun.*

There are, of course, many academic publications regarding these movements and the influences they had on Western history. We consulted many, as will become apparent in the following chapters. The consensus among historians of the Renaissance is that the Hermetic movement

---

*Interestingly, the Jesuit Order was to use virtually the same approach in their missionary zeal to convert the New World, Asia, and Africa to Roman Catholicism.

simply faded away, partly because it was stamped out by the church, and mostly because it was overwhelmed by the scientific age and the Enlightenment of the sixteenth and seventeenth centuries. Thus, according to Frances A. Yates, for example:

> The reign of Hermes Trismegistus can be exactly dated: it begins in the late fifteenth century when Ficino translated the newly discovered Corpus Hermeticum. It ends in the early seventeenth century. . . . Within this period of his reign the new world view, the new attitudes, the new motives, which were to lead to the emergence of modern science, made their appearance. . . . Hermes Trismegistus had to be cast off to free the seventeenth century for its advance.[2]

One of the purposes of our book, but not the main one, is to show that, contrary to what Frances A. Yates and others concluded, the Hermetic movement not only survived but also retained its potency, undetected and dormant—veiled is a better word—waiting for the right time to burst out like the proverbial genie in the lamp. And we aim to do just that: to vigorously rub that intellectual lamp for the Hermetic City of the Sun to pop out *in full view* under the very nose of the Vatican.

We use the term *Vatican* as representing the papacy and the headquarters, from which the pope rules. The Vatican City, an independent state created in 1929 by the Lateran Treaty and which comprises a walled area of about 44 hectares (almost 109 acres) within the city of Rome, is, strictly speaking, not the same as the Holy See, the latter being "the Episcopal jurisdiction of the Roman Catholic Church." According to the British Foreign Office, for example, the Vatican City is seen as the "capital" city of the Holy See, much like London is the capital of England and the United Kingdom, even though it recognizes that the Holy See (actually the pope) acts as the crown in England and the United Kingdom. Both entities, the Vatican City and the Holy See, are regarded as separate entities in international law. There are just under 3,000 employees who work for the Holy See (the Roman Curia), and a further 330 or so on its diplomatic missions. The Vatican City, on the other hand, employs some 1,910 people. The permanent population of the Vatican City is about 800. It is not clear how many beyond this number hold passports from the Vatican City. (The Holy See, not being a "state" itself, only issues "diplomatic passports.") Confused? A statement by the British ambassador regarding the difference between the Holy See and the Vatican City clarifies somewhat this complex relationship: "[The Holy See] is not the same as the Vatican City. . . . [It] is the universal government of the Catholic Church and *operates from* the Vatican City." (italic added)

This seems to also be the position of the U.S. Department of State, which maintains that the Holy See "operates from the Vatican City."

We begin our story where and when it must begin: Alexandria, Egypt, in the first century . . .

THE CITY OF MEMORY

The British author Lawrence Durrell once wrote that Alexandria was the "city of memory!"[3] Such a haunting epithet has a special resonance for me, for I am tied to this city by an invisible umbilical cord that stretches back three centuries. I was born in Alexandria in 1948 from parents of mixed origins—Maltese, Italian, Belgian, and Syrian—that can be traced down to pre-Napoleonic times in Cairo in 1785.* I grew up somewhat oblivious to the rest of the world. My world was the golden Mediterranean beaches of North Africa and the leafy suburb of Alexandria outside the old city walls, the narrow alleyways where Arabs, Armenians, Greeks, Italians, and Maltese displayed their wares,

---

*My family story is told in Robert Bauval and Ahmed Osman's *Breaking the Mirror of Heaven* (Rochester, Vt.: Inner Traditions, 2011, appendix 5).

and where Christians, Muslims, and Jews mingled as friends and lived as neighbors. It was in this cosmopolitan Alexandria that I developed an insatiable appetite for knowledge, especially history, and read whatever books I could lay my hands on. Imported books were too expensive for us to buy, so my father would take me every week to a private library that rented out books. I recall that wonderful feeling of excitement as I carried that sackload of books back home for my weekly reading. I was drawn to ancient history, astronomy, and cosmology. I know now that this was the start of my quest for gnosis, that perennial natural wisdom that once was known to the ancients.

Alexandria—the mere mention of this name evokes memories of my youth and, now more so, the rich and dramatic history that started four centuries before the advent of Christ, with Alexander the Great, Caesar, Cleopatra, Mark Antony, and Ptolemy, and those legendary scholars such as Hypatia, Theon, and Euclid. And magical edifices such as the

Fig. 1.1. Artist impression of ancient Alexandria, looking westward down the Canopus Way. (Jean-Yves Empereur)

Great Serapeum, the Great Library, the Pharos Lighthouse! Yet that is not all that Alexandria evokes for me. There are, too, the romantic characters from Durrell's four-volume novel *The Alexandria Quartet,* modeled on real people from the cosmopolitan society of Alexandria: the love-torn Melissa, the passionate Clea, the beautiful and intriguing Justine, and the mystical philosopher Balthazar. And let us note, too, that it was also in Alexandria that the Hebrew Bible was first translated into Greek, and where St. Mark the Evangelist was martyred. Here, too, legend has it that the Magi of the Nativity had been buried, only for their relics to be stolen by Venetian sailors and displayed in the Cologne Cathedral. But of all these exotic events and tales, the one that has most influenced the *soul* of the world, yet is the least known, is the writing of the Corpus Hermeticum. Alas, today few Alexandrians have heard of these writings, let alone know the amazing effect they had on Western culture.* Alexandria in the first century, then, is where and when we must start, and Garth Fowden, a research professor at the Centre for Greek and Roman Antiquity of the National Research Foundation in Athens and a renowned expert on the Hermetica, drives this point clearly for us: "For any investigation of the milieu of Hermetism, with or without Egypt, Alexandria is the natural point of departure."[4]

So let us mentally time travel to Alexandria in late antiquity, where the Hermetists were busily writing down the perennial theology of old. But before we do that, a veil that has been cast over that ancient city must be lifted.

Today Alexandria, as we would expect, is a large modern city with all the trappings of modern culture. The modern tourist will find it complete with McDonald's fast-food outlets, Starbucks coffee shops, pizza restaurants, and with a population of six million people, made up mostly of Muslims with a minority—about 10 percent—of Christians.

---

*We use here the Hermetica to mean the eighteen so-called *libelli* of the Corpus Hermeticum plus the Latin *Asclepius* and the so-called *Excerpts of Strobaeus* as listed and defined by Walter Scott in his book *Hermetica: The Ancient Greek and Latin Writings,*[5] which contain religious or philosophical teachings ascribed to Hermes Trismegistus.

Ancient Alexandria, however, was a very different place. In the first century it was a magnificent classical metropolis in the best Greek and Egyptian styles, with broad avenues that would make the modern Champs Élysées of Paris look like a common street. Its population, about a quarter million strong, was cosmopolitan: mostly Greeks and Romans. It is a testimony to the magnificence of this ancient city that even though it has disappeared, it nonetheless lives in the collective memory of humanity as the urban jewel of the past.

When the Hermetica was being written in second century CE Alexandria, this metropolis was already five centuries old and had endured dramatic cultural changes since its foundation in 331 BCE by Alexander the Great. Immediately before Alexander's arrival, Egypt had endured a brutal and humiliating occupation by the Persians, who desecrated and even destroyed many of the ancient temples, leaving the country scarred physically and spiritually.

After Alexander defeated the Persian army of Darius III at Issus in Syria and then marched triumphantly into Egypt, this twenty-four-year-old Macedonian king was greeted as a liberator, some even going as far as claiming he was the returning god-pharaoh. The Egyptian

Fig. 1.2. Equestrian statue of Alexander the Great outside the old "Gate of the Sun" in Alexandria. (Robert Bauval)

priests well knew that since childhood Alexander had entertained the belief that his true "father" was Amun, the solar god of Egypt, who the Greeks identified as Zeus-Ammon of the Oracle at Siwa, an oasis deep in the western desert of Egypt.

Zeus-Ammon and Alexander

The belief that the solar god Zeus-Ammon of Siwa was his true father was put into Alexander's young mind by his highly strung and very mystical mother, Queen Olympias. Olympias, a priestess at the Oracle of Zeus at Dodona in Ipirus, which was twinned with that of Ammon at Siwa, was endowed with a deep mystical nature, and believed she was destined to be the mother of a divine hero-son who, like the god Dionysos, son of Zeus, would unite the world. When Olympias married Philip II of Macedonia in 357 BC, Egypt was under Persian occupation, the latter the traditional enemies of the Greeks. Legend has it that on her wedding night Olympias was visited by Zeus-Ammon, who made her pregnant.

Alexander's dream, however, was not just to unite the world but also to create a universal city dedicated to knowledge and wisdom—a great intellectual haven—where scholars and philosophers from everywhere would share their knowledge and discoveries to benefit humanity.

Alexandria: The Universal City

It is probable that the idea of a universal city of learning had been put into Alexander's head by the great philosopher Aristotle, who had tutored the young prince for many years. Aristotle had written the *Politika* [The Politics], in which he examines various systems of *constitutions* and the *ideal state* and which he had surely discussed with the young Alexander. Was Alexandria to be that "ideal state"? For sure it became the universal center of learning for several centuries, as well as the place where the inhabitants called themselves citizens of the world (i.e., cosmopolitans). Here, for a brief but enlightening moment in human history, all religions and races cohabited in relative peace. The term *cosmopolitan* probably comes from Diogenes of Sinope (ca. 415 BC), who, when asked to which state he belonged, answered, "Kosmopolites" (I am a citizen of the world). Alexandria was probably the nearest thing to a cosmopolitan utopia the world has ever known.

Legend has it that the architect Dinoclates of Rhodes, under the guidance of Alexander himself, designed the city plan of Alexandria. The layout of the new city, however, reveals an Egyptian influence that can be termed "solar," a sort of city of the sun to emulate the great solar cities in Egypt, such as Heliopolis, the supreme City of the Sun of the ancient world, or Thebes in Upper Egypt.*

There were two main arteries in Alexandria: the Canopus Way and the Soma. The Canopus Way ran east-west and extended eastward toward Canopus, some twenty kilometers from Alexandria. The Soma ran north-south and intersected the Canopus Way to form a huge cross whose center was an open area known as the Agora.

The Canopus Way was probably named after Kanopos, the legendary Homerian navigator who piloted the fleet of Menelaus in the *Iliad*. According to a Homeric myth, the town of Canopus (modern-day Abukir) in Egypt was founded by Menelaus, who named it after the pilot of his ship, who died on its shore. Homer says that Menelaus built a shrine to his memory there, around which the town was later developed. A temple dedicated to Osiris was later built at Canopus by Ptolemy III. Herodotus, who wrote a century or so before the foundation of Alexandria, claimed that there was a temple dedicated to Herakles in that region. According to some Egyptologists, however, the city was named Canopus because the road led to a temple where pilgrims deposited "canopic jars" used in funerary rituals. Alexander is

---

*A chapel dedicated to Alexander the Great was built within the holy of holies of the sun temple of Luxor in ancient Thebes.

also well known to have claimed descent from Dionysos and Herakles, both of whom were associated with the Egyptian god Osiris by the historian and author Herodotus, whose celebrated books The Histories Alexander had diligently read. So at least since the time of Herodotus it was known that a temple was dedicated to Herakles-Osiris at a town called Herakleon near modern-day Abukir. The Canopus Way axis, when extended toward the eastern horizon, would have passed near Herakleon, something that Alexander would certainly have been made aware of. (Herakleon was submerged after a terrible earthquake but has been rediscovered recently by French marine archaeologists.)

Fig. 1.3. Aerial view of the Canopus Way (today called Abukir Road) looking west, ca. 1950. (*Al Ahram Weekly*)

At both ends of the Canopus Way were gates leading into the enclosed city area. The western gate was known as the Selene (Gate of the Moon) and the eastern gate as the Helios (Gate of the Sun).

Although historians have assumed that the layout plan of the city was based on the classical Greek grid system, the Egyptians had already used such a grid layout—the solar city Akhetaten (Horizon of Aten, the sun disc) at Tell el Amarna is a good example—long before the Greeks. Alexander, after all, had been proclaimed pharaoh of Egypt, a title that directly associated him with the divine genealogy of the sun god of Egypt. As such Alexander was to be seen as the reincarnation of

Fig. 1.4. Sunrise on July 20 (Julia) along the Canopus Way (Abukir Road), ca. 2006. (Robert Bauval)

Horus, the solar falcon god who was deemed reincarnated in the person of the pharaoh. Since time immemorial the births of these Horus-kings were associated with the appearance at dawn of the star Sothis (Sirius). In late antiquity this occurred on July 20 (in the Julian calendar), as observed from the latitude of Alexandria. In ancient Egypt, temples and even whole cities were often aligned to the rising sun to mark an important event.* It would be totally in line with such a tradition that the Canopus Way of Alexandria would also have such a solar alignment to mark some important day related to Alexander the Great.

When I lived in Alexandria I often witnessed the sunrise and sunset along the Shara'a Fuad, the modern tarmac road that today runs directly over the ancient Canopus Way—a fact confirmed by the Egyptian astronomer Mahmoud El Falaki Bey in the 1870s. El Falaki determined that there had been eleven main arteries running parallel along the width of the ancient city, and seven other arteries running parallel along the length of the city. The trial pits and trenches dug by El Falaki established that the Canopus Way was some 2,300 meters long (7,546 feet) and that it was oriented to 24° north of east, within 30 arc minutes accuracy. Seen from the latitude of Alexandria, the sunrise points occur between 28° southeast (winter solstice) and 28° northeast (summer solstice). The first-century chronicler Plutarch, in his *Life of Alexander,* writes, "Alexander was born the sixth of *Hecatombaeon,* which month the Macedonians call *Lous,* the same day that the temple of Diana at Ephesus was burnt" (italics added).

Hecatombaeon was the first month in the Greek year. It was deemed to start on the first new moon following the summer solstice. It can be calculated that in 356 BCE, the year of Alexander's birth, the new moon after the summer solstice fell on July 14 (Julian). Thus Alexander's birth fell six days later on July 20. At this time the sun was in the sign of Leo, which may explain the leonine facial features and hair that ancient writers attributed to Alexander. Alexander or,

---

*See Bauval, *The Egypt Code.*

more likely, his astronomers determined the alignment of the central axis of the city of Alexandria, later to be called the Canopus Way. It is therefore significant that the axis of this road is 24° northeast, and thus targets the rising sun on July 20, Alexander's birthday. Also on that same day would have occurred the heliacal rising of Sirius, the Egyptian star whose rising marked the divine birth of the Horus-kings. All this strongly suggests, if not confirms, that the city of Alexandria was aligned to the sunrise on July 20 to commemorate the birthday of its illustrious founder.

The Canopus Way Alignment Controversy

In 2004 I presented the hypothesis that the Canopus Way of Alexandria was oriented to the rising sun on July 20 (Julian) to mark the birthday of Alexander the Great in my book (coauthored with Graham Hancock) *Talisman: Sacred Cities, Secret Faith*.[6] Eight years later, in 2012, the astronomer Giulio Magli of Milano Politecnico and his colleague Luisa Ferro, an architect from the same polytechnic, confirmed the validity of this theory.[7]

> In the paper "The Astronomical Orientation of the Urban Plan of Alexandria" we have applied rigorous archaeoastronomical and archaeological arguments to show that the Alexandria main axis was deliberately oriented to the sun rising on the day of Alexander's birth and to the king's star Regulus.* After publication we have been informed that a similar solar orientation of the Alexandria main axis also related to Alexander's birth had already been proposed in 2004 in the book *Talisman: Sacred Cities, Secret Faith* by Graham Hancock and Robert Bauval whose priority in elaborating this idea is therefore here acknowledged.[8]

---

*I claim that the alignment was solar and on the same day as the heliacal rising of "Sirius," but Dr. Magli (wrongly, in my opinion) claimed it to be toward the star Regulus.

THE MAKING OF A GOD

No sooner was the city's plan set out than Alexander left Egypt in pursuit of the Persian King Darius III, who had fled to Babylon. Alexander would never return to see the magnificent universal city that bears his name, for he died in 323 BCE in Babylon from a high fever, probably caused by malaria. It was now up to Ptolemy, Alexander's top general, to oversee the construction of Alexandria. Ptolemy, whose name gave rise to the Ptolemaic dynasty, was crowned king of Egypt in 305 BC and took the name of Soter (Savior).

Ptolemy I Soter was a very erudite and wise man. He took council not only from Greek advisors but also from native Egyptian priests. One such advisor was Manetho of Sebennytos, a high priest of Heliopolis, who counseled the king on matters related to religion and history. Ptolemy I also nominated a group of scholars to come up with the most suitable "god" for Alexandria.

The scholars came up with Serapis, the Grecian form of the

Fig. 1.5. Marble bust of Serapis, Vatican Museum. (Robert Bauval)

Manetho and Thoth-Hermes

Manetho was from the delta city of Sebennytos. His name is well known to modern scholars for being the author of a chronology of the pharaohs, *Aegyptiaca,* which is still used for reference today. There is no source to date his birth and death, but most Egyptologists place Manetho in the epoch of Ptolemy I Soter and Ptolemy II Philadelphus. Manetho was highly educated and certainly knew the hieroglyphic language. However he wrote solely in Greek, suggesting that he and other Egyptian priests translated ancient Egyptian sacred writings, such as the celebrated Books of Thoth, into Greek. In a letter by Manetho (attributed to him by a ninth-century monk called George Syncellus of Byzanthium) addressed to Ptolemy II Philadelphus (ca. 285–246 BCE), [he introduces himself as "High Priest and Scribe . . . dwelling in Heliopolis."] Syncellus commented that Manetho knew of the writings that were inscribed in the sacred tongue in hieroglyphic letters by Thoth, the first Hermes, and translated after the flood* from the sacred tongue into the Greek language . . . and set down in books by the son of Agathodaimon, the second Hermes, rather of Tat, in the sanctuaries in the temples of Egypt. . . . [Manetho] dedicated them to Ptolemy . . . writing thus: "since you seek to know what will come to be in the cosmos, I shall present to you the sacred books that I have learnt about, written by your ancestor, Hermes Trismegistus."[9]

---

*The mention of "after the flood" later prompted Christian writers to claim that Hermes Trismegistus was a contemporary of Moses and furthermore that his writings, like those of Moses, were predicting the coming of Christianity.

Egyptian god Wsr-Hapi (Osiris-Apis). Serapis had the appearance of Zeus—a bearded man wearing Grecian garb—but with the addition of a headdress known as a *modius,* a sort of pot used as a dry measure for cereals. Serapis was then given for his consort the goddess Isis. The new cult of Serapis and Isis soon spread far and wide. A great temple dedicated to Serapis, the Serapeum, was built on a promontory in the west of Alexandria. The cult of Serapis and Isis was still hugely popular when the Romans invaded Egypt in 30 BCE. Modern historians have often remarked that had not Christianity become the official religion of Rome a few centuries later, the world would probably still have the religion of Serapis and Isis!

MAGIC IS NOT "RELIGION"

A fact often not well appreciated, sometimes not even by professional Egyptologists, is that ancient Egypt did not have a religion as such, at least not in the way that religion is understood today. Indeed, there was no word for *religion* in the vocabulary of the ancient Egyptians. According to British Egyptologist Alan H. Gardiner, "From the Egyptian point of view we may say that there is no such thing as "religion"; there was only *heka,* the nearest English equivalent of which is "magical power."[10]

In other words, ancient Egypt did not have a religion, it had a *magical religion.* The ancient Egyptians emphatically believed that heka was divine, what we would today term a *sacred science,* a type of *gnosis* brought from heaven by Thoth, the god of wisdom. How heka worked was never revealed, except that it was through intense esoteric teachings, rituals, initiations, and, above all, a thorough knowledge of the sky and its cycles. Having heka meant being a magician who knew the words of power that could control the forces of nature, ward off evil, and heal the sick. There can be no doubt that to the ancient Egyptians, the most supreme of magicians was Thoth. According to British Egyptologist Patrick Boylan, a professor of Eastern languages at University College in Dublin:

Thoth . . . is god of wisdom and orderer of the cosmos. His word has to call things into being . . . [and he is] endowed with magical powers. Magic presupposes always a special gnosis. The magician claims to possess a higher and deeper knowledge of the secret nature of things, and the hidden connection that holds things together. He is the wise one whose words have power to control mysterious forces and to ward off invisible perils. And the magician does all this by the power of his special gnosis.[11]

This *special gnosis*—a magical knowledge of nature and the cosmos—was believed to have been written in the sacred language of hieroglyphs by Thoth himself in books kept in the Great Sun Temple of Heliopolis, the City of the Sun. French Egyptologist Christian Jacq explains:

> The greatest center of magic in Egypt was probably the holy city of Heliopolis, the city of the sun, where the most ancient theology developed. Here were preserved numerous papyri, "magic" in the widest sense of the word, including medical, botanical, zoological, and mathematical texts. Most Greek philosophers and savants traveled to Heliopolis to study some of that knowledge.[12]

Jacq further affirms that Heliopolis was taught a "sacred science that requires specialists trained for many years to grasp the most secret forces of the universe."[13] Essentially, this sacred science or "magic" was used to bring down the power and benevolent influence of the celestial bodies and store it in amulets, statues, shrines, monuments, temples, and even whole cities. We need not see this as hocus-pocus horoscopic astrology, for according to Frances A. Yates:

> The type of magic with which we are to be concerned differs profoundly from astrology, which is not necessarily magic at all but a mathematical science based on the belief that human destiny is irrevocably governed by the stars, and that therefore from the study of a person's horoscope, the position of the stars at the time

of his birth, one can foretell his irrevocably foreordained future. This magic is astrological only in the sense that it, too, bases itself upon the stars, their images, and influences, but it is a way of escaping from astrological determinism by gaining power over the stars, guiding their influences in the direction that the operator desires. Or, in the religious sense, it is a way of salvation, of escape from material fortune and destiny, or of obtaining insight into the divine. Hence "astrological magic" is not a correct description of it, and hereafter, for want of a better term, I shall call it "astral magic."[14]

Frances A. Yates is specifically referring to the type of Hermetic magic that the Renaissance philosophers believed they had discovered in the Hermetica. In fact, a better term for this would be *talismanic magic*. But we are jumping the gun here. We need to remain in ancient Alexandria a little longer to gain an understanding of who Thoth was, that inventor of talismanic magic and archetype of Hermes Trismegistus, or, to be more specific, who the Renaissance philosophers *thought* he was . . .

A PLACE TO FLOURISH

In the few centuries following the foundation of Alexandria, the city was turned into the most magnificent "university" center of the ancient world. Here all the sciences and arts were given free rein to flourish. One of the centerpieces of the city was the splendid mausoleum of Alexander the Great, a small but beautiful Doric temple with a glass sarcophagus containing the mummified body of the hero. There were, too, the famous Pharos Lighthouse and the Great Library, the latter still evoking anger and sadness after nearly two millennia at its senseless destruction by a fanatical Christian mob. The wide avenues of the city were graced with wonderful villas, palaces, and temples, the latter dedicated to Egyptian as well as Greek gods and goddesses. The most splendid of these avenues was, of course, the Canopus Way, which stretched the whole length of the city. Alexandria also had a superb harbor and a great causeway, the Heptastadium, adjoining the mainland with the small island a mile or so offshore called Pharos, on which was built the famous lighthouse, one of the seven wonders of the ancient world. The Great Library was dedicated to the seven muses, the divine patrons of music and the arts, and in its numerous shelves were stored some half-million books and scrolls. Many literary works must certainly have come from the ancient temple-libraries of Egypt, among them the books of Thoth from Heliopolis. Other books were also collected from passing ships, especially from Greece, and copies were made for the library. A copy of the Hebrew Bible was brought to Alexandria and translated into Greek, thus making it available to all literate people. It was in this intellectual milieu and under the aegis of the magical religion of ancient Egypt that the Heremetica was composed. Whoever the authors were, they did not claim the Hermetica as their own but openly attributed it to Hermes Trismegistus, the Greco-Roman alter ego of Thoth.

By the end of the first century BCE, after Cleopatra VII committed her famous suicide, a large part of Alexandria's population was made up of Jews who had drifted in from Judea and other parts of the Levant. These Jews had adopted the Hellenic* language and customs, and were at first welcomed in the Alexandrian cosmopolitan lifestyle.

There was one major problem, however: these newcomers abhorred idols and graven images and repudiated all religions other than their own. To them the ancient gods of Egypt were to be regarded as obscene and their effigies to be vilified. Not surprisingly, soon clashes between the Hellenized Jews and the Hellenized Egyptians became a common occurrence in the streets of Alexandria. But worse was to come.

As the world crossed into the first millennium of the Christian era, things would get very violent and very bloody indeed.

---

*"Hellenic" means of Greek origin or connection. "Hellenized" means converted into Greek form, such as the name of Egyptian kings (i.e., Khufu Hellenized as "Cheops").

Fig. 1.6. Bronze statue in Naples of Octavian, later known as Augustus Caesar. (Robert Bauval)

WHAT HAVE THE ROMANS DONE FOR US?

In late July of 30 BCE the Roman legions of Octavian, the future first emperor of Rome (known as Augustus Caesar), were at the gates of Alexandria. Mark Antony and Cleopatra had challenged the Roman Empire and lost.

Cleopatra committed suicide and, with her death, brought to an end three thousand years of pharaonic civilization. The priests of Alexandria, the intellectuals, and the scientists at the Great Library must have been horrified at seeing their liberal city fall into the hands of the uncouth and violent Romans, who ruled their empire with the sword and an iron fist. For the three previous centuries, Egyptians had enjoyed relative freedom to practice their magical religion unmolested, and their Greek masters had bid well with them. Indeed, the Ptolemies had genuinely embraced Egyptian culture and had generously sponsored the restoration and maintenance of ancient Egyptian temples and had even built quite a few new ones of their own, such the beautiful temple of Isis at Philae, another on Elephantine Island, the dramatic temple of Sobek at Kom Ombo, the temple of Horus at Edfu, the magnificent temple of Hathor at Denderah, and many others along the Nile and in the delta region. But now under Roman rule things were very different. Although the Romans also adopted some aspects of Egyptian culture—the cult of Serapis and Isis was even imported to Rome itself—they did so mostly for political reasons, to keep Egyptians loyal and resourceful for the benefit of Rome. And even if they were genuine about these ancient Egyptian cults, the Romans tended to absorb them and *Romanize* them in their own image. They were, of course, to do the same with Judaic Christianity. But we'll get into that later on. The truth was that unlike the Greeks before them, who had come as liberators, the Romans had come as conquerors, and the Egyptians could not forget this, no matter the cajoling or propaganda applied on them. As Egyptologist Jill Kamil points out:

The institution of sacrosanct monarchy, a cardinal feature of Egyptian life in pharaonic times, which had been maintained by various later dynasties (the Ptolemies, for example), was lost in Roman times. The emperors may have claimed to be divine but it was their prefects who ruled Egypt, reduced the prestige of the priests, and exerted pressure on the people. They siphoned off the wealth of the land to Rome and recruited Egyptians to fight Roman wars in other countries. The Egyptians, who had accepted Ptolemaic rule, resisted the Romans. It is not difficult to see the difference between them. Under the Ptolemies, Egypt had retained its integrity and had a stable economy. Under the Romans the country was shorn of identity and impoverished. It was no more than a private estate for the emperor and a pleasure-ground for the Roman upper classes.[15]

The Alexandrians soon realized that their country's wealth and resources were largely used for the benefit of the Roman treasury. It was inevitable that under such prolonged pressure the Egyptians would revolt. But the several uprisings—in 115 CE, 215 CE, and 297 CE—ended up being brutally crushed by the mightier Romans.* Yet it would not be the mighty hand of Imperial Rome that would attempt to crush ancient Egypt's magical religion but another, far more virulent enemy: Christianity. From the middle of the first century a new breed of Judeans calling themselves "Christians" began to trickle into Egypt. At first the populace of Alexandria ignored their ranting against paganism and idols. But soon they would discover too late that their complacency was a fatal mistake . . .

AN APOSTLE IN ALEXANDRIA

According to Coptic (Egyptian Christian) tradition St. Mark the Apostle came from Rome (allegedly sent by St. Peter) to Alexandria

---

*In 115 CE the Romans nearly annihilated Alexandria's Jews. In 215 BC the Emperor Caracalla, after being mocked by the Alexandrians during a visit to Egypt, ordered a massacre.[16]

circa 45 CE to convert the pagans. He quickly made converts among the Hellenized Jews and the more credulous Egyptians. The first to be converted was a street cobbler who repaired the apostle's shoe when he arrived in the city. But very soon things started to get nasty. Understandably, the "pagans" were not amused to see these conversions taking place. Sometime in 68 CE they decided to get tough. They gathered at the Serapeum, formed an armed mob with sticks and knives, and marched to where the Christians were celebrating Easter with St. Mark. A bloody battle ensued, and the apostle was seized and thrown in prison.* The following is an account of what happened by Severinus, the Christian bishop of Ashmunain,† who wrote the first biography of St. Mark in 955 CE.

And when he awoke, and morning had come, the multitude assembled, and brought the saint [Mark] out of the prison, and put a rope again round his neck, and said: "Drag the serpent through the cattle shed!" And they drew the saint along the ground, while he gave thanks to the Lord Christ and glorified him, saying: "I render my spirit into thy hands, O my God!" After saying these words, the saint gave up the ghost. Then the ministers of the unclean idols collected much wood in a place called Angelion, that they might burn the body of the saint there. But by the command of God there was a thick mist and a strong wind, so that the earth trembled; and much rain fell, and many of the people died of fear and terror; and they said: "Verily, Serapis, the idol, has come to seek the man who has been killed this day." Then the faithful brethren assembled, and took the body of the holy Saint Mark from the ashes; and nothing in it had been changed. And they carried it to the church in

---

*Today there is an Anglican church at the place where St. Mark was supposedly martyred. In 828 CE the relics of St. Mark were stolen from Alexandria by Venetian sailors and taken to the city of Venice. The famous St. Mark's Basilica was built to house the relics. Egyptian Copts, however, claim that the head of the saint remained behind, where it is preserved in the Cathedral of Alexandria.

†Ashmunain was the ancient Hermeapolis, the "City of Hermes," that is, Thoth.

which they used to celebrate the Liturgy; and they enshrouded it, and prayed over it according to the established rites. And they dug a place for him, and buried his body there; that they might preserve his memory at all times.[17]

St. Mark was no ordinary saint. He had been one of the apostles of Christ and the author of the first Gospel. Anticipating his martyrdom, St. Mark had taken precautions to appoint a successor, Anianus (68–82 CE), the first bishop of the Church of Alexandria. This was the beginning of organized Christianity in Egypt.*

EXCURSION ONE, TO ROME, 45 CE

"UPON THIS ROCK I SHALL BUILD MY CHURCH"

About the same time that St. Mark was in Alexandria, another apostle, St. Peter, was in Rome. His Latinized name, Petrus ("rock" in Latin), came from his Aramaic nickname Cephas, meaning "rock." This led to today's San Pietro in Italian and St. Peter in English. According to the New Testament, Jesus told Simon-Cephas, then a humble fisherman on the Sea of Galilee, "I will make you a fisher of men . . . and upon this rock [Cephas] I will build my Church" (Matthew 4:18–19 and Matthew 16:13–20). Tradition has it that St. Peter came to Rome a few years after the crucifixion of Jesus, perhaps sometime around 45 CE. If true, then St. Peter must have been in Rome during the early reign of the emperor Nero.

Nero is Roman Christianity's supervillain. To be fair, he did not deserve all the bad press that was thrown at him by historians. True, he had a warped lust for cruelty, but he was also highly educated. He had been tutored in Greek, philosophy, and rhetoric by the scholar

---

*The title of "bishop of Alexandria" eventually was changed to "pope" or "patriarch" in the third century. It was first adopted by Heraclas, the thirteenth archbishop of the Church of Alexandria. The term *pope* comes from "baba" or "papa" (i.e., Father). The present pope is Theodoros II, the 118th pope of the Coptic Church.

Seneca and, of course, loved to compose songs and even sing them to a select audience. Unfortunately he also had a quirky passion for chariot racing and watching "Christians" being trampled by bulls, eaten by lions, ravaged by wild dogs, and burned on crosses. To this end, he thrilled the Roman people with "games" held in the circuses of Rome. To say that Christians today abhor the very name of Nero is an understatement. Nero is famously known for ordering the senseless burning of Rome in 64 CE just for his whimsical desire to sing with his lyre and, to boot, put the blame on the innocent Christians. Worse, Nero is also accused of ordering the beheading of St. Paul the Apostle and even, according to some, the crucifixion of St. Peter, although granting the latter the wish to be crucified upside down* because, as St. Peter explained, he was not worthy to be crucified in the same manner as his savior.

Fig. 1.7. Crucifixion of St. Peter. Bronze plaque at the Vatican. (Sandro Zicari)

---

*In the New Testament Jesus said to Peter, "You will stretch out your hands, and someone else will dress you and lead you where you do not want to go" (John 21:18–19). This was taken by Christians as a prophecy by Jesus of Peter's upside-down crucifixion in Rome.

Notwithstanding the endless debate among historians whether these are historical realities or were simply made up by Christian propagandists, it has been recently questioned whether it was, in fact, Christians that Nero had martyred in the circuses. It is known that before the Great Fire Nero was a keen follower of the cult of Isis, but then *after* the Great Fire he turned against the followers of Isis, and it was them, not the Christians, whom he accused of arson. It was these followers of Isis, then, who were rounded up and systematically slaughtered in the circuses. Professor Stephen Dando-Collins, an authority on the Great Fire of Rome, explains this abrupt change of heart of Nero toward these followers of Isis:

> Nero had interested himself in Isis, the Egyptian Mother goddess, to such an extent that he had introduced *Isean* feasts to the official Roman religious calendar. But while he retained a fascination with all things Egyptian, his attitude to Isis changed abruptly. It is likely that Nero's disdain of Isis had been sponsored by the death of his infant daughter Augusta the previous year. Feeling let down by this goddess, he had grown contemptuous of her and her cult. Now he found in the followers of Isis, most of whom were slaves and freedmen, easy scapegoats for the Great Fire.[18]

It is certain that Nero's beautiful wife, Poppaea Sabina, was a devotee of Isis. There are coins showing her as Isis that were cast in Rome before the Great Fire. The couple's only child, Claudia Augusta, was born the year before the fire. Her birth had thrilled Nero, who had a temple built in her honor and had a gold statue of a goddess, surely Isis, placed in it. He also had games held in Claudia's honor. But Claudia died when only three months old. Nero was heartbroken and fell into a deep depression. Typically, he blamed his wife, Poppaea, for the death of Claudia or, more likely, her devotion to Isis and, by extension, all those who followed her cult.[19]

Fig. 1.8. Poppaea Sabina, wife of Nero, donning the headgear of Isis.

We are, of course, aware of the well-known reference to "Christians" allegedly made by the Roman Senator Tacitus (ca. 115 CE) regarding the people whom Nero had killed in the circus after the fire.

> Nero fastened the guilt and inflicted the most exquisite tortures on a class hated for their abominations, called Christians by the populace. Christus, from whom the name had its origin, suffered the extreme penalty during the reign of Tiberius at the hands of one of our procurators, Pontius Pilatus.[20]

But the original text was never found, only copies in Latin dating from the eleventh century, shedding doubt on the authenticity of the claim. Stephen Dando-Collins postulated that the word *Christian* was added later, probably to replace the word *Egyptians*.

As we have already pointed out, the followers of Isis were mostly slaves and freedmen, and must have been an easy catch for Peter, the "Fisher of Men," or whoever it was that was filling their heads with passionate sermons about martyrdom, redemption, salvation, and promises of eternal happiness in paradise if only they would change from being followers of Isis to being followers of Jesus.

The transition was not such a big leap after all, for these wretched people could recognize in Christ their own Osiris-Serapis and in the Madonna their goddess Isis. Even the iconography of Mary and the infant Jesus on her lap was the same as Isis with the infant Horus. Indeed, the Romanized Egyptian Isis was almost indistinguishable from the Romanized Jewish Mary. The uncanny similarity of the Egyptian nativity myth with the Christian nativity story—a supernatural pregnancy, the divine birth announced by a star in the east, the martyrdom and resurrection of the Son of God—and, above all, a promise of redemption and everlasting happiness (paradise) must have had much appeal to these poor and oppressed slaves of Rome. A large number of these slaves and freedmen were Jews who could be convinced that their long-awaited "Messiah" was, in fact, Jesus. We do not want to embark further in this issue except to say that we can easily see how this new religion of Christianity preached by Peter and Paul in Rome much appealed to the slaves and the poor who, in their simple minds, syncretized Isis to the Virgin Mary and Horus, "Son of Serapis," to Jesus, "Son of God."

At any rate, this syncretism proved so successful that within a few centuries, as we shall see, Christianity spread like a spiritual virus, not just in Rome, but across the whole empire and, ironically, even in Egypt

Fig. 1.9. Isis and the divine infant Horus. (Robert Bauval)

itself. Mary, the Mother of Jesus, was made Theotokos (i.e., Mother of God) at the Third Ecumenical Council of the Church of Rome in 431 CE, held at Ephesus. It is no coincidence that it was here at Ephesus that the great temple of Astarte, the Greek Artemis and the Roman Diana, had once stood. Astarte, Artemis, and Diana were regarded as alter egos of Isis, the "Goddess of Ten Thousand Names."

According to professors Anne Baring and Jules Cashford, authors of *The Myth of the Goddess:*

> Portraits from the end of the fourth century and beginning of the fifth show Mary seated in the same position as Isis and Horus.
> . . . It had taken less than a century for Mary to take over the role of Isis. . . . Sometime between 400 and 500 CE the Temple of Isis at Soissons in France was dedicated to the Blessed Virgin Mary. Isis and Cybele had been Mother of Gods; Mary was now Mother of God.[21]

Fig. 1.10. Isis and Horus, ca. 100 CE. In Greco-Roman times, Isis began to change into the Christian Madonna.

Fig. 1.11. *The Virgin Mary and the Divine Infant Jesus* by Raphael, sixteenth century.

Returning to Rome and St. Peter, legend has it that his crucifixion took place in the Neronian Gardens, encompassing the present day Piazza St. Peter's in front of the sixteenth-century "new" St. Peter's Basilica at the Vatican, and the area to the south of the piazza.

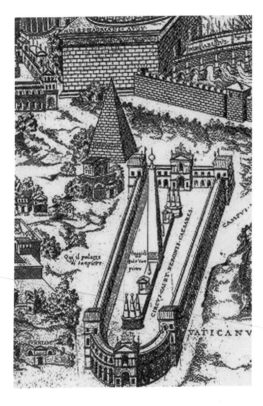

Fig. 1.12. The Circus Nero (construction started by Caligula) with the obelisk in the center. Circa 326 CE, the first, old St. Peter's Basilica would be positioned in the north side of the circus.

Another medieval legend claims that St. Peter's crucifixion took place "between two pyramids," one of which can be identified as the so-called Meta Romuli, an actual stone pyramid that once stood between the basilica and Castello del'Angelo. The "other pyramid" is unknown, and may have been the Egyptian obelisk that was probably seen as a "pyramid" by medieval chroniclers.*

---

*According to another tradition, the place of martyrdom of St. Peter was where today stands the church San Pietro in Montorio, called the *tempietto* (small temple), on the Janiculum Hill. The church was designed by Bramante in the sixteenth century and stands over the ruins of an older, ninth-century chapel.

This obelisk had been brought from Heliopolis, the City of the Sun, in Egypt to Rome in 40 CE, thus just before St. Peter had come to the Eternal City. It was the Emperor Caligula who had brought the obelisk, and it should come as no surprise that, like Nero, he was a keen devotee of Serapis and Isis and, furthermore, that he demanded to be worshipped as the "New Sun." Professor Anne Roullet asserts that from about 37 CE:

> The Isiac religion settled permanently in Rome with the approval and participation of most of the Emperors. Caligula (37–41) rebuilt the Iseum Campense; the cartouche of Claudius (41–54) was inlaid on the mensa Isiaca; Nero (54–68) included festivals in the Roman calendar; Vespasian (69–79) visited the Serapeum in Alexandria; Titus (79–81) visited that of Memphis and officiated at the burial or installation of an Apis [bull] and, back from the Judean War, spent the night before his triumph in the Iseum Campense; Domitian (81–96), who owed his life to a priest of Isis, rebuilt the Iseum Campense after the fire of 80.[22]

The Boat of Isis and the Obelisk

In very ancient times boats had a mystical and sacred significance that is not easy for us to fully appreciate today. In ancient Egypt, from the dawn of its civilization, it was believed that the sky gods traveled across the celestial landscape on boats, and that the means for the soul to reach the heavenly realm after physical death was on a sky boat. Some boats, whether fictional or real, have entered the collective imagination of human history, such as the legendary *Argo* of Jason and his Argonauts, the *Santa Maria* of Columbus, and, more recently, the tragic *Titanic*. But none of these boats acquired the spiritual meaning and fame of the *Boat of Isis*. Since time immemorial the Egyptians had a festival during which effigies of the goddess Isis—she of ten thousand names—were carried from her shrine or temple on a model boat and sailed on a barge along the River Nile.

This festival was later adopted by the Greeks and also the Romans, the latter calling it the Navigum Isidis, literally the "Boat of Isis." This festival, one of the most important in Rome, was celebrated on March 5, during which an effigy of Isis was sailed along the River Tiber. Another "boat" that almost certainly was associated with this festival was the boat-shaped Island Tiberina. Legend has it that in the fourth century BCE a plague ravaged Rome, and that a temple was built on this small island dedicated to Ascelpius, the Greek god of healing and medicine. The prototype of Asclepius was, of course, the Egyptian demigod Imhotep, the quintessential high priest of Heliopolis who invented architecture and medicine. Sometime in antiquity an obelisk was placed at the center of the sacred island, which was intended to represent the mast of the "boat." In 1550 in the garden of the famous Villa d'Este, at Tivoli outside Rome, a symbolic boat with an obelisk as mast was built as part of the so-called Rometta, "Little Rome." Apparently a sort of model Rome with all its important edifices and streets was constructed, with the Island Tiberina built as an actual boat with a small obelisk as its mast. On each side of the obelisk were fountains spurting out water. An obelisk flanked by two fountains that is extremely reminiscent of the obelisk from Heliopolis graces the Piazza St. Peter's, in front of the Vatican. Interestingly, the Ile de la Cité in Paris, on which stands the Cathedral of Notre Dame, is also shaped like a boat and is believed to once have had a temple dedicated to the goddess Isis. Medieval legends abound that the goddess Isis came to Paris on a boat. After his campaign in Egypt, Napoleon went as far as adding an effigy of Isis on the boat of Paris, the traditional coat of arms of the city of Paris.

Fig. 1.13. The boat fountain in the Rometta area in the gardens of the Villa d'Este near Rome, circa 1550 CE. It is supposed to be an allegory of the boat-shaped Island Tiberina in the Tiber. It almost certainly represents the legendary Boat of Isis and the feast of Navigum Isidis, celebrated on March 5 in Rome in ancient times. (Robert Bauval)

All this should make us wonder who exactly was being martyred by Nero: Christians, followers of Isis, or, as the case might be, an amalgam of both. A letter written by the Emperor Hadrian after his visit to Egypt in 130 CE, addressed to his brother-in-law, Servianus, the Roman governor of Alexandria, strongly suggests such a syncretism in full process.

Egypt, which you commended to me, my dearest Servianus, I have found to be wholly fickle and inconsistent, and continually wafted about by every breath of fame. The worshippers of Serapis are called Christians, and those who are devoted to the god Serapis, call themselves Bishops of Christ.[23]

"BY THIS SIGN YOU SHALL CONQUER"

Back in Alexandria, the street slinging between Christians and pagans had turned to street butchering. But things were soon to swing radically in favor of the Christians. This happened in faraway Rome, on October 27, 312 CE, to be precise.

The military legions of Constantine, a Roman general who had been made *Caesar* by his troops while in Britain in 306 CE, were encamped outside Rome and readied for battle against Maxentius, the unpopular coemperor in Rome. Although outnumbered two to one, Constantine's forces would receive a huge dose of moral support, quite literally, from the sky. The legend goes that there was a sudden commotion in Constantine's camp when a bright light appeared in the heavens, shaped like a cross. Someone close to Constantine, probably his old Christian tutor Lactantius, interpreted the celestial sign as being the Christian symbol, telling Constantine, "By this sign you shall conquer." Lactantius is regarded as one of the church fathers, in league with St. Augustine and Clement of Alexandria, and it is well known that he saw Hermes Trismegistus as a great sage and as a prophet of Christian truth.[24]

Highly impressed by this celestial vision, Constantine promptly ordered that the sign—probably the Chi-Rho, or Labarum—be painted on the shields of his soldiers and also fixed on his standard. Constantine won the battle for Rome, known as the Battle of the Milvian Bridge, the Ponte Milvio on the Via Flaminia. He was now virtually supreme master of the whole empire. More importantly, he was very sympathetic to the Christians. With such imperial support, the current "pope" in Rome, Sylvester I, was no longer the underdog of the religious factions in Rome, but now had the upper hand. It also surely must have dawned

Fig. 1.14. Constantine's vision before the Battle of the Milvian Bridge.

There is much doubt to the authenticity of this celestial vision. All manner of theories have been proposed as to what Constantine saw in the sky, if anything at all. Some suggest a cloud formation catching the rays of the setting sun, others think it may have been a meteorite, and still others think the vision was made up by Constantine to encourage his troops by making them believe that they were under divine protection. Christian tradition claims that the sign was the Chi-Rho, the first two Greek letters of the name of Christ. This sign, when used on his standard by Constantine, was called the Labarum. Whatever the truth, there is no doubt that the Battle of the Milvian Bridge set the scene for Christianity to flourish and become the world religion that it is today.

on the various pagan leaders and high priests that they, too, could be Christianized and thus retain their status and cult, even if some serious compromises needed to be made. A sort of "if you can't beat them, join them" approach was thus applied by them toward the Christians. In fact the Christianization of pagan cults had already started, albeit clandestinely, since the time of Nero, but now Christianity had its opportunity served on a golden platter to compete for a total takeover and become the dominant religion of Rome and perhaps even the whole Roman Empire. What made it even more feasible was Constantine's particular notion of Christ, for it was not that of a gentle and compassionate carpenter from Nazareth, but most likely that of a powerful solar god, an Invincible Sun, *Sol Invictus*, akin to Apollo or Serapis. For in Constantine's mind surely only a deity of solar pedigree could have brought him this victory at the Milvian Bridge. At any rate, Christian legend has it that Constantine was "baptized" by "Pope" Sylvester I and the following year, in 313 CE, "legalized" Christianity in the Edict of Milan.*

Emperor Constantine then generously gave the Lateran Palace to Pope Sylvester I and also issued orders for the construction of a basilica at the foot of Mount Vaticanus. This basilica, Constantine insisted, was to have the altar directly over the tomb of St. Peter the Apostle.

ROMAN CATHOLIC CHRISTIANITY

In 325 CE, thirteen years into his reign, Emperor Constantine convened the so-called First Ecumenical Council at Nicaea in Turkey. After weeks of debate among the three hundred or so bishops who had come to the council—some of whom resorted to fistfighting to win their cases—Constantine finally put his foot down and ordered the bishops to get on with it.

---

*In reality Constantine was baptized much later, on his deathbed in 337 CE by Eusebius of Nicomedia. The four popes that ruled during the reign of Emperor Constantine were Miltiades, Sylvester I, Mark, and Julius I.

Fig. 1.15. Emperor Constantine and the bishops holding the
Nicene Creed. (Robert Bauval)

At any rate, they finally agreed that Christianity was now to be regarded as a universal, that is, "catholic," religion, with dogmas and doctrines that should be set on a document, the so-called Nicene Creed, on which the bishops were required to sign their names. Like the founding fathers of the United States of America would do in signing the Constitution and spelling out the tenets of their republic, so did the founding fathers of Roman Catholicism sign the Nicene Creed and spell out the dogmas of their universal Catholic religion. The opening statement was not, however, "We the People," but "We the Bishops," who affirmed that they:

believe in one God, the maker of all things visible and invisible, and in one Lord Jesus, the Son of God. . . . Who for us men, and for our salvation, came down and was incarnate and was made Man.

An edit was then made to this opening statement at the Second Ecumenical Council at Constantinople in 380 CE, so that it now read, "Who for us men, and for our salvation, came down from heaven, *and was incarnate by the Holy Ghost of the Virgin Mary, and was made man*" (italics added).

Most bishops who attended the council complied, and the few who procrastinated were threatened with banishment. And that was that. From now on the original apostolic mission of the gentle carpenter Jesus and his Jewish disciples was taken over by Rome and turned into an organized religion under the authority of the emperor and an infallible pope. Anyone outside Roman Catholicism was either seen as a pagan or, worse, a heretic; the latter was a term applied to Christians who did not embrace the Nicene Creed. Jesus of Nazareth, who had preached love, compassion, forgiveness, and freedom, would have cringed in bemusement and disgust at what was being done in his name.

But this was only the beginning . . .

Back in Alexandria the Christians received the news of the Nicene Creed with jubilation. Now feeling emboldened with the backing of the emperor, the Christians quickly gained the upper hand. The ancient Egyptian religion, its priests and priestesses, its temples, its scribes, and its followers were now officially to be regarded as pagan and thus to be loathed and rebuked. Mostly through coercion, the native Egyptians were converted en masse to Christianity. With fanatical Christians now running amuck, it was evident that the perennial magical religion of Egypt would either be obliterated or become absorbed into Christianity. Indeed, already Osiris-Serapis was beginning to look more and more like Christ, and Isis and the infant Horus like the Virgin Mary and the infant Jesus. By the fifth century CE most Egyptian temples had been turned into churches or monasteries. All the centuries of foreign occupations—Persian, Greek, and Roman—had finally taken their heavy toll on ancient Egypt, and its sacred culture and magical religion were close to their death throes. Something had to be done, and quick.

But what?

THOTH BECOMES HERMES TRISMEGISTUS, AND HIS SACRED BOOKS BECOME THE HERMETICA

In the 1960s, when I was still living in Alexandria, I knew, of course, that I had been baptized in the Roman Catholic Church of Bacos and that at the age of seven I had received my First Holy Communion at the Sacred Heart College in Rushdy Pasha. Roman Catholicism was a way of life in my family, Italian style. A couple of blocks from our home was the cloister of the Clarisse nuns, where some wretched women, many of whom came from poor families, lived in deprivation of all human contact except their own and were only to be seen—actually peeped at—through a grilled window, like caged canaries. During the whole of May, the month Catholics dedicate to the Virgin Mary, my mother used to drag my twin sister and me to the Clarisse for Mass after school. May was the best time of year for fishing and playing with friends outdoors, and here I was in this dreary, dull chapel sitting in silence while my Muslim and Jewish friends enjoyed fun and games at the beach. Things got even worse on Sundays, when the whole family—grandparents, parents, siblings, uncles, aunts, and cousins—attended Mass in one of the many churches of Alexandria. We usually would go to a Catholic church where, to my dismay, the sermons seemed to never end. But on some occasions we also would go to other Christian churches—Greek Orthodox, Armenian Maronite, Egyptian Coptic—where the Mass was more exotic and much less tedious. Christianity, of course, was not the only religion in Egypt, nor was it the main one. Every day, at morning, noon, dusk, and night, I would be reminded by the prayer sung by the muezzins that Egypt was—and has been since the seventh century—a predominantly Muslim country. In those days it never occurred to me to find out how or why the ancient magical religion of the pharaohs had disappeared, only to be replaced by Christianity and Islam. It certainly would not have occurred to me that it had been put into hibernation, only to be reawakened centuries later in Italy!

The American scholar Brian P. Copenhaver, a professor of history at the University of California, explained:

> One set of beliefs [Christianity], eventually labeled "orthodox" by those who held them, displaced other views called "heretical." In Egypt, in the midst of this cultural and spiritual turmoil, over the course of several centuries when the Ptolemies, the Romans, and the Byzantines ruled the Nile Valley, other persons unknown to us produced the writings that we call the Hermetica.[25]

Amid this chaos and tumult the Alexandrian Hermetists translated the books of Thoth into Greek and attributed them to Hermes, a deity known to and highly respected by Greeks and Romans alike. But the "Hermes" they had in mind was an Egyptian one: Hermes *Trismegistus,* "Hermes the Thrice Great." Whether this was a premeditated plan to ensure the survival of their ancient magical religion we will never know. As for the choice of Greek, Egyptologist Jill Kamil explains:

> The languages in official use in Egypt were Greek and Egyptian, Greek being the more widely used. Egyptian literates had learned Greek long before the conquest of Alexander. They also realized that if they transcribed their own language in the Greek alphabet, which was well known among the middle classes and was simpler to read than demotic (the cursive form of hieroglyphic writing in its latest development), communication would be easier. Scribes started translating Egyptian sounds in Greek, adding seven extra letters

from the demotic alphabet to accommodate the sounds from which there were no Greek letters. The emergence of this new script [is] now known as Coptic.[26]

There was, however, one important problem to overcome. Much weight was placed by Egyptians on the sacredness of the hieroglyphs, where each character and symbol was deemed imbued with magical powers. To them it was not just the content of the texts that was important, but also, perhaps more so, the signs and symbols that were used. In the minds of many hieroglyphic purists, translating the books of Thoth into Greek would undermine their effectiveness. A satisfactory solution, however, was eventually found. As the scholar Garth Fowden explains:

> The Hermetists, while insisting that their compositions had indeed been written in Egyptian, and inscribed on stelae in hieroglyphic characters, were also well aware that they could not have been rendered into Greek without losing the authority that [was] attached to sacred texts in the native language, "for the very quality of the sounds and the intonation of the Egyptian words contained in itself the force of the things said." A translation would require, at the very least, the active assistance of the priestly guardians of the originals.[27]

The Hermetists ingeniously proposed that there was not one Hermes but two of them: the first Hermes being the Egyptian god Thoth, the originator of the sacred magical texts in hieroglyphs, and the second Hermes, his grandson, called Hermes Trismegistus, who translated these texts into Greek. With such a lofty pedigree given to the translator, the validity of Thoth's teachings was preserved. This ploy was given much credence by a statement attributed to Manetho, the high priest of Heliopolis and advisor to Ptolemy I Soter and his successor, Ptolemy II Philadelphus:

[There existed] stelae inscribed in the sacred language and with hieroglyphic characters by Thoth, the First Hermes . . . after the flood they were translated into Greek, and deposited in books in the sanctuary of Egyptian temples by the Second Hermes.[28]

THE LAMENT

The demise of paganism in Egypt reached its climax in the middle of the fourth century CE. This was when the spreading of Christianity in Egypt had almost engulfed the whole country. Now Christian monks became more and more intolerant of those Egyptians still practicing the magical religion of the pharaohs. The death blow came when in 391 CE the Roman Emperor Theodosius I issued a decree, which proclaimed all ancient cults *religio ellicita* (illegal religions) and ordered the closure of all the pagan temples.*

In Egypt this was taken by fanatical Christian monks as a license to kill. They began to rouse Christian crowds into hysterical mobs and induce them to go on rampages to cleanse the land from pagans and their sanctuaries. It was then that the Great Library of Alexandria was destroyed and all its precious books thrown to the fire. A large crowd of frenzied Christians were led by the patriarch of Alexandria, Theophilus, to the Serapeum, and, with maddening vigor, they tore the temple down and smashed all its icons and idols, and its books, scrolls, and manuscripts were used for bonfires. A contemporary of these events, Socrates Scholasticus of Constantinople, reported, "Seizing this opportunity, Theophilus exerted himself to the utmost . . . he destroyed the Serapeum . . . and the heathen temples . . . were therefore razed to the ground, and the images of their gods molten into pots and other convenient utensils for the use of the Alexandrian church."[29]

A few years later, in 415 CE, the most despicable act of senseless cru-

---

*In 393 CE Theodosius I also banned the Olympic Games in Greece. It was not until 1896 that they were held again in Athens.

elty by Christian fanatics took place in the main square of Alexandria. This happened to the beautiful and highly educated Hypatia, daughter of the brilliant mathematician Theon, who had received her education in Athens and Rome and now headed the Platonic School in Alexandria. Socrates Scholasticus had written very highly of her.

> There was a woman at Alexandria named Hypatia, daughter of the philosopher Theon, who made such attainments in literature and science, as to far surpass all the philosophers of her own time. Having succeeded to the school of Plato and Plotinus, she explained the principles of philosophy to her auditors, many of whom came from a distance to receive her instructions. On account of the self-possession and ease of manner, which she had acquired in consequence of the cultivation of her mind, she not infrequently appeared in public in the presence of the magistrates. Neither did she feel abashed in going to an assembly of men. For all men on account of her extraordinary dignity and virtue admired her all the more.[30]

On a bright, sunny morning Hypatia rode her chariot to the Great Library as usual. Suddenly a frenzied gang of Christian monks ambushed her, pulled her off her chariot, stripped her naked, beat her senseless, and slowly scraped her flesh off her bones with seashells. She died in the most awful agony.

The mob then ripped her body apart and burned it. A dark and somber mood befell Alexandria. One of the most famous discourses of the Hermetica, known as *The Lament of Hermes Trismegistus,* or more commonly *The Lament,* is found in the tract titled the *Asclepius.* Here Hermes Trismegistus addressed his pupil Asclepius with poignancy and passion to inform him of the terrible calamities and destruction that will befall Egypt, its people, and its magical religion. Hermes Trismegistus opens *The Lament* with a rhetorical question that is as haunting as it is mysterious.

Do you not know, Asclepius, that Egypt is made in the image of heaven? Or, to be more precise, that everything governed and moved in heaven came down to Egypt and was transferred there?

This rhetorical question is most revelatory, for in these words lies the whole idea of a "natural magic" or "magical religion" or "talismanic magic." As we shall see in the next chapter, this is what so much impressed and fascinated the Italian philosophers of the Renaissance. Meanwhile, let us hear more of what Hermes revealed to Asclepius.

If truth were told, our land is the temple of the whole world. And yet, since it befits the wise to know all things in advance, of this you must not remain ignorant: a time will come when it will appear that the Egyptians paid respect to divinity with faithful mind and painstaking reverence—to no purpose. All their holy worship will be disappointed and perish without effect, for divinity will return from earth to heaven, and Egypt will be abandoned. . . . When foreigners occupy the land and territory, not only reverence will fall into neglect but, even harder, a prohibition under penalty prescribed by law—so-called—will be enacted against reverence, fidelity, and divine worship. Then this most holy land, seat of shrines and temples, will be filled completely with tombs and corpses. O Egypt, Egypt, of your reverent deeds only stories will survive, and they will be incredible to your children! Only words cut in stone will survive to tell your faithful works. . . . Asclepius, why do you weep? Egypt herself will be persuaded to deeds much more wicked than these, and she will be steeped in evils far worse. . . . In their weariness the people of that time will find the world nothing to wonder at or worship. . . . No one will look up to heaven. The reverent will be thought mad, the irreverent wise; the lunatic will be thought brave, and the scoundrel will be taken for a decent person. . . . They will establish new laws, new justice. . . . Only the baleful angels remain to mingle with humans, seizing wretches and driving them to every outrageous crime—war, looting, trickery—and all that is contrary to the soul.[31]

The Lament is clearly a prophecy set during the collapsing phase of the ancient Egyptian magical religion and Egypt's pharaonic temples and sacred places. Yet all was not lost, at least not forever, for Hermes Trismegistus also prophesied in *The Lament* that in some distant future the magical religion will be restored.

> When all this comes to pass, Asclepius, then the master and father, the god whose power is primary, governor of the first good, will look on this conduct . . . and in an act of will—which is god's benevolence—he will take his stand against vices and the perversion in everything, righting wrong, washing away malice . . . then he will restore to the world its beauty of old so that the world itself will again seem deserving of worship and wonder, and with constant benedictions and proclamations of praise the people of that time will honor the god who makes and *restores* so great a work. And this will be the geniture of the world: a *reformation* of all good things, and a *restitution* most holy and most reverent of nature itself. The gods who exercised their dominion over the earth will be restored one day and installed in a city at the extreme limit of Egypt, a city, which will be founded toward the setting sun, and into which will hasten, by land and sea, the whole race of mortal men.[32] (italics added)

This utopian solar city at the extreme limit of Egypt—a city of the sun—was surely Alexandria, at least in the minds of those who wrote that text. We recall how Alexandria was indeed founded on the northern limit of Egypt on the Mediterranean coast, which is the northern end of the land of Egypt. We can detect in *The Lament* an echo of the founding of Alexandria in 331 BCE and, more especially, the east-west axis of the Canopus Way, set toward the rising sun at one end and toward *the setting sun* at the other end. This was indeed the city in which the freethinkers, the scholars, and the Hermetists once flourished. Yet the prophecy calls for the restoration of the magical religion in some distant future. For the immediate time, however, the authors of the Hermetica had to save all they could of the precious legacy of their forefathers. They wisely stepped aside to let the Christian monks "convert" their ancient temples and shrines into "churches," and thus in this manner managed to save them from total destruction. The great temples at Edfu, Esna, Kom Ombo, Luxor, Elephantine, and Karnak, all were turned into Christian churches. The last temple to undergo this Christianization was the beautiful temple on the island of Philae dedicated to the goddess Isis. The "conversion" took place in the early fifth century CE. As for the sacred writings inscribed on the temple walls, stelae, obelisks, and columns, these by and large avoided total destruction. Not so, however, for the writings on papyrus and leather scrolls, which, sadly, were burned or torn to shreds. Fortunately, however, copies of the Hermetica were in private hands and thus escaped the destruction. An important clue, however, as to what may have happened to them is given in a dialogue attributed to Isis to her son, Horus, in one of the Hermetic tracts known as the *Kore Kosmou* [The Virgin of the World]. The classical scholar Garth Fowden explained:

> According to the *Kore Kosmou*, Hermes was a god who succeeded in understanding the mysteries of the heavens, and revealed them by inscribing them in sacred books, which he then hid here on earth, intending that they should be searched for by future generations, but found only by the fully worthy. Having finished his task he returned to the abode of the gods.[33]

Surely not in the wildest of dreams of these unknown authors of the Hermetica would they have imagined that their sacred writings would be rediscovered in a monastery in Macedonia more than a millennium later—in 1462 to be precise—by an Italian priest called Leonardo da Pistoia. The simple monks of the monastery, not quite knowing what these books were, probably sold the priceless books to Leonardo for a mere pittance. A few weeks later Father Leonardo rode his donkey into Florence. He immediately took the books to his master, the ruler of Florence, Cosimo de Medici. The latter then handed them to his protégé, a young and brilliant scholar and linguist, Marsilio Ficino.

Fig. 1.16. Cosimo de Medici

Fig. 1.17. Marsilio Ficino

We can perhaps imagine what must have gone through the mind of Ficino as he carefully opened the first page of the first libellus and read, in Greek, the first few words on the worn and yellowed parchment: *Discourse of Hermes Trismegistus . . .* [34]

Here in Ficino's hands were the lost books of the wisest sages and prophets of antiquity, written under the name of the semidivine Hermes Trismegistus! What comes to mind are the famous words of the Egyptologist Howard Carter when, on November 22, 1922, he pushed a candle through a hole in the wall of Tutankhamen's tomb and his mentor, Lord Carnavon, standing behind him, eagerly asked, "What do you see?"

"Wonderful things . . . ," replied Howard Carter . . .

2

THE HERMETIC
MOVEMENT, PART I

He [Giordano Bruno] is thinking of the passage in The
Lament . . . *[and] takes it to mean that the Christian
suppressors legislated against the true Egyptian solar
religion . . . in spite of the suppression, the true religion
did not cease, and Bruno is reviving it.*

FRANCES A. YATES, GIORDANO BRUNO
AND THE HERMETIC TRADITION

*Natural magic, which, by natural things, seeks to obtain
the services of the heavens for the prosperous health of our
bodies.*

MARSILIO FICINO'S OWN DEFINITION OF
"NATURAL MAGIC" IN THE "APOLOGIA"
TO HIS LIBER DE VITA, 1489

NATURAL AND TALISMANIC MAGIC

In our scientific, technological age of 3-D color televisions, cell
phones, iPads, and laptops, the term *natural magic* is as outer-worldly

as the term God. Ask anyone in the street how a cell phone works, however, and at best you will be told that it is something to do with microwaves. Ask a scientist, though, and he will explain in great detail how microwaves are used to transmit sound and image from one cell phone to another anywhere on the planet. Ask this same scientist if he can make a fish or a leaf, and he will smile amusingly. Ask him if he can create a living creature or a living microbe, and you will get a wobbly smile. Ask him yet again what or who can do this, and the smile turns to an annoyed, bewildered grin. A scientific, philosophical waffle may be attempted, but the honest, simple answer, of course, is, "I do not know." A Renaissance philosopher, however, would have replied, "natural magic." Natural magic is all around us all the time. In fact, we people, you and me, are the most wonderful examples of natural magic, at least as far as we know. Yet a bumblebee buzzing about, a flower in your garden, your cat playing on the rug, or a bird flying by, all are wonderful examples, too, of natural magic. But we are merely scraping the surface here. Every breath you take, every move, every emotion, feeling, and sensation is natural magic. Of course, scientists will try to explain all this, and even human feelings are brought down to electrical impulses, neuron transmitters, and chemicals affecting nerves and cells. But to put it very simply, if you hold a flower in your hand and wonder, just wonder without seeking a scientific explanation, then you are experiencing natural magic. And, better still, your soul will also begin to heal.

When Marsilio Ficino began to read in Greek the books of the Hermetica and came across one of the most evocative statements given to Hermes Trismegistus, he must have known, or at least sensed, that he was about to change from being a philosopher into being a magician or, to be more specific, a *natural magician.*

Unless you make yourself equal to God, you cannot understand God.[1]

Fig. 2.1. Dame Frances A. Yates, ca. 1970.
(Warburg Institute, London)

It is my firm belief that it was at this precise moment that the *intellectual* Italian Renaissance truly began . . .

The first time I learned of this peculiar term *natural magician* was back in 1993 when I read a book by a British humanist, Dame Frances A. Yates (1899–1981), titled *Giordano Bruno and the Hermetic Tradition*. If this brilliant scholar were alive today she might prefer the term *Hermetic magician* to *natural magician,* and I would now wholeheartedly agree with her. But back then, engrossed as I was in my engineering career, my initial reaction was to think of Frances A. Yates as an overtly enthusiastic lady scholar, a sort of Madame Blavatsky and Miss Marple rolled into one. But soon I came to realize that I was very wrong about her.

It became apparent to me that the quality of her research and the clarity with which she presented her findings amply justified the high reputation she earned for her deeply intuitive scholarship and intellectual sleuthing of the Hermetic tradition of the Renaissance. But let us not run ahead of our story. I need first to tell you about my visit to Rome and how an ancient Egyptian monument began to work its talismanic magic on me.

THE OBELISKS OF ROME

My first visit to the Eternal City was in the summer of 1978. I had just gotten married in London, and my wife, Michele, and I were on

Fig. 2.2. Blinded by the light: the cross on the Vatican Obelisk. (Robert Bauval)

our way to Iran, where I had taken a job with an international construction company. It was September 29, the day after Pope John Paul I had died. He had been pope for only thirty-three days. Hardly had the celebration of his consecration ended than the mourning of his passing started. Many shops and restaurants were closed, and we were left to wander the streets of Rome with only a guidebook and a Nikon SLR camera strapped around my neck. We walked from the Spanish Steps all the way to the Vatican. When we reached St. Peter's Square we found it packed with people who had come to pay their respects, many displaying overtly their sorrow and others, like us, just curious bystanders. It was a sunny and warm day, and the tall obelisk in the center of the square—it is actually an ellipse, not a square—was casting a shadow on the northern part of the piazza. I raised my eyes and for a moment was dazzled by the strong sunlight. Squinting, I noticed the cross on the top of the obelisk. I vividly recall wondering who had put it there and, more intriguingly, what was this ultimate Christian symbol doing on top of an obviously pagan "solar" monument smack in front of the Vatican!

From my guidebook I found out an interesting fact: the city of Rome has the most obelisks in the world, eight of which were from ancient Egypt, and six of these from Heliopolis, the City of the Sun, near modern-day Cairo.*

The next day we left for Turkey, and then to Teheran, where Michele and I were working. Meanwhile the affair of the Vatican obelisk was put on the back burner of my mind. For the next fifteen years I was involved in my engineering work overseas in Iran, Sudan, West Africa, Saudi Arabia, Australia, France, and England. It was not until I resettled in England in 1993 that it all came back to me and spurred me into the research that has produced several books and reached its climax with this present book. My curiosity about the Vatican obelisk started when I was writing my first book, *The Orion Mystery,* back in 1993. I happened to be browsing in a bookshop at Oxford looking for a copy of

---

*Ironically, only one obelisk today stands on the original site of Heliopolis in Egypt, now a busy and very built-up suburb of modern-day Cairo called Matareya.

the Hermetica, for I wanted to know more about its content and teachings. I found a recent paperback version by Solos Press of Dorset, then owned by Adrian Gilbert. I contacted Gilbert and quickly found that we shared many interests. He offered to publish *The Orion Mystery,* but instead I invited him to coauthor the book with me.*

Gilbert had studied the Hermetica for many years and managed to get me more interested in this subject. A short while before the publication of *The Orion Mystery,* in January 1993, to be more precise, I had the good fortune to meet the Bulgarian scholar Yuri Stoyanov at the Warburg Institute in London. It was Stoyanov who urged me to get a copy of Frances A. Yates's *Giordano Bruno and the Hermetic Tradition.* This I did, and I also obtained a copy of the latest English translation of the Hermetica, by Professor Brian P. Copenhaver, who, I was pleased to find out, had also been introduced to Hermetic studies through reading Yates's book on Bruno. Any remaining doubts I may still have had regarding Frances A. Yates's scholarship were now completely dispelled, for it was now very clear to me that she was a most eminent scholar and was regarded as the authority on the Hermetic tradition and that her findings opened up a new approach to understand the Renaissance and the scientific revolution that ensued. This is what Professor Brian P. Copenhaver had to say about Frances A. Yates:

> Perhaps the most widely read book on Hermes was not about late antiquity; the Renaissance was the period studied by Frances Yates in *Giordano Bruno and the Hermetic Tradition . . .* it was Yates who made Hermes truly prominent once again for students of early modern intellectual history . . . when focusing on figures of the late fifteenth and sixteenth centuries, from Ficino to Bruno and some-

---

*At first *The Orion Mystery* was to be published by Solos Press, run only by Adrian Gilbert. But when the literary agent A. M. Heath of London offered to get me a much bigger deal (eventually with William Heinemann Ltd), Gilbert became my coauthor. *The Orion Mystery* was an instant bestseller and is now published in more than twenty-five languages.

what beyond. . . . Yates' views on the Hermetica became famous for some, notorious for others, especially when, in a 1968 article, she made Hermes a major figure in the preliminaries to the scientific revolution.[2]

I had to find out more about the Hermetic tradition. This, at first, was because the most important tenet of the Hermetists was, "As above, so below," which is precisely the thesis I presented in my book *The Orion Mystery*, namely that the pattern of the three stars of Orion's belt correlated to the pattern of the three Giza Pyramids. We recall the rhetorical question by Hermes Trismegistus, which resonated loudly for me:

Do you not know, Asclepius, that Egypt is made in the image of heaven?

When in February 1994 the BBC aired the documentary *The Great Pyramid: Gateway to the Stars,* which was based on my book, it was also seen in Holland by Joseph Ritman, owner of the Bibliotheca Philosophica Hermetica in Amsterdam.*

Ritman is a keen sponsor of Hermetic and gnostic studies; after seeing the BBC documentary he invited me to Amsterdam to meet him and his colleagues. The meeting took place in Ritman's home. Among the guests was Gilles Quispel, a professor emeritus from Utrecht and Harvard Universities. Quispel was famous in scholarly circles for his work on the so-called apocryphal gospels of Nag Hammadi.

---

*The Bibliotheca Philosophica Hermetica was founded by Joseph R. Ritman in 1957. The purpose was to collect old and new books on Hermetic-Christian studies. A section of the library was open to the public in 1984. Lack of funds recently forced Ritman to put on sale some of the ancient manuscripts, although it seems that he eventually reacquired them. The library has some 450 manuscripts, many of which date before 1550 CE; about 4,000 books published before 1800 CE, and about 11,000 books published after 1800.

The Nag Hammadi manuscripts were discovered in Middle Egypt in 1946. They are mainly gnostic texts but also contained fragments from the Hermetica. A batch was acquired by Quispel in 1952 for the Jung Institute in Zurich, and he was the first to recognize them as "gospels." In 1956 Quispel brought back from Egypt photographs of the original Gospel of Thomas. Speaking at a lecture in Amsterdam in 2000, Quispel made quite a stir when he declared, "Gnosticism is about to become the twenty-first-century world religion." Quispel was a firm believer that ancient religious-philosophical systems such as Hermetism and gnosticism were the way to true salvation. He died at the age of ninety in the Egyptian Red Sea resort of Al Gouna in 2006. As an aside, we note that some modern scholars differentiate between the *Hermetism* of late antiquity in Alexandria and the *Hermetism* of the Italian Renaissance. In this book we make no distinction between the two, as we see them as part and parcel of the same tradition.

After Amsterdam my involvement with the Hermetic tradition was shelved due to other pressing publishing engagements. The years passed. In 2004 my book *Talisman: Sacred Cities, Secret Faith* was published. I followed it with four other books on ancient Egypt.*

Finally, in late 2012, while researching the origins of Egyptian obelisks for an article, I decided to reopen the file on the Vatican obelisk. While casually looking at a satellite image of Vatican City I noticed something that had previously escaped my attention. Fate would have it that I received an invitation to speak at a conference in Tuscany in early November 2012.

The quest for the Hermetic City of the Sun was about to begin . . .

---

*These books are *The Egypt Code,* 2006; *Black Genesis,* 2010; *Breaking the Mirror of Heaven,* 2012; and *Imhotep the African,* 2013.

SYNCHRONISTIC ENCOUNTER

At the conference I met Chiara Dainelli (now Chiara Hohenzollern), an author from Rome. Chiara had published a book titled *Il Codice Astronomico di Dante* [The Astronomical Code of Dante], which she told me had been inspired by my work on the astronomy in the Egyptian Pyramid Texts. Naturally we had much to talk about. Also at this conference I met Sandro Zicari, a professor of applied mathematics and statistics from Sapienza University of Rome. Over breakfast I told Chiara and Sandro of my idea for a book project on the "mysteries" of the Vatican, and I invited them to collaborate with me. Back home in Spain I immediately got in touch with Jon Graham, the acquisitions editor at Inner Traditions. Jon loved the idea, and within a few days we got the okay from the publishers to go ahead. Of course none of this would have happened if Father Leonardo da Pistoia had not stumbled on the Hermetica collection in that monastery in Macedonia and had these books not been handed over to Marsilio Ficino.*

RENAISSANCE

Marsilio Ficino was born at this crucial point in history when, after centuries of medievalism and several senseless Crusades to recapture the Holy Land, Italian scholars were craving a new way forward. Oddly, but perhaps understandably, they looked for it in the past, in the classical age of ancient Greece and Rome and, as we shall now see, in the golden age of pharaonic Egypt. And so it was that the fifteenth century opened with a Renaissance, an intellectual, artistic, and spiritual rebirth in the beautiful and rich city of Florence in northern Italy. Here, a new breed of philosophers, protected and financed by a powerful and enlightened ruler, were able to seek ancient wisdom and knowledge, mainly hoping

---

*Father Leonardo was one of the many agents employed by the ruler of Florence, the great Cosimo de Medici, to scour Europe for ancient manuscripts for his library at the new "Platonic" academy he and Marsilio Ficino had founded in Florence.

to find the pure perennial theology, the *prisca theologia* as they called it, which they believed would revive man's quest for divine knowledge. They were convinced, rightly or wrongly, that the prisca theologia had been recorded in remote antiquity and in its purest form by an Egyptian "Hermes," Hermes Trismegistus, and had somehow been passed down the ages to reach the great philosopher Plato. But then the prisca theologia was corrupted by the advent of Roman Christianity. So these Renaissance philosophers sought to find it in the hope of convincing the Vatican to adopt it and reform Christianity for the benefit of the whole world: a sort of self-Reformation of Catholicism.

One such philosopher—better still, a *sponsor* of philosophers—was the highly enlightened ruler of Florence, Cosimo de Medici. Fate would have it that Cosimo was not just another scholar, but one with vast funds to spare, in other words, a philosopher with firepower. This made him an extremely influential man, not just in Italy but also throughout Europe. Cosimo rubbed shoulders with popes, monarchs, and princes, and was regarded by those he so generously sponsored as a sort of Donald Trump, Bill Gates, and Richard Branson all rolled into one. Cosimo was deeply interested in books, especially old books that expounded ancient philosophies, arcane knowledge, and wisdom teachings.

Cosimo was born on September 27, 1389, on the feast of St. Cosmas (hence his name). He received his education in the monastery of St. Maria degli Angeli in Florence, where he learned French, German, Latin, Greek, and even a spatter of Hebrew and Arabic. He also acquired a profound love for the classics, notably the works of Plato. This came from his tutor, Roberto Rossi, one of the top scholars in Florence. Later, in adulthood, and like his father before him, Cosimo administered the finances of the papacy, which dramatically increased the wealth of the Medici family. In a statement attributed to Pope Pius II in 1458, the pontiff said of Cosimo:

> Political questions are settled in his house. The man he chooses holds office. . . . He it is who decides peace and war and controls the laws. . . . He is king in everything but name.

The word *medici* in Italian actually means doctors (i.e., medics), implying perhaps some links of the Medici family with this profession, which, apparently, one of their ancestors had practiced in Mugello, a town near Florence. But the family preferred a more colorful, although surely mythical, ancestral story that recounted how in the fifth century a knight came to Mugello and saved the townspeople from a terrifying giant that had tormented the region. Eight dents made by the giant on the knight's shield were filled with eight red balls that became symbolic of the Medici family and their family crest. When Cosimo was born in 1389, the Medici family had already acquired much wealth and assets due to their banking activities, especially with the papacy of Pope John XXIII (not to be confused with the "antipope" of the same name), whose real name was Baldassare Cossa. This pope, however, was eventually accused in 1414 of several crimes, including heresy, simony, and murdering his predecessor, Pope Alexander V. It was also rumored that Cossa had seduced dozens of women in Bologna.

The Florentine historian Francesco Guicciardini went even further by saying that Cosimo "had a reputation such as probably no private citizen has ever enjoyed from the fall of Rome to our own day."[3] After Cosimo died on August 1, 1464, Pope Pius II said of him, "His life was full of honor. His honor extended beyond his own city to Italy, indeed to the whole world." The pope died two weeks later, on August 14.

About two decades before the discovery of the Hermetica, Cosimo de Medici had initiated an amazingly bold and inspiring strategy that would launch Italy and the rest of Europe into a new and more liberal form of scholarship. For many centuries the Roman papacy representing Catholicism had been in open conflict with the Eastern Orthodox Church headed by the patriarch in Constantinople. Now at that time the city of Constantinople was the last bastion of Christendom in the East, while the rest had fallen into Muslim hands. It was a matter of time before Constantinople also would face the onslaught on Islam. In the famous words of the Muslim Ottoman Sultan Mehetmet II, Constantinople was "a monstrous head without a body." Sensing the inevitable, in 1438 the Eastern Christian emperor in Constantinople, John VIII Paleologus, appealed to Rome for military aid to protect the city against the Muslims. In response, the pope in Rome, Eugenius IV, called for a great ecumenical council to take place in Italy. Cosimo de Medici grabbed the opportunity and offered to finance the whole event but only if it would take place in Florence. Cosimo wisely threw in a large loan for the Vatican, and in this way managed to clinch the deal.

On a very windy and stormy evening in January 1439 the Eastern emperor and the patriarch of Constantinople rode alongside the pope of Rome, and together they entered the city of Florence in extravagant pomp and amid huge celebrations. Although the coming together of the Eastern and Western Churches did not last for long, there was an indirect benefit that delighted Cosimo de Medici. He convinced a group of Byzantine scholars to stay behind, including the great scholars Bessarion and Gemistos Plethon, two leading authorities on the works of Plato. These scholars were the inspiration to Cosimo, who had long dreamed of establishing in Florence an "academy" modeled on the ancient Athenian academy of Plato, which the Catholic Emperor Justinian I had closed in 529 CE.* It took many years to materialize, but eventually the Florentine Academy, also known as the Medici Academy, was founded in 1462.† The first director appointed by Cosimo was his favorite protégé, the brilliant Marsilio Ficino.

---

*The academy that was closed in 529 CE actually was the neo-Platonic academy in Athens begun by Plutarch of Athens, although this is not certain.

†In 1462 Cosimo de Medici donated a villa, near his own in Careggi, to Marsilio Ficino, so that the young scholar could work from there on the translation of ancient texts and also receive potential members into the "academy" set up in the villa. This can be taken as the date of the founding of what became known as the Florentine Academy.

Ficino had been especially groomed for just such a post by Cosimo de Medici, who treated the young scholar as his own son. Ficino repaid the affection by calling his mentor and protector "my soul father." By making Ficino director of the new academy Cosimo gave the young man a huge boost, which brought him the respect, and envy, of the scholarly elite in Florence. Ficino had only recently become the personal researcher and translator of ancient Greek books for the aging Cosimo, now in his seventieth year and in poor health. Cosimo was eager to read the works of Plato in Latin or Italian before his death, and had thus ordered Ficino to start the translations forthwith. He was in the midst of this task when the Tuscan monk Leonardo de Pistoia delivered the Hermetica to Cosimo de Medici. Stunned by what he realized he might be holding in his hands, Cosimo immediately sent for Ficino to give him new instructions . . .

A BRILLIANT ACADEMIC OF THE CHARMING-UGLY VARIETY

Marsilio Ficino was born in 1433 in a small village outside Florence. His father, Dietifeci, was a physician who became the personal doctor to Cosimo de Medici, a very lucrative position in those days. Although Ficino had been earmarked to follow the medical career of his father, nonetheless two of his personal tutors—Comando Comandi and Luca di San Gimignano—introduced Ficino to Latin grammar and Greek.[4] As trivia, but perhaps a point that might explain his character, there was something special regarding Ficino's appearance and general behavior.

[Ficino] belonged to the charming-ugly variety of male scholars: slight, somewhat hunchbacked, a lanky, curly blond with a lisp and stammer. He was unworthy though not ascetic, sexless, given to melancholy fits and, like many children of doctors, a valetudinarian. Yet [had] . . . great personal attractions. He possessed no doubt that vulnerable charm that stammerers often have. He was modest, gentle, delicate in his tastes, fond of ironic jest, a good companion when the lighter mood was on him . . . he had the ability to shape his own mind without yielding to pressure for conformity, as well as a strong need to impress his own attitudes on others.[5]

Ficino was by no means a guilt-ridden Christian scholar so typical of his times, even though he was deeply religious.* For example, he believed himself to have prophetic powers, which he claimed to have inherited from his mother. Ficino also claimed to have prophetic dreams and was convinced that he had the "gift of interpretation."[6]

After his mentor, Cosimo de Medici, died in 1464, Ficino maintained that he was regularly visited by Cosimo's spirit, who advised him on scholarly matters. Bright, especially gifted for languages, and an avid reader of philosophy and history, from his early twenties and indeed throughout his life Ficino composed long, philosophical, almost romantic letters to friends and colleagues, which clearly showed his ardent love of philosophy, specifically that of Plato.† All in all, this combination of scholarly aptitude and mystical disposition made of Ficino a rather unusual genius who is regarded today as one of the most influential philosophers of the Renaissance and the reviver of neo-Platonism and Hermetism.‡

Ficino saw two kinds of philosophical discourse: one that he approved and dearly loved was the philosophy of Plato, which he deemed "liberal and pleasant, intricate to a degree with hidden art and worthy of a learned and noble man"; and the other type of philosophy was that of Aristotle, which he deemed "dry, terse, garrulous, thick with thorns and cautious reservation about minutiae."[7] Ficino's love and admiration for the "divine" Plato was such that his colleagues and friends would often refer to him as the "Second Plato." It is quite likely that Ficino saw himself as a member of a long line of great sages or philosophers such as Plato

---

*Ficino was ordained as a deacon in September 1473 in Florence by Monsignor Giuliano de Antonio on behalf of Cardinal Pietro Riario, apparently after he had suffered one of his typical "Saturnine" depressions.

†It was apparently Ficino who coined the term "Platonic love," that is, the chaste romantic love for another person of either sex.

‡Ficino was the first translator of the works of Plato from Greek into Latin.

who had contributed in revealing or interpreting the "true philosophy," the prisca theologia, that he, Ficino, believed lead to "divine truth and to God." For Ficino, like many Renaissance scholars, the supreme and wisest of all these ancient sages, the one whose writings had the highest knowledge and magic to reveal, was the Egyptian Hermes Trismegistus.

Although it is true to say that before the discovery of the Hermetica by Father Leonardo da Pistoia in 1462 no one in Florence or elsewhere in Europe had read the complete Hermetica, Ficino had learned of Hermes Trismegistus from the many commentaries made on him and his books in the literature of ancient chroniclers, particularly of the church fathers Clement of Alexandria, St. Augustine, and, more especially, Lucius Lactantius (240–320 CE), who had been the personal advisor to Constantine the Great. There was, too, a tract known as the *Asclepius,* also attributed to Hermes Trismegistus, which had survived in Latin, and with which many Renaissance scholars, including Ficino, were very familiar. On the whole, Hermes Trismegistus was regarded as one of the most important, if not *the* most important, and most ancient of the "gentile prophets" of Christianity. As one of Ficino's most recent biographers, Angela Voss, explained:

> Hermes was already known to Renaissance scholars through the Latin *Asclepius** and the Church Fathers Lactantius and Augustine by the former favorably as a prophet of Christian truth, by the latter unfavorably as a magician. Hermes, who was supposed to have lived a few generations after Moses, was considered by Ficino . . . to be the fount of the *prisca theologia,* the initiator of an esoteric religion.[8]

The Renaissance scholars had not only heard of this all-wise Hermes Trismegistus from the church fathers and had gotten to know of his philosophy and magic from the *Asclepius,* but they had also read the classics and had learned that the great Greek philosophers such as

---

*The Latin translation of the *Asclepius* was in circulation since the third century and is now considered an integral part of the Hermetica.

Solon, Pythagoras, and Plato had gone to Heliopolis in Egypt to learn the philosophies and the sciences of the Egyptians from their priests and sages. The great Plato had called the Egyptians a "race of philosophers" and had recounted in his *Timaeus* how Solon, even though highly esteemed by the Egyptian priests, was nonetheless interrupted by an older Egyptian priest, who put him straight with these words:

> O Solon, Solon, you Greeks are all like children, and there is no such thing as an old [wise] Greek. . . . You are all young in mind . . . you have no belief rooted in ancient tradition and no knowledge hoary with age.[9]

Let us note in passing, too, that it was the priests of Sais who narrated to Solon the story of the destruction of the fabled Atlantis and how all civilization had been wiped out except Egypt. It was thus only in Egypt that the prediluvian records had survived because they had been inscribed on the temple walls and obelisk walls, and were now in the keep of Egyptian priests. Many other classical authors—Herodotus, Plutarch, Diodorus, and Proclus, to name but a few—had come to Egypt to marvel at the great wisdom, magic, and knowledge of the Egyptian priests, especially their high understanding of the heavens and the cycles of the sun and stars. To them Egypt was the true and original repository of magic and sacred science, and where the secrets of immortality were known. And all this arcane wisdom and knowledge had been revealed to Thoth, the archetype or predecessor of Hermes Trismegistus. There was encrusted in the minds of Greek philosophers and also church fathers such as Lactantius that in some very remote past this perennial wisdom, magical religion—and what later the Renaissance philosophers called the *prisca theologia*—had been written down and inscribed by Thoth himself in the magical hieroglyphic signs, the "language of the gods." But with the passing of time and, especially, with the protracted occupation of Egypt by foreigners, the ability to read the sacred writings was lost. We recall from chapter 1 the poignant words of Hermes

Trismegistus to his pupil Asclepius in *The Lament,* which are perhaps worth quoting again here.

> When foreigners occupy the land and territory, not only reverence will fall into neglect but, even harder, a prohibition under penalty prescribed by law—so-called—will be enacted against reverence, fidelity, and divine worship. Then this most holy land, seat of shrines and temples, will be filled completely with tombs and corpses. O Egypt, Egypt, of your reverent deeds only stories will survive, and they will be incredible to your children! Only words cut in stone will survive to tell your faithful works.

But we recall, too, how in the *Kore Kosmou* Isis tells her son, Horus, that Hermes Trismegistus had hidden the sacred writings of Thoth, *"intending that they should be searched for by future generations, but found only by the fully worthy"* (italics added).

Starting with the fall of Alexandria in the first century BCE and up to the opening of the Italian Renaissance in the early fifteenth century, there was a general belief among philosophers that the books of Thoth had survived in Greek translation made by his "grandson" Hermes Trismegistus. Great hopes were pinned on the possibility of finding a copy someday. The Hermetica became the holy grail of the literary world. So when Cosimo de Medici announced to the scholars of Florence that he had miraculously come into possession of an (almost) complete copy, it was the same as announcing that NASA had found an inhabited planet in our solar system! Frances A. Yates shared her own perception of the importance and sense of excitement this find had for the Renaissance philosophers.

> From early Christian writers, more about Hermes Trismegistus could be learned, particularly from Clement of Alexandria, who, in his striking description of the procession of the Egyptian priests, says that the singer at the head of the procession carried two books

of music and hymns by Hermes; the *horoscopus* [astrologer] carried four books by Hermes on the stars. In the course of this description Clement states that there are forty-two books by Hermes Trismegistus, thirty-six of which contained the whole of the philosophy of the Egyptians, the other six being on medicine. It is very improbable that Clement knew any of the Hermetica, which have come down to us, *but the Renaissance reader believed that he had in the Corpus Hermeticum and the* Asclepius *precious survivors of that great sacred library of which Clement speaks.*[10] (italics added)

Many of these scholars, including Ficino—indeed, especially Ficino!—believed that the divine Plato himself had been tutored from the books of Hermes Trismegistus. We can understand why Cosimo, now in possession of the Hermetica in Greek, immediately instructed Ficino to put aside the works of Plato and get cracking instead on translating the Hermetica. Frances A. Yates again sets us in the scene.

It is an extraordinary situation. There are the complete works of Plato, waiting, and they must wait whilst Ficino quickly translates Hermes, probably because Cosimo wants to read them before he dies. *What a testimony this is to the mysterious reputation of the Thrice Great One.*[11] (italics added)

It took about a year for Ficino to get a translation of the fourteen books of the Hermetica into Latin. Cosimo was now on his deathbed with Ficino constantly by his side, as well as his fifteen-year-old grandson, Lorenzo—the future Lorenzo the Magnificent, the great patron of Leonardo da Vinci, Verrocchio, Michelangelo, and Botticelli. The dying Cosimo asked Ficino to read to him from Plato and, we can now also safely add, from the Hermetica. The title that Ficino gave to his Latin translation was *Mercurii Trismegisti Liber De Potestate Et Sapientia Dei* [Hermes (Mercury) Trismegistus, the Book of the Power and Wisdom of God], but it was better known as *Pimander* for short—a name only found in the beginning of the first book (*liber*) of the Hermetica, and one that symbolized the "universal mind." It was this universal mind that supposedly had revealed to Hermes Trismegistus the truth of creation and the role of man and, more importantly, the wisdom or gnosis by which knowledge of God and the immortality of the soul could be attained.*

In Ficino's preface to the *Pimander* the great reverence that Ficino had for Hermes Trismegistus can clearly be discerned.

> At the time when Moses was born flourished Atlas the Astrologer, brother of the natural philosopher Prometheus and maternal grandfather of the elder Mercurius (Thoth-Hermes), whose grandson was Mercurius (Hermes) Trismegistus. . . . They called him Trismegistus or Thrice-Greatest because he was the greatest philosopher and the greatest priest and the greatest king . . . just as he outdid all philosophers in learning and keenness of mind, so he also surpassed every priest . . . in sanctity of life and reverence for the divine . . . thus he was called the first author of theology.[12]

But how did a devout Roman Catholic such as Ficino reconcile his unshakable faith in Christianity and the "truth" of the Holy Scriptures when he also openly expressed his veneration of an Egyptian sage and called him the "first author of theology"?† The answer to this apparent paradox lies in the following claim, also made by Ficino in his preface to the *Pimander.*

> Mercurius [Hermes Trismegistus] wrote many books pertaining to the knowledge of divinity . . . speaking not only as philosopher but

---

*It has been suggested that the name Pimander, which is derived from the original Greek *poimadres,* is a Grecian distortion of the ancient Egyptian word *Peime-n-Re,* meaning the "knowledge of Re," who was the supreme Egyptian sun god.

†Here Ficino is obviously basing himself on the authority of the church father Lactantius, "who honored Hermes for pagan prophecies that supported Christian revelations."

also as prophet . . . the ruins of the old religion, the rise of the new faith [Christianity], the coming of Christ.[13]

Ficino thus made Hermes Trismegistus acceptable by saying that, like Moses, he was a prophet who foretold the coming of Christianity. Better still, unlike Moses, Hermes Trismegistus was a gentile. I have often wondered at this simplistic explanation given by Ficino, and later embraced by other Renaissance philosophers, to justify their admiration and reverence for the Hermetica. It may also be that the Hermetica extolled the virtues of freethinking and the quest for divine knowledge. Indeed, the Hermetica proclaimed that man can get to understand God and also achieve divinity. This was something that Renaissance philosophers desperately wanted the church to also proclaim, instead of oppressive and repressive doctrines and dogmas. The idea inevitably came to the Renaissance philosophers that if the Hermetica could somehow be made part of the teaching of the church or, as some even dared to hope, if they could have it canonized and placed alongside the Gospels, then the quest for knowledge, divine or secular, could be liberated for the betterment of humankind.

At any rate, whatever the deeper motives of Ficino and his patron, Cosimo de Medici, soon handwritten copies of the Latin Hermetica began to circulate among the learned of Florence and slowly in other parts of Italy and Europe. The first printed edition of the Hermetica appeared in 1471, seven years after Cosimo's death, and became a huge bestseller. Soon several other editions followed. It is a testimony to the effort and quality of Ficino's work, as well as the interest in Hermes Trismegistus, that no fewer than fifty separate editions of the Hermetica were in circulation by the mid-1500s. Hermes Trismegistus, to employ a cliché, was definitely the talk of Florence and even beyond. Inevitably, the ancient Egyptian sage would also soon be—as such things always were in those dangerous times—the talk of the Vatican.

Serious trouble was about to start . . .

3

THE HERMETIC MOVEMENT, PART II

I hope to show that both Bruno's proposed moral reform and his philosophy are related to his Hermetic religious mission—a mission which Ficino's magic becomes expanded into a projected full restoration of the magical religion of the pseudo-Egyptians of the Asclepius.

FRANCES A. YATES,
GIORDANO BRUNO AND THE HERMETIC TRADITION

For even if the Corpus Hermeticum was written down very late, its concepts could easily be very old and Egyptian. And in fact the basic principles of emanations, of the world as an overflow from God, and of man as a ray of sunlight . . . are typically ancient Egyptian.

GILLES QUISPEL,
INTRODUCTION TO THE WAY OF HERMES: THE CORPUS HERMETICUM

COSMIC AMBIENCE

Sometimes there is but one way to explain something, and that is to have the courage to lay bare your soul to others. I need to do this now to be able to explain what talismanic magic is and how it works.

Let me begin by saying that whenever I am in Egypt I always feel that I am touched by an unseen and immeasurable emanation, something magical in the air, a sort of divine flux or cosmic ambience that envelops me and then prompts me to seek another truth about my existence. In this ancient land where a perennial magical religion left its fingerprints on monumental pyramids and temples, it was perhaps inevitable that I would become receptive to such otherworldly perceptions. Yet it was not always so. Having been trained as an engineer to think and reason in a tangible and practical manner, I felt uncomfortable every time such ephemeral perceptions took hold of me. Gradually this uncomfortable feeling became an inner conflict that pulled me to and fro, from the metaphysical to the physical. This conflict intensified when I published my first book, *The Orion Mystery,* in 1994. For several years I experienced a tug-of-war between two opposing mental forces, two ways that the human mind deals with existence: the empirical and the intuitive. It was, for lack of better words, slowly tearing me apart. Such a conflict was bound to take its toll, and ten years later, when I was writing my eighth book, my mind, thoughts, and emotions froze. I felt a strong sense of defeat, of being beaten at my own game. Yet precisely what that game was, I could not tell. For several months I found myself battling an unknown and unseen demon, and I nearly lost. I was living at that time in an apartment on the fourth floor of a small building directly opposite the Great Pyramid. This ancient monument that I once so much loved now overwhelmed and terrified me until I could no longer look at it. It was as if the pyramid had sucked out my soul, leaving me like an empty shell. Finally one morning, after a turbulent, sleepless night, I found myself uttering two words: "I surrender." I got up and walked out on the balcony, exhausted but elated by something familiar stirring in me—my soul. It had come back to me or, perhaps aptly, was waking up from a very deep and deathlike sleep. I looked intensely at the pyramid. It was lit up with the pink light of sunrise. A feeling of peace and kindness was all around me. I felt a love I had never felt before: love for myself. I filled my lungs with the pure air coming from the desert beyond. The inner conflict that had torn me apart and that had nearly destroyed me was over. I was now ready to understand what talismanic magic is.

EPIPHANY

It all happened a few months later, not in Egypt as I would have once expected it, but rather in a small town in the Abruzzi region of Italy. Circumstances had brought me to spend the night in Campotosto, a quiet little hamlet that was a minor holiday resort for the elderly. The small family-run hotel where I stayed overlooked a small artificial lake set in a tree-barren valley. It happened that I was the only guest in the hotel. I had dinner early and went up to my unnecessarily large room. Tired from the long hours of driving, I quickly fell asleep. When I woke up, it was still dark outside. Desperate for a cup of hot coffee, I went down to the reception area. No one was there. The whole household was fast asleep. The silence was deafening.

I decided to go out for a walk along the lakeside. Dawn was slowly breaking as I entered a little wooded area near the shore of the lake. It suddenly got dark again. As I emerged on the other side of the *bosco* and into the predawn light there, a few feet from me and to my great surprise and horror, a wild boar was grazing. Jolted by this unexpected encounter the boar, a fully grown male with large tusks, handed me a most ferocious stare. He snorted and pounded the ground with his fore-leg, readying himself to charge. For a moment that seemed a lifetime I stood there, motionless, and all I could do was to gaze intensely into the eyes of the wild creature. And, I know not how, but I am certain that I spoke to it, not in words or with sounds, but in a silent language, the language of nature. I was "telling" the angry animal that I meant him no harm. The boar suddenly relaxed his tense demeanor, his gaze softened, and, to my great relief, he wagged his little tail and trotted away. Bemused, I just stood there and smiled.

At that precise moment I became acutely aware of all things and sounds that surrounded me, the trees rustling in the gentle, early morning breeze, the birds chirping, the frogs croaking in the shallows, the wildflowers shedding their dew, and the tiny summer flies swirling in clouds like desert *djins* in the soft light of the morning. Then a flash of golden sunlight momentarily blinded me. I looked at the orb of the sun rising from behind a low mountain range. For a few seconds—or perhaps it was minutes, I cannot recall—I stood there, motionless, frozen in a time warp, sensing an epiphany coming strongly onto me. For the first time in my life I felt totally connected, umbilically linked to nature, to the world, to the universe. I was no longer the *observer* but an integral, active part of it all. I felt as if I had suddenly been plugged into the network of the cosmos. I did not quite know what this feeling was, let alone give it a name. But now, after so many years of researching and questing, I know that I had experienced "natural magic" or, as I will henceforth call it, *talismanic magic*. I also know that it was this same magic that I sensed when I looked at the Great Pyramid and the sky above it. At last I fathomed what had so long escaped my understanding, the link between the macrocosm out there and the microcosm in me, that great Hermetic axiom: *As above, so below.*

TALISMANIC MAGIC

When Marsilio Ficino published the Latin translation of the Hermetica, he did not include another Hermetic tract known as *Logos Teleios* [The Perfect Discourse], better known as the *Asclepius*. The reason was that the *Asclepius,* even though regarded as an integral part of the Hermetica, had already been translated into Latin, probably in late antiquity, and had been widely circulated in Italy and Europe since it was printed in

1469, two years before the publication of Ficino's *Pimander*. Ficino saw no good reason to attach it to the *Pimander*. Nevertheless, it soon became customary to attach the *Asclepius* to the main body of the Hermetica.

Ficino, of course, was fully conversant with the *Asclepius*. But not just that: he was totally besotted by the magic that he saw in it. It is well beyond the scope of this present book to discuss in detail how Ficino applied such magic.[1] But let me say that what is often called the "natural magic" of Ficino is, in my own understanding of it, *talismanic magic*. Frances A. Yates also gave it another name, which, I think, is also quite appropriate.

> The type of magic [Ficino's] with which we are to be concerned differs profoundly from astrology, which is not necessarily magic at all but a mathematical science based on the belief that human destiny is irrevocably governed by the stars, and that, therefore, from the study of a person's horoscope, the position of the stars at the time of his birth, one can foretell his irrevocably foreordained future. This magic [in the *Asclepius*] is astrological only in the sense that it, too, bases itself upon the stars, their images, and their influences, but it is a way of escaping from astrological determinism by gaining power over the stars, guiding their influences in the direction the operator desires. Or, in the religious sense, it is a way of salvation, of escaping from material fortune and destiny, or obtaining insight into the divine. Hence "astrological magic" is not a correct description of it, and hereafter, for want of better term, I shall call it "astral magic."[2]

The "astral magic" or "talismanic magic" required a trained operator or magician who knew the special invocations, music, herbs, incense, stones, potions, objects, lighting, and places—a sort of complex ergonomics, homeopathy, ritual, feng shui, art, music therapy, and special architectural environment all rolled into one. A good singular term for this would be, in my opinion, *cosmic ambiance,* that is, the ideal conditions set up in order to attract and house the beneficial influ-ence of the heavenly bodies—the sun, moon, stars, and planets. One of Ficino's many ardent adepts, his mentor and friend, Lorenzo de Medici, simply saw Ficino's magic as "natural magic, which, by natural things, seeks to obtain the services of the heavens for the prosperous health of our bodies."[3] As Yates further explained:

> The material of lower things being intimately related to the *spiri-tus* material in the stars . . . [Astral] Magic consists of guiding or controlling the influx of *spiritus* into material [i.e., the "spirit" of a star into the material of an object], and one of the most important ways of doing this is through talismans, for a talisman is a mate-rial object into which the spiritus of a star has been introduced and which stores the *spiritus*.[4]

"It was a 'mild form' of this astral or talismanic magic," says Frances A. Yates, "which Ficino cleverly sanitized by calling it a 'natural magic.' This was because he feared that his 'deep interest in the Egyptian magical religion' could be construed as 'heretical' by the Inquisition."[5] Calling this form of magic "natural magic," Ficino thus made it acceptable for Christian usage and somewhat shielded himself from unwelcome accusations of paganism or heresy. As an example:

> [Ficino] thinks that the use of the cross [the Egyptian ankh symbol or *crux ansata*] was not so much on account of its power in attract-ing the gifts of the stars, but as a prophecy of the coming of Christ, made by them [the Egyptians] unknowingly. Thus the sanctity of the Egyptians as prophets of Christianity through the use of the cross as a talisman comes in an appropriate introduction to the list of talismanic images.[6]

A TALISMANIC IMAGE OF THE UNIVERSE

In a book that Ficino published in 1486, *De vita coelitus comparanda,* he lists various images, mainly of planets and astrological signs, as legitimate talismans that can be used in a religious Christian context.

Ficino's book *De vita coelitus comparanda* is, in fact, the third in a three-volume opus titled *Libri de Vita* [Books of Life] that is a treatise on medicine typical of his epoch, when it was believed that astrological signs ruled different parts of the human body and that the temperament and mood of a person were related to different planets, such as "mercurial," "saturnine," and so forth. Although, like his father before him, Ficino practiced medicine, this can hardly have been regarded as a "science" as such but rather as a form of natural magic. Indeed, Ficino was later, in 1489, accused of heresy by the Roman Curia because they saw what he had written in *Libri de Vita* as magic and thus unacceptable by the church. Ficino subsequently wrote an *apologia* explaining that it was natural magic and thus acceptable.

"In short," writes Yates, "by devious means, Ficino has extracted his use of talismans from blame."[7] It is in *De vita coelitus comparanda* that Ficino advances an extraordinary idea to actually make a talisman of the "universe."

> Why, then, should we not permit ourselves a universal image, that is an image of the universe itself? From which it might be hoped to obtain great benefits from the universe itself.[8]

Ficino here is offering to make a sort of model of the universe as a talisman to obtain great benefits from the universe itself. We must bear in mind, of course, that Ficino is writing in the late fifteenth century, half a century or so *before* the Polish astronomer Nicholas Copernicus published the heliocentric theory in *De Revolutionibus orbium caelestium* [Revolution of the Celestial Bodies], in which he revealed the new "image" of the visible universe, that is, a sun-centered universe with the Earth and other planets orbiting the solar orb. But Ficino was a humanist and priest, not a scientist or astronomer. His perception of an image of the universe, or *mundi figura* as he called it in Latin, was highly symbolic and allegoric. It also involved alchemical ideas such as planetary metals, celestial colors, and suchlike notions. Even poor Frances A. Yates was at a loss to comprehend Ficino's image of the universe, and refreshingly admits:

> There is a good deal that I have not been able to understand in this description. The figure seems to refer to a New Year as a new birthday of the world, or even the first birthday of the world, *the creation.* . . . The object described, or hinted at (for the description is very vague) would seem to be *a model of the heavens constructed so as to concentrate or drawing down the fortunate influences of Sol* [the Sun].[9] (italics added)

The prevalent scientific image of the universe in the late fifteenth century would have been the Ptolemaic vision, what today we call the geocentric model, namely the belief that the Earth, not the sun, is at the center of the visible universe, with all the other celestial bodies orbiting around it. To represent in diagram the geocentric model, that is, to make a drawing or *talisman* out of it, one would have to draw a series of concentric circles representing the various celestial bodies, whose common focus would be the Earth. Although Ficino's own vision is intensely symbolic and intended to be a talisman, there can be but little doubt that when he was thinking of an "image of the universe," he was thinking of the passage in the *Asclepius* where Hermes Trismegistus reveals with a rhetorical question to his pupil Asclepius that Egypt and its temples are a talisman made "in the image of heaven": "Did you not know, Asclepius, that Egypt is made in the image of Heaven?" The word *heaven* is given as *caelo* in the Latin text, but would surely have been *cosmos* (universe) in the original Greek text, which Ficino would have surely known.*

Ficino and his contemporaries, of course, were not to know of Copernicus's heliocentric theory, for this would not be made public for another fifty years. We, today, also know that even the Copernican circular orbit model would be replaced by Johannes Kepler's elliptical model or, as it is technically known, Kepler's first law of planetary motion. We shall return to this idea of making a talisman in the image of the universe using these scientific models when we discuss other Hermetists and Renaissance philosophers living at a time when heliocentrism was common knowledge.

Meanwhile so very popular was Ficino's Latin translation of the Hermetica that it was "hungrily read and studied throughout the sixteenth century by Renaissance scholars and magicians."[10] In this highly animated revival, or Renaissance, of Hermetism and magic of the late fifteenth century in Italy, with all the talk of rediscovery of ancient philosophies, of the prisca theologia and "natural magic," it was but a matter of time before some more enthusiastic and forceful philosophers would take Ficino's ideas a few levels higher and, in doing so, not unexpectedly force the Vatican into debating the issue, with dramatic consequences.

MESSIANIC HERMETIC MISSIONS

The great Swiss psychiatrist Carl Jung has shown that we all respond to archetypes, either by design or unconsciously. Our very nature as well as our cultural upbringing induces us into various forms of role-playing. Our natural roles can be one or more, such as daughter, sister, mother,

---

*What Ficino could not have known, but perhaps intuited, was that the ancient Egyptians did, in fact, make various "images of heaven," namely, the "heaven," or "duat of Osiris," in the constellation of Orion, by having the layout of the Giza Pyramids set like the pattern of the belt of Orion. See my book *The Orion Mystery.*

son, brother, father, and so on. But some of us take on more dramatic cultural roles—hero, loser, winner, leader, seducer, priest, nun, healer, and so on—that often are modeled not just on well-known historical characters but also on legendary or mythological ones. The archetype adopted may be so strong that it leads the role-player to think or even be convinced that he or she is the *reincarnation* of the archetypal original. The Dalai Lama and the pope are good examples of this. In my line of business I have been told by seemingly very balanced and highly educated individuals that they think they are the reincarnation of this or that Egyptian god or goddess, or pharaoh, or queen.

There is an ultimate archetype or role, however, one that has been successfully claimed only once in Western history (even though others tried in vain to appropriate it): this is the role of the Messiah. In Christianity this role, of course, is firmly pegged on a Jewish carpenter from Nazareth in Judea called Jesus.*

Indeed, so solidly established was—and still is—Jesus's tenure of this archetypal role that anyone even hinting at being a "new Messiah" would face derision and, worse, accusations of profanity. In the fifteenth century such a pretender would either have been deemed mad or quickly incarcerated by the Inquisition on charges of blasphemy and probably burned alive in a public square. We want here to drive home the point of how incredibly dangerous it would have been for anyone in Renaissance Italy to make such a claim, let alone make this claim in Rome outside the Vatican. Yet this is precisely what one such Italian philosopher did after reading the Hermetic writings! This extraordinary event concerns the very eccentric but also highly educated gentleman from Bologna, signore Giovanni di Correggio, also known as "Mercurio." The incredible bravado—some may say suicidal behavior—of signore Giovanni is worth recounting, for it exemplifies the tremendous impact that the Hermetica had on some individuals and, in an opposing manner, on the Vatican.

---

*Actually in Roman Catholicism and the Orthodox Church, the role of "Mother of God," passed on to the biological Jewish mother of Jesus, Miriam, is far more popular.

In 1471, the same year Ficino's Latin Hermetica appeared in print, on a cold day in November in Rome, Giovanni da Correggio, a.k.a. "Mercurio" (the name Italians gave to Hermes Trismegistus), suddenly appeared in the streets of the Eternal City and went about loudly preaching apocalyptic sermons. Modern scholars on the whole have not paid much attention to this oddball and his strange ranting, but it is clear that this "reincarnated" Hermes-Mercurius not only caused somewhat of a rumpus at the Vatican but even gained the protection of a few powerful monarchs, notably King Ferdinand I of Naples and the French King Louis XII. Several historians, including Frances A. Yates at the Warburg Institute, Professor Jean-Pierre Mahé at the Sorbonne in Paris, and Professor Wouter Hanegraaff at the University of Amsterdam, gave vivid narratives of some of the activity of this rather exotic philosopher, Mercurio of Bologna.[11] Hanegraaff, for example, went as far as saying that Giovanni, a.k.a. "Mercurio," was "one of the most enigmatic figures that one might have encountered in Italy in the second half of the fifteenth century."[12]

In November 1481 the humanist and astrologer Ludovico Lazzarelli met "Mercurio" by chance when the latter was again preaching in the streets of Rome. So impressed was Lazzarelli by what he heard that he decided there and then to become Mercurio's pupil and disciple. It was after this encounter that Lazzarelli and his master Mercurio found more of the lost writings of Hermes Trismegistus, known as the *Definitions of Asclepius*. Here is Lazzarelli's own account of this astonishing discovery:

It was by chance, while scrutinizing relentlessly the old books of those who inspired me, and while over a cup full of the most suave nectar, which, I do not doubt, had flowed from the huge crater [bowl] of Hermes Trismegistus, by which I mean a small book in Greek having the title of the *Definitions of Asclepius*. As soon as I read it, its conciseness and the mysterious authenticity of its wisdom enchanted me and filled me with admiration.[13]

Among the many public appearances of Mercurio, the most bizarre was in Rome during the pontificate of Sixtus IV. On Palm Sunday of 1484, Mercurio, then thirty-three years old, entered Rome on a donkey guided by two servants and wearing a white, blood-stained linen mantle and a crown of thorns on his head,* clearly intended to evoke the entry of Jesus the Messiah in Jerusalem.[14] On Mercurio's chest was fixed a silver plaque in the form of a lunar crescent, on which were written these words:

> This is my son Pimander, whom I personally chose. From early childhood he has grown to sublime heights, and I have empowered him with all my compliance to cast away demons and to install my truth and my justice upon all nations. Be warned not to oppose him! Heed his words and obey him with fear and reverence. These are the words of the Lord of all the sanctuaries of the world, Jesus Christ.[15]

Incredibly, Mercurio was making his way via St. John's of the Lateran and the Campo dei Fiori to the Vatican. Soon a crowd began to gather behind Mercurio, and they enthusiastically followed him to the gates of St. Peter's. Mercurio then pulled out a wad of leaflets from his bag and threw them at the crowd, presumably saying the same thing as that written on the silver plaque on his chest. Some must have thought him insane, but most, oddly enough, were thrilled at this colorful and dramatic display of piety and promptly acclaimed him a prophet. The guards at the Vatican† were clearly baffled by this odd sight, and in their confusion stood aside and let Mercurio enter the basilica.

Mercurio managed to walk unopposed all the way to the altar, and there, facing a bewildered congregation, announced that he was the reincarnated Pimander, the entity that had imparted divine wisdom to Hermes Trismegistus. And when Mercurio returned to Bologna, he

---

*Other versions of this story have Mercurio riding a black stallion and wearing a black cloak, a golden belt, and purple shoes.

†They were not of the Swiss Guard, who only came a few years later, in 1506.

was hailed as a hero and a prophet. In 1486 Mercurio made another dramatic appearance in Florence, shouting again his bizarre apocalyptic sermons and making his outrageous claims about being Pimader. But Lorenzo de Medici, the ruler of Florence, was having none of this. He promptly ordered that Mercurio be arrested and thrown in jail. Lorenzo then handed Mercurio to the Inquisition, who immediately accused him of blasphemy. Luckily for him, King Ferdinand I of Naples, who had become Mercurio's sponsor, used his influence to obtain his release. Far from being discouraged by this incident, Mercurius again in 1492 preached in Rome, proclaiming that he was "the younger Hermes," that is, Hermes Trismegistus. Then sometime later, (1497–1499) he did the same in Venice and in Milan. In 1501 Mercurio traveled to Lyon in France and was received by King Louis XII, "whom he had managed to impress with his erudition as well as promises of revealing 'sensational alchemical and magical secrets.'"[16]

In 1506 Mercurio wrote a manuscript titled *de Quercu,* which also bore the subtitle *On the Oak of Pope Julius or on the Philosopher's Stone,* which he dedicated to Pope Julius II (1503–1513). The text is a long praise of the pontiff, whose real name was Giuliano della Rovere, literally "Giuliano of the Oak," hence the pun in the title. In his dedication Giovanni Mercurio wrote:

And what is even more, and much, much greater, the greatest of all things most great, that which vanquishes the triumph of all the grandeurs of this your most triumphal oak: on top of it, on the highest and most fruitful place of its loveliness . . . [sits] the truly mercurial, trismegistical, wise, amiable, and most happy Phoenix . . . the one that, crowned with the triple crown, burns itself in the city of Heliopolis [City of the Sun] in Egypt.[17]

The "Phoenix" is clearly an allegory for Hermes Trismegistus, for the expression "the truly mercurial, trismegistical, wise" is clearly a euphemism for "the truly wise Mercury Trismegistus," the phoenix that burns and is regenerated at Heliopolis. Yet the Phoenix is the "the one with the triple crown," that is, Pope Julius II, whose papal coat of arms contains an oak tree with a triple crown above it.*

The legend of the Egyptian phoenix flying to Heliopolis to begin a new astrological age is found in classical books such as Herodotus's *The Histories* (book II) and also in Tacitus's *Annals* (book VI. 28). The myth was well known to humanists of the Renaissance and, obviously, to Giovanni Mercurio. Incredibly, Mercurio is also telling Pope Julius II not only that he is the Egyptian phoenix but also that his teachings are "the triumph of all the grandeurs." We cannot know what Pope Julius II made of all this, but he surely must have been aware that only a few steps from the Vatican, inside the ruins of the ancient Circus Nero, stood a genuine Egyptian obelisk from Heliopolis, the only one still standing in Rome. Was Mercurio alluding to this obelisk when he spoke of the "triumphal oak" on whose top the Hermetic phoenix, that is, the symbol of the pope or of Christianity, should be placed? And did the pope understand this allegorical message? Probably yes, because Pope Julius II had in fact commissioned Michelangelo to paint the Sistine Chapel, and while the great artist was still at work, one of Julius's successors, Pope Paul III, asked him to bring the Heliopolitan obelisk of the Circus Nero to the Vatican so that it could be placed in front of the St. Peter's Basilica. Presumably Pope Paul III would also have then placed his own symbol on the apex of the obelisk. Michelangelo, however, declined, saying, "What if it should break?" The honor of bringing that obelisk to the Vatican, as we shall see later, would go to Domenico Fontana during the pontificate of Sixtus V in 1586, who, predictably, also had his own symbol, "three mounds surmounted by a cross," placed on its apex.

It is not known what end signore Mercurio met. By 1610 he and his wife and their five children were living in total poverty. Yet it

---

*The triple crown was actually worn by all popes until 1963, after which it was abolished. Its origin is in the Phrygian hat worn by the solar god Mithras. The triple crown is still used by popes on their heraldic insignia and also on the flag of the Vatican State (see postscript).

would not be the last time we would see such eccentric behavior from a Renaissance Hermetist, and it would not be the last nor, indeed, the only time that a pope would be implored to adopt the role of Hermes Trismegistus or some other Hermetic character to bring about a reformation of the Vatican . . .

HERMES TRISMEGISTUS IS SLIPPED INTO THE VATICAN

It should be clear by now that for the Renaissance philosophers, Hermes Trismegistus was a real historical person who had lived in ancient Egypt and had been the author of the Hermetica. This was especially the view held by Marsilio Ficino. However, like Ficino, most also wisely claimed that the Egyptian sage came *after* Moses—or at least *not before* Moses—and that like Moses, was also a prophet of Christianity. This was no doubt a ploy by some to avoid antagonizing the Vatican any more than was necessary. The Renaissance philosophers based their chronology on the huge authority of St. Augustine (354–430 CE), one of the most popular of the church fathers, who had written that Hermes Trismegistus "came after Abraham, Isaac, Jacob, Joseph, and even Moses. Because Moses was born in the time of Atlas, brother of Prometheus [who] was the grandfather of the older Hermes, himself the grandfather of Hermes Trismegistus."[18]

The Renaissance philosophers also felt covered on this matter by the church itself, for in the great Cathedral of Siena, which is dated to the late fifteenth century, there is encrusted on marble flooring a scene showing Hermes Trismegistus handing—or receiving—a book on which is written "*Suscipite O Licteras Et Lege Egiptii*" (Take up thy letters and laws O Egyptians) and a plaque under the figures that states, "*Hermes Mercurius contemporaneus Moyse*" (Hermes Trismegistus contemporary to Moses).

Still, saying that Hermes Trismegistus was a contemporary of Moses was one thing, but no one dared to suggest, of course, that Hermes

Fig. 3.1. Hermes Trismegistus probably handing the "law" to Moses. The inscription below Hermes reads "Hermes Trismegistus contemporary to Moses." (Robert Bauval)

Trismegistus had lived *before* Moses, as this would give the Egyptian sage precedence, and thus authority, over Moses and the Scriptures, which was something that the church could not readily accept. Yet in spite of this cautionary advice, some Hermetists pushed their luck to the limit. Ludovico Lazzarelli, and probably also his master Mercurio, openly argued:

> It was not at the times of Moses that Trismegistus had lived, but long before, as one can easily ascertain from the works of Diodorus Siculus. The latter reported, in his chronology of the kings of Egypt, it was first gods that ruled then human beings. Hence it is evident that Mercurius (Hermes) Trismegistus lived in the times of the gods

... whereas Moses lived at an epoch where the Bible and many other ancient writings known in Egypt clearly state when ruled pharaohs.[19]

The controversy about whether Hermes Trismegistus had lived before or after Moses enhanced the already spectacular popularity that the Hermetica had attained by the early sixteenth century. Indeed, such was the fame of Hermes Trismegistus in Italy, France, Germany, Holland, and England that Frances A. Yates, in reference to the depiction in the Cathedral of Siena, felt it necessary to drive home this point:

> The representation of Hermes Trismegistus in this Christian edifice, so prominently displayed near its entrance and giving him so lofty a spiritual position, is not an isolated phenomenon but a symbol of how the Italian Renaissance regarded him and a prophecy of what was to be his extraordinary career throughout Europe in the sixteenth century and well on into the seventeenth century.[20]

The influence of the Hermetica in Europe was indeed immense and prolific. In 1554 the French scholar and humanist Turnebus published in Paris the first edition of the original Greek text of the Hermetica, accompanied by Ficino's translation in Latin. The theologian Petrus Paulus Vergerius wrote in the preface:

> Hermes Trismegistus was an Egyptian by race. . . . He flourished before the time of pharaoh. . . . Some, among whom is Cicero, suppose that he is the person whom the Egyptians called Thoth. . . . He must have lived, therefore, before pharaoh, and consequently, before Moses.[21]

In 1574 Francois Foix, the duke of Candalle as well as bishop of Aire but better known as Flussas, published a new edition of the Hermetica that he dedicated to the Holy Roman Emperor Maximilian II. In the dedication he informs the emperor that Hermes Trismegistus was privy to knowledge of "divine things," which he first wrote in Egyptian, then in Greek, and which surpassed the knowledge

> which was revealed to the Hebrew prophets, and equaling that of the Apostles and Evangelists. . . . What more is made known to us by those who were instructed by our Savior himself? And yet this man [Hermes Trismegistus] was anterior in time not only to the disciples of our Lord, but also to all the prophets and teachers of our law and, as the ancients say, to Moses himself.[22]

In 1591 the Italian scholar Francesco Patrizzi published an edition of the Hermetica in his work *Nova de Universis Philosophica.* In the preface he beseeches Pope Gregory XIV to give instruction that the Hermetica, among "five philosophies," which included *Aegiptiam aliam mysticam philosophia* [The Other Mystical Philosophy of the Egyptians], should actually be taught to everyone, even to the Jesuits, as a "conversion" tool for the papacy.

> I hope that you and your successors will adopt this new restored religious philosophy and cause it to be studied everywhere. . . . I would have you then, Holy Father, and all future popes, give orders that some of the books, which I have named, shall be continually taught everywhere as I have taught them in the last fourteen years at Ferrara. You will thus make all able men in Italy, Spain, and France friendly to the Church; and perhaps even the German Protestants will follow their example, and return to the Catholic faith. It is much easier to win them back in this way than to compel them by ecclesiastical censures or by secular arms. You should cause this doctrine to be taught in the schools of the Jesuits, who are doing such good work. If you do this, great glory will await you among men of future times. And I beg you to accept me as a helper in this undertaking.[23]

THE DIGNITY OF MAN

THE MANIFESTO OF THE RENAISSANCE

When Ficino was fifty-one and at the peak of his successful career, he was now ready to have printed his Latin translation of the complete works of Plato. It was then that a brilliant young Italian scholar entered Ficino's life and, in a stroke of genius, would take Ficino's natural magic, extracted from the Hermetica, and turn it into a new philosophy that would have huge implications on Christianity. His name was Pico della Mirandola. In the words of Frances A. Yates:

> Pico della Mirandola, a contemporary of Ficino, though younger, began his philosophical career under Ficino's influence and imbibed from Ficino his enthusiasm for *magia naturalis* which he accepted and recommended much more forcibly and openly than did Ficino.[24]

A synchronistic event created in Ficino the strong belief that his encounter with Pico was the result of some celestial providence.

First there was Pico's year of birth: he was born in 1463, the year that Ficino began translating the Hermetica. Then Ficino met Pico the

Fig. 3.2. Pico della Mirandola (Robert Bauval)

same day in October 1484 when Ficino's translation of the *Complete Works of Plato* went to print—a day chosen because of favorable astrological signs. Ficino and his wealthy sponsor Lorenzo de Medici took an instant liking to Pico and invited him to join the Florentine Academy. While a student at the University of Ferrara, Pico had developed a sort of compendium of various philosophies, including Platonism, neo-Platonism, Aristotelianism, Hermetism, Kabbalah, and Chaldeanism, commonly known as the *900 Theses,* which Pico intended to have published in Rome. He also hoped to debate these *900 Theses* in an "international congress" with scholars from all over Europe. So keen was Pico to have this debate that he offered to pay all expenses for the scholars and the cost of the congress. To this end, Pico also composed, as an introduction to his *900 Theses,* his famous *Oration on the Dignity of Man,* which he intended to read at the opening of the congress. The *Oration* begins with these very evocative words, which leave little doubt which philosophy Pico wanted to promote:

> Most esteemed Fathers, I have read in the ancient writings of the Arabians that Abdala the Saracen on being asked what, on this stage, so to say, of the world, seemed to him most evocative of wonder, replied that there was nothing to be seen more marvelous than man. And that celebrated exclamation of Hermes Trismegistus, *"What a great miracle is man, Asclepius!"* confirms this opinion.[25] (italics added)

Pico, who was planning his journey to Rome in 1485, was probably aware of the commotion that signore Mercurio had caused at the Vatican just the year before. But whether he knew of this or not, Pico's bold plan to go to Rome to debate his *900 Theses* with scholars who, in effect, would have been mostly Jesuits from the Collegio Romano, was not such a brilliant idea given the circumstances. Yet apparently oblivious to any possible dangers, Pico departed for Rome in the summer of 1486 with a group of friends. On the way, passing through the town of

---

In the *Oration on the Dignity of Man* Pico della Mirandola speaks of the primary role of humans. He maintains that God has given humans the ability to choose for themselves their own destiny, which is what separates them from all other creatures. Whereas other creatures and "angels" come into existence full developed mentally and thus are unchangeable, humans, on the other hand, can and must change because they are gifted with these possibilities by God. He says the philosopher is supreme in this ability, but all humans have the potential to be philosophers. Pico argues strongly in favor of nature and scorns those who denigrate it for not understanding it. He ends the *Oration* by promising to always speak in favor of the free pursuit of knowledge and one's own personal development, and asks everyone to do the same.

Arezzo, Pico fell madly in love with donna Margherita, the beautiful young wife of Giuliano Mariotto de Medici, a cousin of Pico's mentor, Lorenzo de Medici. It seems that Pico and the promiscuous lady attempted to run away together but were quickly apprehended by an armed band sent in hot pursuit by the enraged husband. In the scuffle than ensued some of Pico's companions got killed. As for Margherita, she claimed in her defense that Pico had taken her against her will.[26]

Margherita got off lightly with a reprimand, while Pico was thrown in jail. It was only thanks to the intervention of Lorenzo de Medici and Ficino that Pico was released. Pico then spent several months in Perugia recovering from his botched-up love affair.

It was in Perugia that Pico was introduced to Kabbalah, and which he then also added to his *Theses*. Kabbalah is an ancient Jewish mystical tradition involving the interpretation of sacred Hebrew scripts for magical purposes, and it is deemed to have been handed down orally by Moses himself. It was about that time that Pico had a brilliant idea. Ficino had tried to Christianize the Hermetica and its magic; Pico would do better: he would not only Christianize Kabbalah but also merge it with Hermetism. To this end Pico made use of his extraordinary knowledge of Hebrew, Greek, and Latin. Pico's reasoning went something like this: since Moses was both founder of Judaism and a prophet of Christianity, then Jewish Kabbalah surely must also be regarded as a *Christian Kabbalah.* In Pico's versatile mind the merging of Kabbalistic magic coming from Moses and Hermetic magic coming from Hermes Trismegistus, both of whom were believed by some to be contemporaneous, would create a powerful new form of magic that could be embraced by the Vatican for the advantage of Christianity. So Pico, using words as a magician would use potions, concocted an intellectual brew that can be regarded as "Christian Hermetic-Kabbalistic magic." One example of Pico's technique was a sort of etymological propaganda, where he showed that the four letters of *Jesu* (Jesus) as written in Hebrew could signify "God," "Son of God," or "wisdom of God," in other words, the Christian Trinity: God the Father, Jesus the Son, and the Holy Spirit. In simplistic terms Pico was able to convince many that the Hebrew religion was but the foundation of Christianity, which was the true and final religion of the world. This type of semantics, curiously enough, apparently induced many Jews in Italy to convert to Christianity.

At any rate, Pico arrived in Rome in the winter of 1486, full of hope that Pope Innocent VIII would support his idea of a congress to debate his *900 Theses.* While he waited Pico had his *900 Theses* published in December 1486 as *Conclusiones philosophicae cabalasticae et theologicae.* But he got the opposite reaction that he had expected from the Vatican: in February 1487 the pope stopped Pico's motion and asked the Inquisition to examine Pico's publication for possible signs of heresy. The inquisitors, of course, had no trouble in doing that. Pico was promptly arrested. After a valiant defense of his *900 Theses,* Pico was told by the inquisitors that there were still thirteen of them that were deemed heretical. Pico offered to remove them from his list, but the Inquisition demanded also a full and total recanting. Pico refused. Instead he wrote an apologia defending them. The cardinals rejected

Pico's apologia and instead declared his work to be "in part heretical, in part the flower of heresy, several are scandalous and offensive to pious ears; most do nothing but reproduce the errors of pagan philosophers ... others are capable of inflaming the impertinence of the Jews; a number of them, finally, under the pretext of 'natural philosophy' favor arts that are enemies to the Catholic faith and to the human race."[27]

With such a verdict from the Inquisition, not even Pico's powerful patrons in Florence could save him now. Taking their advice, however, Pico quickly escaped to France. There he asked the protection of the French King Charles VIII. Pico stayed in exile in France until 1492. After Pope Innocent VIII died, the new pope, Alexander VI, allowed Pico to return to Italy. This cranky "bad pope" was the infamous Rodrigo de Borgia, a hot-blooded Spanish nobleman who was quite unlike anything the Vatican had known. Among other things, this pope was openly interested in Hermetic magic and Kabbalah. He was also openly interested, unfortunately, in many other divertissements of the carnal variety. At any rate, in June 1493 Pope Alexander VI not only absolved Pico of all the charges against him but also wrote him a letter in which he termed Pico a faithful son of the church who was inspired by a *divina largitas* (divine bounty). Pico, however, died the next year at the early age of thirty-one, probably by poisoning.

Pico della Mirandola was buried in Florence at San Marco. Ficino was to write, "Our dear Pico left us . . . Florence might perhaps have never seen a more somber day than that which extinguished Mirandola's light."[28] In 2007 a team of scientists exhumed his remains and confirmed that he had died from arsenic poisoning.

It was in this year that Pope Alexander VI allowed Hermes Trismegistus to creep into the Vatican and, like some giant gecko, fix himself on the ceiling of his apartments.

THE CEILING OF THE BORGIA APARTMENTS

Rodrigo Lanzol was born in 1431 in the kingdom of Valencia, Spain, into a hugely rich and powerful family. His uncle, Alfonso de Borgia, who was then the bishop of Valencia, was to become Pope Callixtus III in 1455. It was the uncle who personally supervised Rodrigo's education in Bologna in Italy, shrewdly grooming him to be his successor. So close was Rodrigo to his uncle that he adopted his family name, and thus became Rodrigo de Borgia, a name, as fate would have it, that would live in infamy forever.

Hardly a year into his pontificate Callixtus III made Rodrigo a cardinal of the Roman Church. He was only twenty-three years old. In 1492—some historians say through bribery and manipulation—Rodrigo de Borgia was elected pope and took the name Alexander VI, this in spite of Rodrigo having already fathered four illegitimate children with one of his many mistresses, the beautiful Vannozza dei Cattani.*

We do not propose to review the many intrigues at the Vatican during the pontificate of Alexander VI, especially those proliferated by his promiscuous daughter Lucrezia de Borgia, the quintessential femme fatale of the Renaissance. We are much more interested in another intriguing matter that, in our opinion, raises huge questions about this particular pope's association with the teachings in the Hermetica.

The Italian scholar and historian Giovanni Nanni, a Dominican monk, was the personal secretary of Pope Alexander VI. In a thesis he published covering the alleged "history from the Deluge to the fall of Troy," Nanni concocted a most bizarre theory that Pope Alexander VI was a direct descendant of the Egyptian god Osiris, whom Nanni called

---

*Vannozza is reputed to have also had a passionate fling with Cardinal Giuliano della Rovere, the future Pope Julius II. Rodrigo was later to drop Vannozza for the even more beautiful Giulia Farnese, wife of Orsino Orsini. La Bella Giulia, as she was known, was pregnant by Rodrigo the year he actually became pope. She bore him a daughter. Rodrigo is also rumored to have fathered many more illegitimate children, although documented proof is lacking.

the "Father of the Egyptian Hercules." Basing this odd conclusion on his interpretations of classical chroniclers such as Herodotus, Plutarch, and Diodorus Siculus, signore Nanni was totally convinced, and what is more managed to convince the pope, that the "wisdom of the Egyptians" (which in his context meant the Hermetica) had been brought to Italy in very ancient times by Osiris himself. According to Danish scholar Erik Iversen, a specialist on the "Egyptomania" that much inspired Western traditions, "[Nanni] provided a heroic genealogy for his papal patron by demonstrating that the Borgia family descended directly from the Egyptian Hercules [Horus], the son of Osiris, and that the bull on the family crest was, in fact, the Osirian Apis [Serapis]."[29]

Before we pursue this curious connection between the Borgias and the "Osirian Apis," let us take note that when Marsilio Ficino worked his opus, the *Libri de Vita,* in 1489, hardly three years before Rodrigo de Borgia became pope, he strongly recommended to his readers that they should consider drawing "on the domed ceiling of the innermost cubicle of the house, where most live and sleeps," various figures of the "universe" to act as talismans. Bearing in mind that Ficino had derived his talismanic magic from the Hermetica, the "figures" he had in mind no doubt were to be Egyptian-Hermetic ones. About this matter Frances A. Yates commented, "I understand this to mean a painting on the ceiling of the bedroom . . . artistic objects, which are to be used magically for their talismanic virtue . . . works of art [that] are functional; they are made for a purpose, for magical use."[30]

We recall how Pope Alexander VI had shown his support and admiration for Ficino's favorite and most talented student, Pico della Mirandola. We also recall how Pico had openly recommended Ficino's *magia naturalis* to the Vatican. It is thus surely not unrelated that no sooner did Alexander VI begin his pontificate than he commissioned the famous painter Pinturicchio to decorate the ceiling of the Borgia Apartments at the Vatican with scenes showing Hermes Trismegistus and Isis, and most especially Serapis as the Apis Bull of Memphis.

Fig. 3.3. The paintings on the ceiling of the Borgia Apartments at the Vatican. (Sandro Zicari)

According to the scholar Jurgis Baltrusaitis, an authority on this specific subject, in those painted scenes of the Borgia Apartments:

> We can see the queen of Egypt [Isis] teaching the sciences and the laws; Isis finding the pieces of the dismembered body of Osiris, the coffin of Osiris, a pyramid decorated with lace having geometrical patterns, the apparition of Apis next to a pyramid . . . the scene represents the fabulous ascendance of Alexander VI. We can identify in compositions the *toro* [bull] symbol of the Borgias with the Apis which glorifies the heroic origins of the family of the pope.[31]

Another of those painted scenes is clearly an allegory of the Hermetic astral magic found in the *Asclepius,* for in this scene Hermes Trismegistus is standing under a huge sky globe with a large star over his head, and he is surrounded by various sages representing the classical philosophers, who stand in reverence and receive his teachings.

All this is testimony of how deeply the Hermetists had managed to influence Pope Alexander VI and persuade him to introduce the teachings of Hermes Trismegistus into the Vatican. Nonetheless, with the death of the Hermetists' supreme patron, Lorenzo de Medici, in 1492, followed by the deaths of Pico della Mirandola in 1494, Ficino in 1499, and Pope Alexander VI in 1503, all in the course of a single decade, the thrust of the Hermetic movement began to wane. Fifty years were to pass before the Vatican would be again shaken by a Hermetic magician. This time, however, the Hermetic magician would strike with such force that it would inflict a near knockout blow to the papacy, one from which it has not yet fully recovered—and probably never will.

THE HERMETIC MISSION
OF GIORDANO BRUNO

The year is 1548. We are some five years after the death of the Polish astronomer Nicolas Copernicus, who devised the earth-shattering

Fig. 3.4. Giordano Bruno

heliocentric theory. In faraway southern Italy, Giordano Bruno is born in the small town of Nola near Naples. In adulthood this verbose and astonishingly courageous "Nolano" would not only promote Copernican heliocentrism but would also very cleverly combine it with the Hermetic movement, creating a potent, intellectual brew that would rattle the very foundations of the Vatican. For unlike Ficino's pussyfooting with natural magic and Pico's roundabout attempt to Christianize it, Bruno went all out, head on, right for the jugular of the papacy by calling for a full restoration of the magical religion of the Egyptians to actually replace Christianity! As Frances A. Yates so put it:

> He is taking Renaissance magic back to its pagan source, abandoning the feeble efforts of Ficino to do harmless magic whilst disguising its main source in the *Asclepius,* utterly flouting the religious Hermetists who tried to have a Christian Hermetism without the *Asclepius,* proclaiming himself a full Egyptian who . . . deplores the destruction by the Christians . . . of the religion of the Egyptians through which they approach the divine ideas, the intelligible Sun.[32]

Ironically, Giordano Bruno began his adult life within the Catholic Church by enrolling in the Dominican Order in the year 1563. But six years later he got into trouble with his fellow monks at the monastery, who accused him of reading pagan books and reported him to the Inquisition. When Bruno found out that he was about to be arrested and charged with no less than 130 heresies against the Catholic Church, he disrobed himself of his priestly garments and escaped from the monastery. It was at this point in his life that he probably formulated his mission in his mind: *the full restoration of the Egyptian religion of Hermes Trismegistus.* Thus began Bruno's mission, which would bring him to a head-on collision with the Vatican, with disastrous consequences for both . . .

EXCURSION TWO, TO ROME, 1542

THE BIRTH OF THE SOCIETY OF JESUS

Like the Freemasons in many ways, the Jesuits have been regarded on the one hand as diabolical propagandists and manipulators of men's souls and, on the other hand, as saints and brilliant scholars. This perception depends, of course, on which side of the fence you stand. The truth of what the Jesuits really are, as is often the case with such extreme views, lies somewhere in the middle. When Giordano Bruno was born in 1548, the Society of Jesus, or the Jesuit Order as it is better known, had only just been created by a small group of Spanish monks led by Ignatius de Loyola (1491–1556), a soldier turned priest. It all started in 1521 after he was wounded in battle at Pamplona; Ignatius de Loyola decided he wanted to devote his life to "help souls." To this end he first decided to educate himself, then learned Latin, and finally went to France to get a doctorate at the University of Paris. There he stayed for seven years, from 1528 to 1535.

It was also there that he and his few companions got the idea to form a company or society of Jesus that would help souls. This lofty mission meant, in practical terms, converting heathens to Roman Catholicism. After Paris, Ignatius and his companions went to Venice, where they received Holy Order and were ordained as Catholic priests in 1537. They then went to Rome, where they were given official approval to form the priestly order of the Society of Jesus by Pope Paul

Fig. 3.5. The logo of the Society of Jesus, also known as the Jesuits. (Robert Bauval)

Fig. 3.6. Ignatius de Loyola

III in 1540. A year later, in 1541, Ignatius also founded the Collegio Romano, which recruited Jesuit priests to teach them various subjects in the sciences and the humanities that would serve them as "tools" for conversion. In other words they were taught propaganda. Interestingly, the favored subjects were mathematics, physics, natural science, and, most notably, astronomy.

It was astronomy, that is, the science of the heavenly bodies, that most served the Jesuits in their conversion missions to the New World. Advanced knowledge of the sky and the ability to make accurate predictions of eclipses and other impressive celestial events tended to much impress the credulous native populations. Since time immemorial these populations had been led by shamans and priests of various "sun religions" who saw the celestial bodies—the sun, the moon, and the constellations—as gods that directly influenced events on Earth and, more especially, the fate of humans. The Collegio Romano was also linked to the Propaganda Fide, the Vatican's official body to promote Catholicism around the world. Interestingly, the Propaganda Fide was made into a pontifical department in 1622 by Pope Gregory XV, who, in the same year, canonized Ignatius de Loyola as St. Ignatius (see postscript). In fact the term *propaganda* was first coined when Pope Gregory XV established the Propaganda Fide, whose full official title is Congreagatio de Propaganda Fide (the Sacred Congregation for Propagating the Faith). It is no secret that the Jesuit Order was originally used as a main proponent to the Counter-Reformation against the Lutheran Protestants. Since the early 1500s many European countries had converted en masse to Lutheranism, provoking eventually the Thirty Years' War, which devastated much of Northern Europe, and propaganda was as much a tool of warfare as open military conflict. Indeed it proved to be far more effective in the long run. When Bruno began his long and arduous Hermetic mission in 1570, the Reformation and Counter-Reformation were in full swing, and many scholars, particularly the Jesuits at the Collegio Romano, were devising schemes of propaganda to propose to the Vatican. One approach, which we will discuss in greater detail in chapter 5, was the use of monumental art, particularly architecture, as sort of permanent, giant "billboards." Professor Franco Mormando is one of the few specialists on Bernini who realized that Bernini was the master of this type of propaganda art. In the same way a political leader today will court the top media for his political propaganda, to use a nicer term, it was perhaps like "public relations," points out Mormando, "as monarchs and popes would court the top artists to confirm, advertise, and enhance his public status."

> It was art as political propaganda . . . the tried-and-true strategy for all power wielders in the Age of Absolutism. For awe-inspiring propaganda—or public relations if you will—Bernini, "Image Maker of the Popes," was one of the very best in Europe.[33]

Bernini, in other words, was the artistic equivalent of CNN, Fox News, the *New York Times,* and the *Herald Tribune* all rolled into one—a sort of artistic Rupert Murdock of the Renaissance. Indeed, all we have to do is see the daily hordes of tourists and visitors that come to his Piazza St. Peter's and are subliminally awed at the amazing architectural mood this place exerts on the mind and the soul to realize the power of the amazing artistic genius that was Bernini. He was, of course, not alone in the heyday of the Counter-Reformation in Rome. Others—Bramante, Michelangelo, Della Porta, Fontana, Maderno, Borromini, Sacchi, to name but a few—did their part. It was Bernini, however, who, with his unique Baroque style, used symbolic art in its most subliminal form. But more on Bernini in chapter 5.

Another tool for conversion was rhetoric, which, in simple terms for the Jesuits, was the science of eloquent and persuasive speech making and preaching to "win the souls of men." It was rhetoric, inter alia, that was mostly used by Giordano Bruno on his solitary mission of world reform. Indeed, Bruno would have made a devastatingly effective Jesuit had his methods and objectives not been so extreme and deemed "heretical." In any case, it is in the context of the Reformation and Counter-Reformation that Bruno set along his ambitious but ultimately doomed mission . . .

THE HERMETIC MISSION

After a brief and turbulent sojourn in Geneva, where Bruno ended up quarrelling with the Calvinists, this volatile but brilliant magician from Nola made his way to France. There, at the University of Toulouse, Bruno obtained a doctorate and, in 1581, made his way to Paris, where he gave lectures on "natural magic." So popular were these lectures that the curiosity of King Henry III was pricked, and Bruno was summoned at his court. In Bruno's own words, "I gained such a name that King Henry III summoned me one day . . . whereupon he made me an endowed reader at the Collége de France."

Henry III was keen on all things exotic, especially magic, hence his interest in Bruno. It was said that Henry III's very domineering and influential—and very Catholic—Italian mother, Catherine de Medici, was herself also addicted to magicians and astrologers. And although Bruno's type of natural magic is too complex to elaborate here, suffice it to say that he made use of Ficino's talismanic and Hermetic magic but with a twist to it: Bruno linked it to the Copernican heliocentric system, which he saw as a powerful talisman, a sort of celestial portent that was signaling the imminent reform of the world. Bruno, however, took his own Copernican vision much further than the solar system. He also advocated the existence of infinite "worlds" in the universe, which, as it would turn out later, would be fatal for him when in the hands of the Roman Inquisition. Bruno, however, saw Copernican heliocentrism not merely as a mathematical reality but more as a propitious religious symbol, a great astrological and cosmological logo or talisman in the heavens that convinced him that the solar Egyptian Hermetic reform of the world was at hand. And because of this, Bruno desperately needed a powerful and enlightened monarch to help him bring it about. The volatile, slightly unhinged, and effeminate Henry III of France clearly was no such monarch. In any case, Henry III was more preoccupied with serious religious conflicts in France, not to mention his personal and weird debaucheries at court.*

So Bruno turned his ever-searching eyes toward England, where such a monarch, or so he thought, was in the making: the Virgin Queen Elizabeth I. In March 1583, Bruno left for England. Frances A. Yates was to write of this, "Giordano Bruno, Hermetic magician of a most extreme type is now about to pass into England to expound his 'new philosophy.'"[34]

A letter from Sir Henry Cobham, the English ambassador in Paris, to Sir Francis Walsingham, the personal secretary of Queen Elizabeth I, dated March 1583, reveals the very serious concern that Bruno's forthcoming visit to England was already causing: "Doctor Giordano Bruno

---

*Historians debate whether Henry III's effeminate tendencies, dressing as a woman and having sexual liaisons with his *mignons* at court, were true or made up by his enemies; it was probably a bit of both. Henry III was also prone to take part in extremely bizarre religious processions in the streets of Paris.

Nolano, a professor in philosophy, intends to pass into England, whose religion I cannot comment."[35]

Cobham had attended Bruno's lectures in Paris, and thus in his dispatch to Walsingham he is obviously referring to Bruno's extreme Hermetic ideologies, which Cobham saw as a religion he could not commend. Even if we take into account the stiff-upper-lip language used, we can see that Cobham is much alarmed of Bruno's likely intentions: to push this "religion" at the highest of levels, perhaps even to the middle-aged Queen Elizabeth I. The latter was well known to be harboring fanciful, messianic visions of herself as the Virgin Queen or Virgin of the World, spreading Anglican Protestantism as far as the New World, the Americas.[36]

These epithets for Elizabeth I must have struck a chord in Bruno's brilliant, scheming mind. He was surely acutely aware that the second epithet was the title of a Hermetic tract, the *Kore Kosmou,* which in Greek meant "Virgin of the World" and was applied to the Egyptian goddess Isis. He also would have known of the *Fourth Eclogue* of the Roman poet Virgil, who also prophesied the return of the "virgin" at the end of the Iron Age to initiate a new golden age (see Excursion Three below). Finally Bruno also would have known that Virgil's contemporary, the poet Ovid, in his *Metamosphosis* spoke of the virgin as being Astraea, the last of the immortals who had abandoned the Earth at the end of the Iron Age. All these ancient prophesies of a new golden age brought about by a returning Virgin of the World could be transferred on the person of Elizabeth I by a master of propaganda such as Bruno.[37]

All these thoughts were probably in the mind of Bruno as he crossed the English Channel on his way to London.

EXCURSION THREE, TO ROME, FIRST CENTURY BCE

Virgil (70 BCE–19 CE) and also Ovid (43 BCE–17 CE) were both poets laureate to the Emperor Augustus Caesar (63 BCE–14 CE). Both, too, are regarded as ancient Rome's greatest poets, and were indeed legends in their own time. Virgil's *Fourth Eclogue* is a prophecy of an imminent golden age brought about by a virgin and her son.

> Now comes the last age of the Cumaean song; the great order of the ages arises anew. Now the Virgin returns, and Saturn's reign returns; now a new generation is sent down from high heaven. Only, chaste Lucina, favor the child at his birth, by whom, first of all, the Iron Age will end and a Golden Race will arise in all the world; now your Apollo reigns.[38]

The birth of a male child from the returning virgin as prophesied by Virgil was meant to be seen as the birth of Octavian, the first Roman Emperor Augustus Caesar, who had claimed direct descent from the virgin goddess Venus and furthermore was also regarded as having ushered in a golden age for the new Roman Empire. But later Christian propagandists in Rome latched on to the Virgilian prophecy and tagged it on their own Virgin Mary and her divine child, Jesus, who ushered in the golden age of Christianity. Amazingly, and against all odds, this type of propaganda had worked beyond anyone's expectation. What was very appealing in such a propaganda strategy were the "Egyptian" links that could also be made. The poet Virgil had been in Rome when Queen Cleopatra of Egypt had stunned the Romans with her famous entry into the Eternal City in 44 BCE as the "New Isis" or the "Returning Isis" (in her Egyptian language, Ast), and next to her was the young Caesarion sired by Julius Caesar. This event took place in the electrifying political situation in which Julius Caesar had adopted Octavian as his son, and had also placed a statue of Cleopatra as Isis in the temple of Venus, clearly identifying his Egyptian queen with the Roman Venus.[39]

Such acts sent conflicting messages to the Roman senate and ultimately brought about the assassination of Julius Caesar. Although Virgil, like most high-ranking Romans, had definitely not approved of Cleopatra, his *Fourth Eclogue* may have unintentionally opened the way later for the Christian propagandists to metamorphose Isis into the Virgin Mary.

VIRGO CELESTE

In Elizabethan England, the bad press that Roman chroniclers had given to Cleopatra—branding her as a power-hungry opportunist and femme fatale—was now changed by the English poets, who crafted an image of a warrior-queen filled with love and devotion for her people and her kingdom, a theme that certainly must have appealed to Elizabeth I. Shakespeare, in the play *Anthony and Cleopatra,* used his prose to turn the Egyptian queen into a tragic sovereign who had heroically battled the mighty and hated Romans. Elizabeth I was, of course, Shakespeare's most generous patron, and the famous bard, like many other poets of his age, well knew how to flatter the confident but also flirtatious Virgin Queen. The aura of such a legendary character as Cleopatra was something that the highly versed Elizabethan poets and writers could easily pin on Elizabeth I. But Giordano Bruno, Hermetic philosopher par excellence, could do a lot better than this. It would have been intellectual child's play for someone like Bruno, for example, to realize that the mythological Greek Astraea—literally the "star maiden"—the last of the immortals and the Virgin of the World, could easily be shown to be the constellation of Virgo. Indeed, this connection had long ago been made by the Greek astronomical poet Aratus (315–240 BCE) and later by many of the Roman poets, who also identified her with Justitia, the personification of Justice.[40] There was, too, an uncanny similarity between Astraea and Isis that could not have escaped an astute Hermetist such as Bruno. On the famous Zodiac of Dendera, said to be from the Greco-Roman era, Isis is shown holding ears of corn and following the constellation Leo; this celestial iconography clearly depicts Isis as the constellation Virgo. Although it is unlikely that Bruno knew of the Zodiac of Dendera, he, like many of his scholarly contemporaries,

Fig. 3.7. Athanasius Kircher's Isis-Virgo in the *Oedipus Aegyptiacus*.

was nevertheless conversant with the Greek classical writers and chroniclers such as Eratosthenes (276–195 BCE), who had identified Isis with the constellation Virgo, and knew that many others had done the same.*

The name Isis in ancient Egypt was Ast. Isis, or Ast, was the oldest and best-known star goddess, and there can be little doubt that her name of Ast is at the root of the Greek word for "star," *astro,* from

---

*The connection is clearly shown by Athanasius Kircher in his *Oedipus Aegyptiacus* (1653, tome IIA, 160) in the diagram of the so-called Hieroglyphic Zodiac, where under the sign IX of Virgo is written "Isis."

which comes the name Astraea for the starry virgin of the world. The scholar Margarita C. Stocker, an authority on Elizabethan iconography and poetry, showed the links that can easily be made between the Virgin Astraea, the constellation Virgo, the Virgin Mary, and finally, the Virgin Queen Elizabeth I, links that, quite plainly, were exploited by the Elizabethan poets to shower praise on their beloved virginal queen.[41] It would also seem that in ancient Roman, the "assumption" of the Virgin Astraea into heaven was celebrated on August 15 on the old calendar. It is surely not a coincidence that this same date of August 15 was chosen by the Christians to celebrate the Feast of the Assumption of the Virgin Mary.[42]

Finally, and perhaps less obvious, was the link that could be made between Iside (the name given to Isis by the Italians) and the name Eliza given to Elizabeth I. Iside is pronounced "ee-zeede" in Italian, and it may well be that Bruno, who was also a master of semantics and loved to make linguistic associations, may indeed have noted the phonetic similarity between the two names. At any rate, be that as it may, whatever Bruno might or might not have been conjuring in his mind for the role of Elizabeth I, we shall now see that the association of the English queen with the quintessential astral queen of Egypt is not as farfetched as it first may appear.

Let us see why . . .

EXCURSION FOUR, TO LONDON, 1581

THE COURT OF THE VIRGIN QUEEN

The scholar John N. King, in a detailed study of the representations of Elizabeth I as the Virgin Queen, seriously considers the possibility of an association of Elizabeth I with the Egyptian goddess Isis. To make his point King points at the various representations of Elizabeth I in the later part of her life wearing a lunar crescent that could well be the commonly seen moon crescent on the Egyptian goddess Isis.

The emergence of the queenly moon cult typified the Petrarchism and Platonism of royal circles, where courtiers paid homage to Elizabeth as an ever youthful yet unapproachable object of desire. The cult originated in Giordano Bruno's praise of Elizabeth during his mid-1580s residence in England . . . thus jeweled crescent moons appear . . . in the queen's hair in miniatures . . . [which] raises the intriguing possibility that Elizabeth's crescent moon imagery may derive from Isis. . . . The *rich mitres shaped like the moone* worn by the priests of Isis correspond to the moon devices that appear in the queen's portraiture during her last decade.[43] (italics added)

King was referring to the epic ode *The Faeire Queene* by the Elizabethan poet Edmund Spenser. This poem has been the subject of hundreds of commentaries, critiques, and debates, some enlightening, others obtuse, and it is not our wish or indeed within our scholarship to deal with all of them here. Most would agree, however, that the poem is a eulogy of Queen Elizabeth I and is directed at her sexuality, or rather lack of it, and the hope that she would produce an heir while somehow retaining her maidenly innocence, her glorification, and perhaps even deification, all weaved and veiled in an intricate pseudomythological and imaginary realm. We are specifically concerned here with book V, canto VII of *The Faerie Queene,* in which the heroine, the virgin-knight Britomart (one of the many alter egos of Queen Elizabeth I), spends the night in a temple of Isis that Spenser calls "Isis Church." Spenser titled this part of the poem thus:

> *Britomart comes to Isis Church*
> *Where she strange visions sees:*
> *She fights with Radigund, her slaies,*
> *And Artegall thence frees.*

In book V, canto VII, it is plain to see that Spenser is very familiar with the myth of Isis and Osiris, probably from classics such as Plutarch's

Iside et Osiride and Apuleius's *The Golden Ass.** Spenser focused on that part of the myth where Isis rescues Osiris from an earthly doom by her special magic and posthumously becomes pregnant by him and bears him a heir, thus retaining her virginity in some miraculous way. What is more to the point is that Spenser clearly equates Britomart with Isis and sees this combined entity as Queen Elizabeth I. Spenser wrote the poem sometime in the late 1580s and published it in two parts in 1590 and 1596, when Queen Elizabeth I was in her early fifties, and thus incapable of bearing children. Yet there was hope that somehow in some supernatural way she would, like Isis, produce a male heir to rule her kingdom. It had been well known that Elizabeth I had once proclaimed that if she did ever marry then her choice of consort would be a man of the highest of virtues. Spenser, in the following excerpt from *The Faerie Queene,* seems to be suggesting someone like the god-king Osiris, husband-consort of Isis.

> *Calling him great Osyris, of the race*
> *Of the old Egyptian Kings, that whylome were*
> *With fayned colours shading a true case*
> *For that Osyris, whilest he lived here,*
> *The justest man alive and truest did appeare.*
> *His wife was Isis, whom they likewise made*
> *A Goddesse of great powre and soverainty*
> *and in her person cunningly did shade*
> *That part of Justice, which is Equity*
> *Whereof I have to treat here presently*
> *Unto whose temple when as Britomart arrived.*

Britomart is presented as the Knight of Chastity, a sort of virginal warrior woman, a Briton heroine evoking the well-known scene

---

*See the excellent thesis by Stephanie Danis, "The Amalgamation of the Character of Britomart in Edmund Spenser's *The Faerie Queene:* A Study of Classical, Medieval, and Renaissance Influence on the Knight of Chastity," Honors Program, St. Peter's College, New Jersey, May 4, 2011.

of Queen Elizabeth I in full knightly armor riding her steed and giving her famous speech to the troops at Tilbury in August 1588, the year before Spenser wrote *The Faerie Queene*. Being also a beautiful maiden, Britomart cannot help falling desperately in love with a reflection of the handsome Artegall in a magical glass ball in the cave of Merlin. Britomart then begins an epic quest to find her future lover. The poem goes on to narrate how Britomart during her epic search ends up spending the night in the temple of Isis, becomes herself a priestess of Isis, and is presented with an idol of the goddess. Britomart then falls asleep and has a "strange dream." The "vision" in her dream is of herself *becoming* Isis.

> *There did appeare unto her heavenly spright*
> *A wondrous vision, which did close implie*
> *The course of all her fortune and posteritie*
> *Her seemed, as she was doing sacrifize*
> *To Isis, deckt with Mitre on her hed*
> *And linnen stole after those Priestes guize*
> *All sodainely she saw transfigured*
> *Her linnen stole to robe of scarlet red*
> *And Moone-like Mitre to a Crowne of gold*
> *That even she her selfe much wondered*
> *At such a chaunge, and joyed to behold*
> *Her selfe, adorn'd with gems and jewels manifold.*

The famous scholar and writer C. S. Lewis undertook an in-depth analysis of *The Faerie Queene* and commented on the character of Britomart with these words:

> Britomart . . . rescues him [Artegall] from slavery. And if, as I think, she becomes Isis in her dream (the "crown of gold") then Artegall is to her as the crocodile is to Isis . . . thus in a sense she rescues or saves him eternally in the Church of Isis.[44]

In the "church" or temple of Isis, Britomart is presented with a female idol standing with one foot on a crocodile and holding a long scepter or lance.

> *Thence forth unto the Idoll they her brought . . .*
> *And at her feete a Crocodile was rold, That with her*
> *   wreathed taile her middle did enfold.*
> *One foote was set upon the Crocodile,*
> *And on the ground the other fast did stand . . .*
> *She stretched forth a long white slender wand.*

The patron saint of the Copts, the Egyptian Christians, is St. George, who, oddly enough, is also the patron saint of England. This much-loved warrior saint was often depicted in Coptic iconography as Horus, son of Isis and Osiris, slaying a crocodile with a lance, much in the same way that St. George of England is depicted slaying the dragon. There are, too, many depictions of Horus stepping on a crocodile. Could Edmund Spenser have known of this? Or Bruno? At any rate, after her dream in the temple of Isis, Britomart-Isis subdued and tamed the crocodile and copulated with it and became pregnant and gave birth to a male lion.

> *For grace and love of her to seeke*
> *Which she accepting, he so neare her drew*
> *That of his game she soone enwombed grew*
> *And forth did bring a Lion of great might.*

It is obvious that this episode in Spenser's poem is culled from the myth of Isis and Osiris, where the goddess goes on an epic search to find her lover-companion Osiris, copulates with him in a magical way, becomes pregnant, and gives birth to Horus, Egypt's first king, the "Solar King," whose symbol is the lion. Spenser composed *The Faerie Queene* sometime from 1588 to 1589, a short while after the visit of

Giordano Bruno in England at the court of Elizabeth I. Surely the hidden hand of the Italian magus can be felt here. The same is felt by the author M. Isidora Forrest, who wrote:

> It may have been Bruno's *Spaccio* that influenced the Elizabethan poet Edmund Spenser. . . . The political motivation behind *The Faerie Queene* appears to have been the association of England's Queen Elizabeth with an ancient Golden Age ruled over by another strong queen: Isis, the divine queen of Egypt. Spenser tells us that Isis was "a goddess of great power and sovereignty." Elizabeth is further associated with Isis—and with Egypt's Queen Cleopatra—by the fact that *The Faerie Queen* of the title lives in "Cleopolis."[45]

When Giordano Bruno was in England in the mid-1580s, Britain and the rest of Europe were already caught in a frenzy of religious hatred. The terrible Thirty Years' War (1618–1648) was but a few decades away. Soon Protestants and Catholics would clash in a terrible, bloody, and protracted conflict across the continent. The Lutheran Reformation and the Catholic Counter-Reformation had the common people—Protestant Christians against Catholic Christians—turn against each other in isolated acts of cruelty rarely seen before or since. As for the poets, painters, sculptors, writers, scholars, and philosophers, they directed their talents in the "other," more powerful war: the psychological war of words and symbols. Using myths, prophecies, legends, Holy Scriptures, and powerful symbolism, they subjected the superstitious, poorly educated, and gullible populaces to what today we would call brainwashing. Protestants tried to convert Catholics and vice versa, not through the obvious means of coercion, threats, torture, and fear but through that invisible but very effective psychological weapon: *propaganda*. It is in this dangerous and devious atmosphere of Reformation and Counter-Reformation propaganda that we must view the mission of the Society of Jesus, the *Jesuits*. But there was, too, a much more ephemeral but equally, if not even more effective society of individuals, one in which Bruno excelled: the Hermetic philosophers. For they, too, joined in this struggle with their own intellectual arsenal of propaganda to bring about not just a religious reformation but also a social reformation, a reformation, no less, of the collective human mind. Although these Hermetists operated alone and often were not aware of each other, they nonetheless shared a common mission: to unshackle the "soul of the world" from religious bigotry and launch it again on its rightful path of knowledge and enlightenment.

The propaganda surrounding the persona of Elizabeth I as Virgin Queen, Astraea, Britomart, Gloriana, and especially Isis fed the populace with their hopes of a new golden age brought about by a "returning virgin of the world," a Christianized new Isis of messianic magnitudes. The cult of the Virgin Mary had drawn pagans en masse into Christianity by veiling her with the mythology and iconography of Isis and by converting Isaic temples into churches dedicated to the Madonna. It surely must have crossed the minds of astute rulers and their propagandists that such devastatingly successful conversion methods could be used again to bring heretics back to the fold. We will see in chapter 5 how another Protestant virgin queen would be flaunted to the masses as a new Isis in Rome by the Vatican itself. Meanwhile we take another excursion to Rome to see a pope lose, quite literally, ten days of the year 1582 . . .

EXCURSION FIVE, TO ROME, 1582 CE

POPE GREGORY XIII AND THE CALENDAR

While Bruno was traveling to England he must have known, as everyone else in Europe probably did, of the huge controversy that the current pope in Rome, Gregory XIII, had just caused throughout the Christian world by the reformation of the old Julian calendar. Acting on the advice of the German Jesuit priest-mathematician Christopher Clavius of the Collegio Romano, the pope issued a bull to delete ten days from the year 1582. This, on face value, was apparently to restore the calendar in line with the true astronomical year.

It would seem that several motives were at play: first the so-called *ecclesiastical* vernal equinox, an arbitrary date used by the church to compute Easter, had drifted some ten days prior to the true *astronomical* vernal equinox, such that now in 1582 the *true astronomical* vernal equinox fell on the Julian calendar date of March 11 instead of March 20 when this calendar was originally established. Although this couldn't have really mattered that much to the common people, it did matter quite a lot to the pope and his cardinals because it affected the all-important question regarding the "incarnation" of the "Son of God."

THE TROUBLE WITH MARY

To understand why the reformation of the calendar mattered so much to the Vatican, we must bear in mind that the pope regarded himself as the legitimate successor of St. Peter the Apostle, and that it was, quite literally, on his throne that he sat. St. Peter's Basilica was believed to stand at the very spot that St. Peter the Apostle had been buried in 69 CE. Indeed, the authority of the Roman Catholic Church rested on the statement made by Jesus Christ to Simon (Peter) the Apostle: *Tu es Petrus et super hanc petram aedificabo ecclesiam meam* (You are Peter [the Rock], and upon this rock I will build my Church; Matthew 16:18). It was Constantine the Great, the "Father of Catholicism," who had built the basilica in the fourth century CE and had defined the dogmas and canons of Roman Catholicism in 325 CE at the First Ecumenical Council at Nicaea. It was also at this council that the Catholic Easter was defined: the first Sunday after the so-called Pasqual Moon, the latter being the full moon after the true astronomical vernal equinox, which, at the time of the council at Nicaea fell on March 20. Apparently the true astronomical vernal equinox was established in Alexandria in 325 CE as being March 20 of the Julian calendar. At any rate, from 325 CE onward March 20 came to be regarded as the *ecclesiastical vernal* equinox. But because the Julian calendar of 365 days (adjusted by adding one day every leap year, i.e., every four years) drifted forward from the true astronomical year (tropical year of 365.2412 days) by one day every 131 years, by the time of Pope Gregory XIII in 1582 it had drifted such that the *ecclesiastical* vernal equinox now fell ten days after the *true astronomical* vernal equinox. So to "pull back" the ecclesiastical equinox to where it had been at the time of the Nicaea council, Pope Gregory XIII declared that the next day after October 4 would be October 15.

Christian tradition has it that the old basilica built by Constantine the Great was supposedly built on the very spot where St. Peter the Apostle was martyred and buried. It would have been directed, as was the custom then, toward the rising sun on the vernal equinox. But since then the date of March 25 was regarded as the Day of Annunciation when, according to Christian tradition, the Archangel Gabriel had announced (hence "annunciation") to the Virgin Mary that she would be the "Mother of God"—March 25 to December 25 (birthday of Jesus) being, of course, the nine months of human "gestation."*

In Roman Catholicism this supremely important feast was also called the Feast of the Incarnation, that is, when the "spirit" became "flesh." This all-important feast day on March 25 was now used for determining the date for Easter, instead of March 20.† All these religious feasts, however, were locked into the Julian calendar. But as we saw earlier, the problem was that this *Julian* calendar drifted away from the true astronomical year. The Jesuit astronomers at the Collegio Romano, however, had been aware of this for some time.

In early 1582 the top Jesuit astronomer Christopher Clavius persuaded Pope Gregory XIII to reform the Julian calendar by deleting ten

---

*The Annunciation event supposedly happened while Mary was reading the Book of Isaiah in which is found the prophecy, "Behold, a virgin shall conceive, and bear a son, and shall call his name Immanuel."

†Confusingly, the *Eastern Orthodox* Church still used the vernal equinox established at the time of the First Ecumenical Council at Nicaea in 325 CE, being March 20, to work out the Easter date.

days in that year. The purpose was manifold, but it was done mainly to create a universal calendar (it was given the name Gregorian in honor of the pope) so that all Christians, both in the East and West (and presumably as well people in Protestant countries) would be encouraged to celebrate Easter at the same time, but also, perhaps more so, to pull back the liturgical Feast of the Annunciation (also called the Incarnation) as it had been at the time of Constantine in 325 CE (Gregorian) and when the sun still rose in alignment with the basilica of the Vatican. The ploy to convert other non-Catholic Christians did not quite work, at least not immediately. Many countries, especially the Protestant ones, rejected the Gregorian calendar for many years. (The United States of America did not officially adopt it until 1752, nearly two centuries later.)

Since the fourth century, the Feast of the Annunciation (also known as the Incarnation), when supposedly the Archangel Gabriel announced to Mary that she would become pregnant and bring forth a son,* had been fixed on March 25, which is nine months, that is, the period of human gestation, before December 25, which supposedly marked the birthday of Jesus. Since time immemorial the common folk of Europe celebrated their feasts, especially the divine birth cycle of nine months from vernal equinox to winter solstice, according to the true astronomical solar year. This meant that any dislocation of the feast days relative to the position of the sun could cause a deep psychological disturbance in a populace still very superstitious and still very susceptible to heavenly events. The Virgin Mary, after all, was the queen of heaven, and surely her gestation cycle had to be fixed to the true cycle of the sky. Let us retain this thought, for as we shall see in chapter 5, the alignment of the old basilica, which was aligned to the true vernal equinox and was still standing in 1506 when work began on the new basilica, was to cause a curious confusion with the architects concerning its layout.

---

*And the angel said unto her: "Fear not, Mary: for thou hast found favor with God. And, behold, thou shalt conceive in thy womb, and bring forth a son, and shalt call his name Jesus" (Luke 1:30–31).

Let us state in passing that we see the "Reformation" of the calendar and calling it the Gregorian calendar, with the pope's name, as yet another clever act of Counter-Reformation propaganda by the Vatican aimed at the Protestants. This is made evident by the immediate rejection of the Gregorian calendar in Protestant countries; indeed Britain and the colonies, including North America, introduced it only in 1752. But more than the calendar, we also see the grandiose embellishment projects of Rome, starting with the building of a new St. Peter's Basilica in 1506, the Sistine Chapel, the raising of ancient obelisks by Pope Sixtus V in 1586, and many other impressive projects as part of this propaganda warfare. But we will read in more detail about these matters in chapter 5.

Meanwhile let us return to Giordano Bruno and his arrival in Elizabethan England . . .

THE "PEDANTS" OF OXFORD

In London Bruno took up residence in the house of the French ambassador through the recommendation of Henry III of France. In June 1583, just a few months after his arrival, Bruno somehow got himself invited to the University of Oxford to debate his radical views with a group of scholars. It was to be an evening of scholarly dispute, a sort of intellectual gladiator fight to entertain a Polish prince visiting the university. Bruno gave a passionate oration on "the immortality of the soul," adding his own religious vision of the Copernican heliocentric theory. It didn't go well at all, and he was constantly interrupted by the Oxford scholars; some even booed him down. After this fiasco, Bruno's high hopes to convert the English scholars, let alone the English queen and her bishops, to his ideas of reforming the world went pear-shaped. Bruno later lamented at the coarseness and rudeness of the Oxford scholars, calling them, inter alia, "pedants." He felt pride that he had taken their abuse with "patience and humanity . . . showing himself to be indeed a Neapolitan, born and bred beneath a kindlier sky . . . ," while they, on the other hand, had behaved like pigs.[46]

Bruno had an intense dislike of stiff, dry, narrow-minded scholars who, in his opinion, simply parroted their peers and were completely shut to any new ideas. He saw such type of scholars as "'pedants' and 'Aristotelians'"—the last a kind of "insult" as far as Bruno was concerned since Aristotle was practically revered by the church and the Jesuits. He lamented that such pedantic scholars "understood but did not dare to say what they understood . . . saw but did not believe what they saw." To Bruno such scholars were pompous men with impressive titles that disguised their lack of humanity and understanding, in other words, the opposite of what he was or, more to the point, what the ancient Egyptian sage Hermes Trismegistus inspired him to be. It is not that Bruno did not approve of science and logic; his strong defense of the Copernican heliocentric theory clearly shows that he did. However, to Bruno, science alone was useless if it was not part of a Hermetic philosophy, that special gnosis or prisca theologia that could benefit not just the physical world but also its *soul*.

On that fateful day when Bruno had confronted the scholars at Oxford, there had been present at the academic brawl the dashing Sir Philip Sidney, nephew of the earl of Leicester, the late Sir Robert Dudley, the latter once Queen Elizabeth's favorite and, some historians believe, her secret lover. Sidney was a refined scholar and a sensitive poet, and very likely conversant with the Hermetica. Perhaps because of this, and also in the hope of gaining favors with the queen, Bruno dedicated his most important book, *Spaccio della Bestia Trionfante* [The Expulsion of the Triumphant Beast], published in England in 1584, to Sir Philip Sidney. Although Bruno explains in the dedication that the "triumphant beast" was a metaphor for the vices that predominate and oppose the divine part of the soul, it was obvious that the triumphant beast was none other than the Vatican, the pope, and all that they stood for. According to Bruno the triumphant beast has to be removed, expulsed, thrown away in order for the true religion of the world, the Egyptian Hermetic religion, that *good religion, which was overwhelmed in darkness when the Christians destroyed it, forbade it by statutes, substituted worship of dead things, foolish rites, bad moral behavior, and constant wars,* to be fully restored and embraced by all. It is clear that Bruno's *Spaccio della Bestia Trionfante* is unabashedly flaunting the Hermetic, talismanic, astral magic of the *Asclepius,* for in it are many references to stars, the zodiac, the constellations, the sun, and how their powers or spiritus can be brought down to create talismans through "the magic and divine cult of the Egyptians." Frances A. Yates clearly saw Bruno's ambitious Hermetic motives when she wrote:

> Bruno's intention was clear enough. He wanted to show that Egyptian wisdom came earlier than that of the Greeks, and certainly much earlier than that of the Christians and, therefore, must be regarded as "the best religion and the best magic and the best laws of them all.[47]

In the *Spaccio della Bestia Trionfante* Bruno drives his point by quoting a passage from *The Lament* in the *Asclepius* where Hermes Trismegistus predicts that although the true and magical religion of ancient Egypt will fall under the cruel and oppressive rule of foreigners, there will come a day when it will be restored in a wonderful solar city, a talismanic city, in which the powers of the heavenly bodies have been brought down. Here Bruno's battle cry is heard loud and clear.

> The marvelous magical religion of the Egyptians will return, their moral laws will replace the chaos of the present age, the prophecy of the Lament will be fulfilled . . . the sign in heaven proclaiming the return of Egyptian light to dispel the present darkness was . . . the Copernican sun.[48]

To Giordano Bruno the Copernican heliocentric diagram—the planets orbiting the sun in concentric circles—was none other than a perfect solar talisman, a magical Hermetic seal that he understood at its deepest levels. He also must have realized the huge implication regarding the impact that the heliocentric theory might have on the Vatican once it was proved mathematically and through observations to be true, not just from a scientific viewpoint but also, and perhaps even more so, from a religious viewpoint, because of the acrimonious opposition it had received from the Vatican. A huge revolution was in the brewing, and Bruno must have sensed it and wanted to ride the intellectual and spiritual tsunami that it would generate. Thus by attaching the Hermetic magical religion of the Egyptians to this imminent Copernican upheaval, Bruno hoped that his own ideas would also be pulled along with it. It was a brilliant strategy—if he could pull it off . . .

Did Bruno also have in mind the building of a city of the sun as prophesied in the *Asclepius?* We will discuss this issue in chapter 4. Meanwhile let us just note that after he left England and while he was temporarily back in France, Bruno had a conversation in late December 1585 with the librarian and diarist at the Abbey of St. Victor in Paris, Guillaume Cotin, with whom Bruno had resided while in France. During this conversation Bruno narrated to Cotin how the duke of Florence had expressed the wish to build a *civitas solis,* a city of the sun. In Cotin's own words, "[Giordano Bruno] heard it said that the Duke of Florence wished to build a *Civitas Solis* in which the sun would shine every day of the year."[49]

Meanwhile things in Paris had taken a turn for the worse. A religious war was in the making between the Catholics and the Protestant Huguenots. The Protestants were headed by Henry of Navarre, the legitimate next in line to the throne of France, and also the duke of Condé. Both had been branded heretics by Pope Sixtus V, who also threatened them with excommunication. The Catholic priests, especially the Jesuits, inside Paris were making passionate sermons to rouse the people against the Protestants. As for King Henry III, once the keen supporter of Bruno, he was cowering in his chambers. Henry III would come out only at night, wearing monk's attire and joining bizarre penitent processions in the streets of Paris. In these extremely muddled and dangerous circumstances, Bruno wisely decided not to tarry in Paris. In September 1586 he left France. But soon he would make the most unwise decision that would cost him his life . . .

EXCURSION SIX, TO ROME AGAIN, 1586

ST. PETER'S BASILICA

In September 1586, around the time that Giordano Bruno was leaving Paris, there was taking place a very odd ritual in Rome outside the Vatican. A cardinal from the Curia stood near the ancient Egyptian obelisk that had just been raised in front of the St. Peter's Basilica and, in a dramatic gesture, sprinkled holy water on the obelisk while reciting these words:

> Behold the cross of the Lord. Flee you adversaries. The Lion from the tribe of Judah won. Christ wins. Christ reigns. May Christ defend his people against any evil.[50]

This nearly four-thousand-year-old Egyptian obelisk had once graced the sky above ancient Heliopolis, the City of the Sun, the religious capital of pharaonic Egypt, for three millennia. It was brought to Rome in 37 CE by the infamous Emperor Caligula (37–41 CE). Caligula had erected it in front of the Iseum—the temple of Isis—in the center of the circus that he was having built, and was later to be finished by the Emperor Nero, hence also known as the Circus Nero. By the Middle Ages, the Circus Nero was in ruins. The obelisk, however, was still standing,* but now partially covered in mud.[51]

The task of erecting the Egyptian obelisk in front of the new St. Peter's Basilica was perhaps the most dramatic engineering event in the history of Rome. The construction of the new basilica, which had begun

---

*In the fourteenth century an English prelate named Gegorius saw the obelisk in a dark, narrow alley, its base covered by garbage and standing next to old houses that were butting against the south wall of the old basilica.

in 1506, was still in progress, and the area was cluttered with stone debris and derelict old houses in the Rione di Borgo, know as the old Borgo, the district adjacent to the basilica. Early in 1586 Pope Sixtus V had commissioned the Swiss-Italian architect Domenico Fontana to oversee the delicate operation that entailed transporting the obelisk from the Circus Nero and repositioning it some 280 meters further away in the open space (the future Piazza St. Peter's) in the east of the basilica. It actually took Fontana six months to complete the task, using an army of nearly one thousand men, seventy-five horses, and forty wooden cranes. The final ceremony took place on September 26, 1586, with a huge crowd come to witness the event. It has often been said that the raising of the obelisk in front of the basilica was to symbolize the glory of Christianity over paganism. Sixtus V was surely aware that this obelisk was from Heliopolis, the City of the Sun, that it was brought to Rome by Caligula, a devotee of Isis, and that it was a sun symbol. The original idea, however, was first suggested much earlier by Pope Nicholas V (1447–1455), who wanted to have the obelisk stand on four bronze statues of the evangelists and have a bronze statue of Jesus holding a golden cross at the top. But nothing came out of it. Then later Pope Paul III (1534–1549) had asked Michelangelo to do the job, but the great artist had declined. "What if it breaks?" Michelangelo is said to have asked the pope. Finally Pope Sixtus V took the risk with Domenico Fontana. The obelisk was placed over four bronze lions—the "lion of Judea" and also the symbol of the Perettis, the family of the pope—and at the top, the symbol on the pope's coat of arms: three mounds surmounted by a star, and above this, a Christian cross. When a few years later the Inquisition interrogated Giordano Bruno about the meaning of the cross, he replied:

I think that I have read in Marsilio Ficino* that the virtues and holiness of this symbol is much more ancient than the time of the

---

*The book of Ficino to which Bruno was referring is *De vita coelitus comparanda,* where Ficino asserted that the Egyptian crux ansata or ankh was a powerful talisman, but also a presage of the coming of Christ.

Incarnation of Our Lord, and that it was known at the time in which the religion of the Egyptians flourished, about the time of Moses, and that this sign was affixed to the breast of Sarapis.[52]

We shall see in chapter 5 how the Jesuit scholar Athanasius Kircher would say the same thing to two other popes, Urban VIII and Alexander VI, and, more specifically, that the cross on the Vatican obelisk from Heliopolis was but a variation of the "Egyptian magical cross foreshadowing the Christian cross."[53] We shall also see how—and more importantly *why*—Domenico Fontana did not align the obelisk with the extended axis of the new basilica but four meters to the left of it. But we are again moving ahead of our story.

Let us stay with Bruno in the final stage of his Hermetic mission . . .

INTO THE HANDS OF
THE PAPAL INQUISITION

After a sojourn in Germany and Poland until 1591, Bruno was about to make a fatal mistake. Thinking that a new pope, Clement VIII, could be induced to look favorably on his ideas of universal Hermetic reform, and probably also seized by a deep nostalgia for his native land, Bruno decided to return to Italy. A Venetian nobleman, Zuane Mocenigo, somehow contacted Bruno in Germany and invited him to come to Venice, all expenses paid. Either shunning or oblivious to the great danger of such a move, Bruno accepted the invitation. After a short stay at Padua, where he taught at the University of Padua from November 1591 to March 1592,* Bruno moved into Mocenigo's home in Venice.

Signore Mocenigo proved to be a very possessive man. He hounded

---

*Interestingly, Galileo was also teaching at the same university in 1591 and 1592, although there is no record of him meeting Bruno. Considering their mutual interest and support of the Copernican theory, it would seem odd, however, that they did not meet.

Bruno to teach him "the art of memory and invention," but Bruno kept dodging the issue. In fact Bruno was far more interested in completing a book he hoped to dedicate to Pope Clement VIII. When Mocenigo found out, he became furious with jealousy, locked Bruno in his room, and called the Venetian Inquisition, who promptly arrested Bruno on charges of heresy. Bruno immediately offered to renounce whatever they wanted him to renounce, but the inquisitors decided instead to have him taken to Rome to be questioned by the more experienced Papal Inquisition.

For the next eight years Bruno was imprisoned in the papal dungeons in Rome. He was regularly tormented, humiliated, and probably endured torture during Gestapo-like interrogation sessions by the Papal Inquisitors. Bruno, however, now took a harder stance and refused to recant or withdraw anything from his works. Finally, on February 8, 1600, "the months and years of suffering reached their dreadful close."[54] He was taken to face his inquisitors for the last time, to hear the terrible sentence they were to pass on him: to be burned alive in public. Legend has it that Bruno bravely stared defiantly into the eyes of the inquisitors and pronounced these immortal words:

Perchance you are more afraid in passing judgment on me, than I
am in receiving it.

A young Jesuit novice from Breslau, Germany, named Kaspar Schoppe was present at Bruno's trial. It was Schoppe who reported these famous words by Bruno. Schoppe, a Protestant, had recently converted to Catholicism. Pope Clement VIII had shown his appreciation by making Schoppe a Knight of St. Peter and a count of the Sacred Palace. And so it was that on a cold and damp winter's morning in Rome, February 17, 1600, according to most accounts,* Bruno was taken from his cell, chained, and escorted to Campo de Fiori, a small, open space not far

---

*The dates of February 19 and 20, 1600, are also quoted by various biographers of Giordano Bruno.

from the Vatican. With Bruno were a few priests from the Company of Mercy and Pity, whose morbid duty was to lead heretics to their place of execution. Also in this morose procession were two Dominicans and two Jesuit monks who goaded Bruno and reminded him of his errors and heresies. At one stage Bruno cried out, "I die a willing martyr and my soul will rise with the smoke to paradise." To shut him up a metal spike was pushed through his cheeks and another spike through his lips. Blood then gushed all over him. He then was tied to a wooden stake and burned alive.[55]

According to Schoppe, "When the image of our Savior was shown to him before his death he angrily rejected it with averted face."

Apparently when Bruno was agonizing in the flames one of the Dominican monks brandish a crucifix (Schoppe's "image of our Savior") in his face. But Bruno, in an act of amazing defiance, managed a last surge of energy while his limbs were roasting in the flames: he swung his head away in total revulsion.*

A while before, Bruno had written these words, which would fit well as an epitaph for him:

> I have fought . . . it is much . . . victory lies in the hands of Fate. Be that with me as it may, whoever shall prove conqueror, future ages will not deny that I did not fear to die, was second to none in constancy, and preferred a spirited death to a craven life.[56]

The Vatican got rid of Giordano Bruno the man, but as the flames that consumed his corpse went skyward, a martyr was created, not for Christianity but for the free will of humans. Because Bruno, in spite of

---

*Some trivia: the approximate cost for one public burning at the stake was budgeted as follows: large wood, 55 sols, 6 deniers; vine branches, 21 sols, 3 deniers; straw, 2 sols, 6 deniers; stakes, 10 sols, 9 deniers; ropes, 45 sols, 7 deniers; executioner, 20 sols. This adds up to a total of 155 sols, 7 deniers, which was worth approximately 2.3 grams of gold, at today's price about $42. The price could be much less if four victims were burnt together on one stake. The priests who went along to witness the burning offered their services for free.

Fig. 3.8. Statue of Giordano Bruno in Campo de Fiori. (Robert Bauval)

his impulsive ways, was a real Renaissance philosopher who spoke the truth, albeit as he understood it, and whose deepest desire was to free the human spirit from the bondage of an intolerant and cruel clergy that carried out acts of untold brutalities in the name of "God." Bruno's horrible death was not to be a fatal blow to the Vatican, but rather a dark stain that, to this day, has not gone away. In 1887, nearly three centuries after Bruno's death, a group of wealthy anticlerics donated funds for Italian sculptor Ettore Ferrari to sculpt a statue of Giordano Bruno cast in bronze. Ferrari was a deputy in the Italian Parliament and also the Grand Master of Grande Oriente D'Italia, the supreme rank in Freemasonry. This must have sent a chilling message to the Vatican. The statue was raised on the spot where Bruno was burned.

There he broods, that amazingly stubborn, amazingly brave, and amazingly erudite Renaissance philosopher who only wanted all men and women to be "lovers of knowledge" and to reawaken them to the beauty of nature and its magic. Bruno's statue is a potent talisman, a defiant one, directed at the Vatican. It is a grim reminder that the price of freedom can be very high, but it is also a reminder that freedom is an indelible part of the collective human spirit that cannot be destroyed.

Still, in the year 1600 the chilling message from the Vatican was directed at anyone who might be considering defying its tenets and dogmas. One would have thought that no one in his right mind living in Italy, especially someone from within the church itself, would preach again about the Hermetic magic and the "true religion of the world," let alone openly promote the idea of a city of the sun as prophesied in the *Asclepius*. But as incredible as it may seem, someone actually did.

And he did so even louder than Bruno . . .

4

THE CITY OF THE SUN

At that time, there will be five cities [that will] swear allegiance to the Lord of the Heavenly Armies. One of them will be called the City of the Sun.

ISAIAH 18:19

Few things so much contributed to overthrow the medieval ideal of human existence and to introduce the modern one as the astronomical theory of Copernicus.

THOMAS DAVIDSON,
"GIORDANO BRUNO AND THE RELATION OF
HIS PHILOSOPHY TO FREE THOUGHT,"
LECTURE AT THE NEW YORK LIBERAL CLUB,
OCTOBER 30, 1885

Campanella spent the rest of his life trying to find the contemporary representative of the Roman Empire who would build his City of the Sun.

FRANCES A. YATES,
"CONSIDERATIONS DE BRUNO ET DE
CAMPANELLA SUR LA MONARCHY FRANCAISE"
(CONSIDERATIONS OF BRUNO AND CAMPANELLA
ON THE FRENCH MONARCHY)

PASSING THE TORCH

Since my late teens I have been fascinated by the strange coincidences that often happened in history and that indelibly changed the course of human existence. Lately I have wondered if perhaps something else, which cannot be explained, is at play. I am becoming convinced that there exists a universal law that cannot for now be fathomed, and perhaps never will. But this is the great beauty of this unseen and immeasurable law, that, indeed, it cannot be understood, but only experienced. For want of a better name to give it, for now let us settle for synchronicity.

At the same time that Giordano Bruno was being burned alive in Campo de Fiori, another rebellious and heretical Dominican monk was being tortured by the same Inquisition in a dungeon in Naples. His name was Tommaso Campanella. Although Bruno and Campanella never met,* there is much about their lives that is uncannily similar: both were from southern Italy, both were Dominican monks, both were branded heretics, both had missions to reform the church, both were Hermetists, and both were arrested and imprisoned by the Inquisition. Indeed so similar were the lives of these two men that it led Frances A. Yates to wonder—with typical scholarly caution nonetheless—whether Bruno's mission had not in some way passed on to Campanella.

> Obviously, it would be going too far to view Campanella's movement as resulting solely from the impact of Bruno's return to Italy . . . but when due allowance has been made for other influences, and precaution taken against overstatement, it does look very much as though a torch may have passed from Bruno to Campanella.[1]

---

*Bruno and Campanella almost did meet in Padua in 1592. Fate would have it that Bruno left Padua in March, and Campanella arrived in October, when he met Galileo.

Plate 1. Robert Bauval in Piazza St. Peter's. (Robert Bauval)

Plate 2. Robert Bauval with Sandro Zicari checking alignments at Piazza St. Peter's.
(Robert Bauval)

Plate 3 and Plate 4. Alignment of obelisk with the Maderno facade and cupola of St. Peter's Basilica. These two photographs show the "error" in the alignment of the Vatican obelisk with the cupola of St. Peter's Basilica (plate 3), and the uneven size of the triangles on the Maderno facade in plate 4 when the obelisk aligns with the cupola. (Robert Bauval)

Plate 5. View from St. Peter's Basilica looking due east along the main axis. (Google Earth)

Plate 6. View of St. Peter's Basilica looking due west. (Google Earth)

Plate 7. Statue of St. Peter welcoming the faithful to St. Peter's Basilica. Note the statue of Christ at the top of the Maderno facade. (Robert Bauval)

Plate 8. The Vatican obelisk from Heliopolis, the "City of the Sun." (Robert Bauval)

Plate 9. Overhead view of the Vatican City. Top of page is due east. (Google Earth)

Plate 10. Andrea Sacchi's fresco *La Sapienza Divina* at the Palazzo Barberini in Rome. (Robert Bauval and Sandro Zicari)

Plate 11. Divine Wisdom on her throne. Note the two lions flanking the throne, and also the solar disc on the goddess's breast. (Robert Bauval and Sandro Zicari)

Plate 12. Robert Bauval and Sandro Zicari in the Palazzo Barberini, Rome. Note the reduced size model of the Sacchi fresco on the wall. (Robert Bauval)

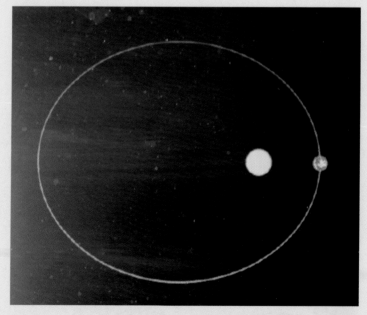

Plate 13. Diagram showing Kepler's first law of planetary motion. Note only one of the foci is shown. (Robert Bauval)

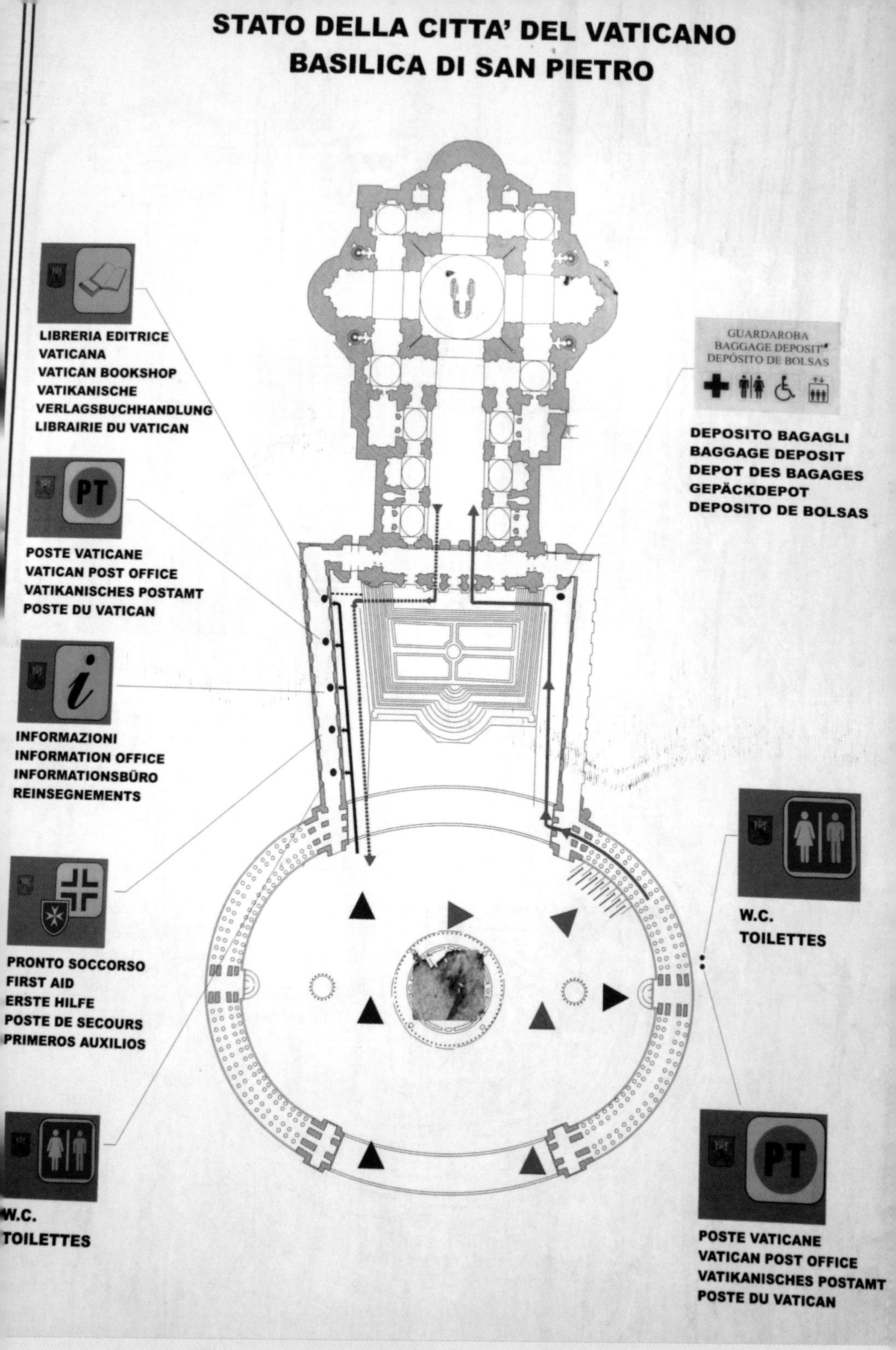

STATO DELLA CITTA' DEL VATICANO
BASILICA DI SAN PIETRO

LIBRERIA EDITRICE
VATICANA
VATICAN BOOKSHOP
VATIKANISCHE
VERLAGSBUCHHANDLUNG
LIBRAIRIE DU VATICAN

POSTE VATICANE
VATICAN POST OFFICE
VATIKANISCHES POSTAMT
POSTE DU VATICAN

INFORMAZIONI
INFORMATION OFFICE
INFORMATIONSBÜRO
REINSEGNEMENTS

PRONTO SOCCORSO
FIRST AID
ERSTE HILFE
POSTE DE SECOURS
PRIMEROS AUXILIOS

W.C.
TOILETTES

GUARDAROBA
BAGGAGE DEPOSIT
DEPÓSITO DE BOLSAS

DEPOSITO BAGAGLI
BAGGAGE DEPOSIT
DEPOT DES BAGAGES
GEPÄCKDEPOT
DEPOSITO DE BOLSAS

W.C.
TOILETTES

POSTE VATICANE
VATICAN POST OFFICE
VATIKANISCHES POSTAMT
POSTE DU VATICAN

Plate 14. Official Plan of St. Peter's Basilica. (Vatican Poster,
The Vatican Tourist Information Office)

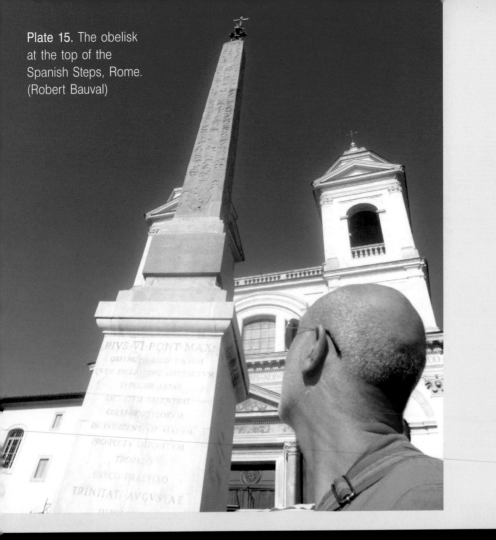

Plate 15. The obelisk at the top of the Spanish Steps, Rome. (Robert Bauval)

Plate 16. The Piazza and St. Peter's Basilica at night. (Robert Bauval)

Plate 17. Robert Bauval near the Maderno Fountain north of the obelisk. (Robert Bauval)

Plate 18. The coat of arms of Pope Alexander VII on the top of the Bernini Colonnade. (Robert Bauval)

Plate 19. The Bernini Fountain in the Piazza St. Peter's. (Robert Bauval)

Plate 20. Castel Sant'Angelo, Rome. It was once a prison used by the Vatican, where Giordano Bruno was incarcerated. (Robert Bauval)

Plate 21. The god Mithras killing the bull. It is possible that the many figures (bull, dog, scorpion, snake) are symbols of constellations: Vatican Museum. (Robert Bauval)

Plate 22. The she-wolf feeding Romulus and Remus, the founders of Rome.

Plate 23. Bust of the goddess Isis in black granite. Roman period: Vatican Museum. (Robert Bauval)

Plate 24. The "Boat of Rome" in the Villa D'Este, Rome. Note the fountains on each side of the obelisk. This arrangement may have inspired Maderno and Bernini for the fountains at Piazza St. Peter's. (Robert Bauval)

Plate 25. Statue of Ptolemy I Soter outside the Bilbliotheca Alexandrina, Alexandria, Egypt. (Robert Bauval)

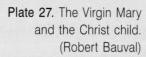

Plate 26. Pope Francis I and his coat of arms. (Vatican Official Photo)

Plate 27. The Virgin Mary and the Christ child. (Robert Bauval)

Who was Campanella? What connection might he have had with Giordano Bruno and his Hermetic mission? Again Yates senses a synchronistic event.

> Tommaso Campanella was the last of the Italian Renaissance philosophers, of who Giordano Bruno was the last but one. Like Bruno, Campanella was a magician-philosopher, in the line of the Renaissance magi descending from Ficino. Campanella is known to have practiced the Ficinian magic up to the end of his life. Like Bruno, too, Campanella was a magus with a mission . . . in touch with the cosmos and destined to lead a universal magico-religious reform.[2]

Was Campanella "another Bruno?" Yates does emphasize two important differences between the two men. First, unlike Bruno, Campanella had savoir faire and was far more astute and diplomatic, and he thus avoided being burned at the stake, but died in bed of old age. Second, also unlike Bruno, Campanella *very nearly succeeded* in bringing off the project of a magical reform within the Catholic framework"[3] (italics added). Yates's conclusion, however, that the "magical reform" never happened was probably premature. We intend to show in the next two chapters that a powerful spiritual and intellectual idea in the form of a Hermetic time

Fig. 4.1. Tommaso Campanella

bomb whose fuse was meant to be lit when the right conditions prevailed was cunningly placed at the very doorstep of the Vatican.

First let us try to understand what exactly was this magical reform that Bruno and, after him, Campanella "very nearly succeeded in bringing off." Bruno wanted to bring about the full restoration of the true religion of the world by persuading a powerful monarch, Catholic or Protestant, to embrace his vision of the Hermetic philosophy and the heliocentric truth. Campanella, as we shall see, also wanted to bring about the restoration of the true religion of the world by persuading a contemporary representative of the Roman Empire, preferably the pope, of his vision of a universal solar republic administered from the City of the Sun, *la città del sole,* roughly modeled on the heliocentric truth.

Clearly Bruno and Campanella had similar missions, albeit one being far more radical than the other. Nonetheless the goal was the same, and both of them made use of Hermetic philosophy and magic to bring it about. But whereas Bruno's objectives were vague, Campanella's

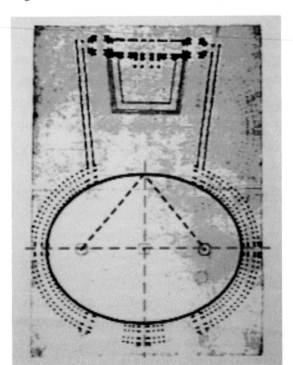

Fig. 4.2. Campanella's vision of the City of the Sun. (George L. Hersey)

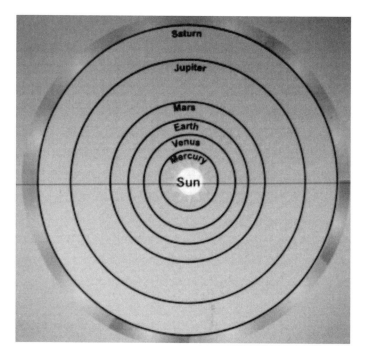

Fig. 4.3. The Copernican model. (Robert Bauval)

objectives were clear: to find a Catholic monarch to build the City of the Sun. Yates, however, did not see the City of the Sun as being anything other than an idea, and she did not try to find out if *a contemporary representative of the Roman Empire* actually built it. But her studies open the way for us to search for it. Perhaps unintentionally Yates let out this important clue: "The City of the Sun is heliocentric in a religious and magical sense. . . . Is its plan also heliocentric in an astronomical sense, that is to say, is it Copernican? Campanella's *Città del Sole* was ultimately Egyptian in origin."[4]

Combining Bruno's and Campanella's ideologies, we are to imagine a sort of religious "sun city" designed to represent the heliocentric Copernican model of the world, whose focal point is the sun or, more precisely, the Egyptian sun or a symbol thereof.

For these Hermetic thinkers the City of the Sun—Heliopolis in Egypt—would have been a talismanic city that could bring down the benevolent influences of the heavens. Bruno and Campanella were obviously thinking of the kind of talismanic magic expounded by Marsilio Ficino in his *De vita coelitus comparanda,* which he, in turn, had culled from the *Asclepius.* We are reminded of Ficino's strange cry—a cry perhaps aimed at the Vatican—to actually make such a talisman.

> Why, then, should we not permit ourselves a universal image, that is an image of the universe itself? From which it might be hoped to obtain great benefits from the universe itself.[5]

But what great benefits were Ficino—and also his more radical followers, such as Pico della Mirandola, Bruno, and now Campanella—hoping to obtain? Frances A. Yates again gave a clue.

> It is also in these strange magical realms that Campanella's ideal republic or City of the Sun must be placed, with the astral religion and sun worship [of the Hermetica] . . . [in order to bring about the] ethic of social utility and public service, and the use of learning and invention for the public good which both Bruno and Campanella teach as a necessary part of their reformed society.[6]

So let us now look more closely at Campanella and his strange vision of the City of the Sun . . .

THE FIRST CELEBRITY OF EUROPE

Campanella was born on September 5, 1568, in the small town of Stilo in Calabria in southern Italy, then under the Spanish viceroyalty of Naples.* This was twenty years *after* Bruno was born in the small town of Nola, also in southern Italy. Like Bruno, Campanella entered the

---

*Even Campanella's birthday, September 5, would play a curious prophetic coincidence later in his life when he predicted the birth of the "Sun King," Louis XIV of France, who was also born also on September 5 (in 1638).

Dominican Order in his youth, and, also like Bruno, he walked away from its austerity and repression six years later.

In 1591 Campanella published his first book in Naples, *Philosophia sensibus demonstrata* [Philosophy as Demonstrated by the Senses], which brought on him accusations of heresy. Campanella was thrown in the dungeon of the Dominican monastery for several months but released a year later. Campanella then traveled to Rome and from there to Florence, where he arrived in early October 1592. He was received by the grand duke of Tuscany,* who called Campanella "a man of great learning" and personally recommended him to the librarian of the Medici Library. Campanella returned the compliment by describing the library as "a wonder of the world."[7]

Campanella then went to Padua, where he met the soon-to-be-famous astronomer Galileo Galilei. Galileo had come from Florence bearing a letter for Campanella from the grand duke. Both men were still in their twenties, Galileo being the older by four years. The meeting with Galileo much impressed Campanella, and years later he would defend the great scientist against his accusers by writing an *Apologia per Galileo* [A Defense for Galileo].[†]

In Padua, Campanella resided in the Convent of St. Augustine. He shared a room with a fellow monk. The master of the convent clearly did not approve of Campanella and accused him of sodomy. But this was a typical, trumped-up charge common in those days, and Campanella was acquitted due to lack of proof. Eventually other heretical charges were brought against him, and Campanella was arrested and jailed. The charges included writing a poem against Christ, keeping a book of magic (the *Asclepius?*), refusing to adhere to the doctrine of the church, and,

---

*The grand duke was Ferdinando I de Medici, the son of Cosimo I de Medici (not to be confused with Cosimo de Medici, who had died in 1464).

†It was in 1616 while incarcerated in the papal dungeons that Campanella wrote the *Apologia per Galileo*. This was at the time that Galileo was being criticized for his support of Copernicus's theory. The *Apologia* was published later in Frankfurt in 1622 and stands as testimony to the great audacity and scholarly honesty of Campanella, who was obviously risking the wrath of the church by defending the heretical ideas of his friend and colleague.

oddly, discussing the Christian faith with a "Judaiser" (a person who favored Jews) and not denouncing this "Judaiser" to the Inquisition.

In February 1594 Campanella suffered his first physical agony at the hands of the official torturers of the Inquisition. Not satisfied with Campanella's desperate pleas of innocence, the inquisitors transferred him to the Vatican in Rome for more expert interrogations.[8] In October 1594 Campanella was put in the papal dungeon at the Tor di Nona in the Ponte region of Rome. This, ironically, was where Giordano Bruno and another famous Florentine heretic, Francesco Pucci, were also being kept. Pucci had been charged for being a sympathizer of heretics (Protestants), and he, too, was condemned to death by the Inquisition. But his death was more humane: Pucci was first beheaded in the dungeon, *then* his headless corpse was burned in Campo dei Fiori.

Beginning in October 1594 a curious push-and-pull, morbid, and sinister relationship developed between Campanella and his inquisitors-*cum*-torturers. We will pass, however, over the gruesome details. Suffice it to say that records show that in only a period of one year, 1594 to 1595, Campanella endured no fewer than twelve sessions of horrible torture, with the last session lasting nearly two days. In May 1595 Campanella was released on the grounds of very poor health: excruciating pain from hernia, sciatica and partial paralysis, and consumption. But he was again arrested and imprisoned in December 1596, released in January 1597, rearrested in March 1597, and finally released in December 1597 after abjuring his heresies under extreme torture. Campanella's books were henceforth put on the official prohibition list, the *Index Librorum Prohibitorum*. He was then ordered to return to his birthplace in Calabria and stay out of trouble. Campanella, of course, did nothing of the sort. In fact, while in prison, he had been planning a most unusual revolution . . .

THE CALABRIAN REVOLT

Campanella had barely resettled in Calabria, then under Spanish rule, when he again got into very serious trouble with the powers that be. His writings were now taking a highly political tone against the Spanish authorities, and he also hinted that he possessed "prophetic powers," which did not please the clergy. In early 1599 Campanella wrote, "It occurred to me that revolution ought to happen soon." Apparently he had consulted several astrologers who confirmed that "political revolution ought to occur for us. . . . If a general transformation should impend for us, certainly it will happen on a crucial date, thus in the next seven-year period following the year 1600."[9]

In the first few months of 1599 Campanella preached to the public his vision of general transformation and upheavals, and soon he found himself leading a conspiracy to overthrow the Spanish rulers. But Campanella and his followers were badly organized and had very unclear objectives and, to be practical and realistic, no chance to overthrow their powerful Spanish lords. From what can be made of Campanella's half-baked plan, after toppling the Spanish authorities, he intended to replace them with a theocratic republic governed by highly enlightened and benevolent priest-scientists, whom, he, Campanella, would preside over.

It all very quickly went pear-shaped after two of his followers reported the conspiracy to the Spanish authorities. Campanella was captured along with many of his followers—about 150 of them, mostly students—and they were taken to Naples in four galleys. When the ships arrived at the port, sixteen conspirators were hanged on the yardarm of the galleys, and others were slaughtered and disembowelled on the wharf. On January 11, 1600, Campanella was questioned by inquisitors appointed by Pope Clement VIII. Ironically, this was the same time that Giordano Bruno was being questioned in Rome by inquisitors also appointed by the pope. Campanella was imprisoned and again suffered brutal torture. This went on for several months, with the inquisitors trying to extract a confession from him.

Hoping to avoid the death penalty, Campanella pretended he was insane by setting his cell on fire. But this only provoked the inquisitors to use a more persuasive method of torture called *la veglia* (the awakener). The objective was that if he admitted to his pretense of madness he would be burned at the stake for heresy, but if he endured the pain for forty hours and did not confess, he would be judged insane and just imprisoned for life. The la veglia torture was applied on Campanella on June 4, 1601. The wretched man was suspended on ropes such that he could, by using his shoulder muscles, prevent his body from hitting sharp wooden spikes beneath him. When his muscles could no longer bear him up, his body would slump, and his thighs and buttocks would be gashed by the spikes. Campanella would then pull himself up. And so it went on, for hours, this gruesome torture. When he could no longer hold his tongue, rather than confess Campanella cried unintelligible things such as "ten white horses," "I am slaughtered," "enthrone and shut up," and "the soul is immortal." At other times he would howl in pain. Campanella held on for forty hours, and his torturers were obliged to declare him "officially insane." He was thrown back in his cell.

This unsinkable, unbeatable, and resilient man, rather than rot in the Neapolitan papal dungeon, applied his brilliant mind to composing poetry, corresponding with a huge number of scholars around Europe, and even managing to write several books. By 1607 Campanella had become a huge celebrity, and everyone in the scholarly world wanted to visit him. One such visitor in 1607 was none other than the German priest who had witnessed the burning of Giordano Bruno, Kaspar Schoppe.[10]

Schoppe, a Protestant converted to Catholicism and now a zealous promoter for the Counter-Reformation, had come to see Campanella about a book described as a "volume against politicians and Machiavellians," which the latter had recently written. Campanella was impressed by Schoppe and dedicated the book to him. Campanella had intended the title of the book to be *Recognoscimento della vera religione universale* [Identification of the True Universal Religion], but Schoppe convinced him to change the title to *Atheismus Triumphatus* [Atheism Conquered], which would go down better with the pope. Schoppe also convinced Campanella to let him have the manuscript, which he promised to have printed in Germany.*

---

*Campanella kept the original Latin version of *Atheismus Triumphatus* and gave the Italian version to Schoppe. The Latin version was printed in Rome in 1631 and in Paris in 1636.

We recall that Schoppe had witnessed the trial and burning of Giordano Bruno a few years before. But there is no mention of Bruno in their discussion. Campanella perhaps did not wish to discuss Bruno with a zealous Counter-Reformist such as Schoppe. This may also be why Campanella did not hand over to Schoppe another, far more explosive manuscript: *La Città del Sole* [The City of the Sun]. At any rate, Schoppe never kept his promise to publish Campanella's *Atheismus Triumphatus*. Instead he ended up plagiarizing much of its content in a book he wrote himself in 1611.[11]

It is not our intention to review the many scholarly theses dealing with Campanella's writings and philosophy, but we are, however, very interested in his book, *The City of the Sun*. In a letter he wrote to a colleague from prison Campanella gave a major description as to what such a city might be used for by claiming that he could "*make a city in such a wonderful way that by only looking at it all the sciences may be learned*"[12] (italics added). Campanella is visualizing a city that will work as a giant talisman, a sort of *talismanic city* designed, decorated, and administered in such a way so that "all the sciences" could be learned by just being inside it. This magical city Campanella would call Heliaca—clearly a take on Heliopolis.[13]

THE SOLARIANS AND THE CITY OF THE SUN

Like many of the philosophical tracts of the Renaissance, especially when the author wishes to dissimulate his own thoughts behind fictional characters, Campanella's *The City of the Sun* is in the form of a poetic dialogue. We are to understand, however, that one of the characters is Campanella himself. Should the dialogue be deemed heretical or offensive to the Vatican, then the author could always claim that the work is fictional and that, in any case, it does not represent his own views. The dialogue here is between the grand master of the Knights Hospitaller and a Genoese sea captain, his guest for dinner.

The first scene opens with the captain telling the grand master that during his many travels he happened across a wonderful community living in a city of the sun. Eager to know more, the grand master questions the captain, who is more than happy to answer. The captain goes on to explain that the City of the Sun is circular and is about three kilometers in diameter. It stands on a mound, at the center of which is a circular temple (seemingly representing the sun). Around this temple are seven concentric walls, with habitations, said to represent the "seven planets," the farthest one being at the foot of the mound. Seen on plan, this city layout is clearly based on the Copernican diagram, with the seven visible planets orbiting the central sun. The concentric walls act like an encyclopedia in stone, for on them are painted images and scenes imparting knowledge of the sciences and humanities, including botany, zoology, astronomy, physics, history, geography, and so forth. The city of the sun is headed by a high priest called Sol, the "Sun."[14]

The high priest's symbol is, therefore, the sun (a circle with a dot in the center, used in ancient Egypt to denote Re, the sun god). Campanella calls Sol also "Metaphysic." Sol was elected for his vast wisdom, knowledge, and benevolence—a sort of King Solomon and high priest of Heliopolis rolled into one.*

The high priest is assisted by three collaborators called Power (a sort of minister of war), Wisdom (a sort of minister of education and culture), and Love (a sort of minister of welfare and health and "unity between men and women"). Under them are magistrates with names like Liberality, Justice, Truth, Gratitude, and so on. As for the religion of this magical, utopian solar city-state, even though it includes some benevolent doctrines of Christianity—Christ and his apostles are "held in great esteem"—there is no doubt that Campanella envisages a

---

*This wise, priestly ruler may have inspired Francis Bacon for his Salomon, the benevolent ruler of Bacon's *New Atlantis,* published in 1627. Bacon's Salomon's House much resembles Campanella's City of the Sun, a place "dedicated to the study of the works and creatures of God." It is believed by some that it provided the idea of the Royal Society. The name Solomon, Salomon (the French derivative), or Solamon has been seen by some as the combination of Sol, that is, the sun, and Amon, the Egyptian sun god.

natural religion, which Frances A. Yates says "is saturated through and through with astrology; its whole way of life is directed in achieving a beneficial relationship with the stars, the sun, the planets, and the zodiacal constellations."[15] Indeed, the grand master is informed by the captain that "priests over the age of twenty-four" reside in the high part of the city, which acts as a sort of astronomical observatory, and their task is to constantly observe the sky and measure the cycles of the orbs with instruments; this is done in order to advise on propitious times for planting, breeding, festivities, stately decisions, and so forth. As for the citizens themselves, they all share a common purpose, which is for the benefit of all, and are all dressed, men and women, in white robes or togas. We would much agree with Frances A. Yates, who concluded that Campanella's *The City of the Sun* is somewhat modeled on the magical solar city described in the *Asclepius,* where Hermes Trismegistus declares that in some future times, when the magical religion of Egypt is finally restored, "The gods who exercised their dominion over the earth will be restored one day and installed in a city . . . which will be founded toward the setting sun, and into which will hasten, by land and sea, the whole race of mortal men."

"Once one sees this," writes Yates, "it becomes obvious that Campanella's white-robed Solarians are really Egyptians, that is to say, Hermetic pseudo-Egyptians." Thus Yates goes on to say, "The deepest, the primary layer of influence behind the City of the Sun is, I suggest, Hermetic . . . and its first model [is] the description in the *Asclepius* of the religion of the Egyptians."[16]

Although Campanella does not specifically mention the Hermetica in his commentaries about the City of the Sun, he nonetheless lets out certain clues. For example, we find drawn on the exterior wall of the City of the Sun the prominent inventors of science and laws, and Campanella lists among them Osiris and Mercury (Hermes). In another of his tracts, the *Theologia* (also composed in prison in 1614), Campanella praises Hermes Trismegistus as a prophet of Christianity and says in the doctrine that "the world is a living creature first taught by (Hermes) Trismegistus" and, in support, quotes a passage from book XII of the Corpus Hermeticum. This attempt to Christianize the Hermetica is also made for the inhabitants of the City of the Sun, who although they "praise Ptolemaeus and admire Copernicus nevertheless follow the 'law of nature' i.e. 'natural religion' that is 'so close to Christianity' that it may as well be 'Christian' and that 'when its (Christianity's) abuses are taken away, *it will rule the world*'" [17] (italics added).

Campanella is here proposing a Christian Hermetism based on the theology of the Egyptians as found in the Hermetica. Yet he, too, like Bruno, sees the Copernican heliocentric discovery as the portent for an imminent reform of the Christian world. As Yates also puts it, "I would think that the City of the Sun represents something like the magical and Ficinian reform of religion and morals of which Bruno foresaw the imminent return, through Copernicanism as a portent, a sign in the sun." [18]

STRANGE VISITORS

During his long imprisonment Campanella was visited in 1613 by two German scholars, Tobias Adami and Rudolph von Bunau, who were on their way back from the Holy Land. Campanella handed to Adami several of his manuscripts, including the Italian copy of *The City of the Sun*. Although Adami had *The City of the Sun* published in Frankfurt in 1623, copies were later passed around to scholars in Germany and other parts of Europe. [19] Why did Campanella hand over his most important work to Adami, apparently a total stranger, and not to Kaspar Schoppe, the envoy from the Vatican? A statement by Campanella may give us a clue. In one of his descriptions of Heliaca, Campanella wrote, "All kings and people will unite in a city, which they will call "Heliaca" ... a temple will be built in the midst of it, *modeled on the heavens* ... and the sceptres of kings will be placed at the feet of Christ" (italics added).

Why was Campanella imagining a temple "modeled on the heavens" and "placed at the feet of Christ"? Could the explanation be that in 1613, when Campanella handed the manuscript to Adami, a life-size statue of Christ was being placed on the facade of the new basilica of the Vatican, looking down in the open space, where at its center, since 1586, soared the Egyptian obelisk from Heliopolis, the City of the Sun? We shall discuss this issue in more detail in chapter 5. Meanwhile let's note in passing that Campanella's *The City of the Sun* inspired one of Adami's colleagues, the founder of the Rosicrucian Order, Johann Andreas, to propose his own utopian city called Christianapolis, which, like Campanella's vision, was governed by philosopher-priests and with also a circular temple at the center, a city that was to be called Civitas Solis.[20]

The City of the Sun was a huge bestseller, turning Campanella, who was still in prison, into a literary celebrity, a sort of Renaissance Birdman of Alcatraz. But what was about to happen could not have been foreseen by anyone, least of all Campanella.

ECLIPSING THE POPE

In June 1626, after having spent twenty-seven years in prison, something short of miraculous happened to Campanella. Out of the blue, he was suddenly freed and summoned to Rome by order of the new pope, Urban VIII. He arrived in Rome only to be imprisoned for another two years. While in prison in Rome he wrote an astrological tract, *De Siderali fato vitando* [How to Avoid Fate Dictated by the Star]. Now it seems that the pope had become ill and feared for his life, something to do with the ill-boding effect of a forthcoming eclipse of the sun, which his Spanish enemies had said would cause his death. Having been told of Campanella's natural magic, it was the pope's hope that Campanella could ward off this dire astrological prediction.*

---

*The magic that Campanella intended to use was the one that Ficino had concocted from the *Asclepius*. This is made clear from one of Campanella's books, *Metaphysica*, where he "gave a complete summary of Ficino's magic in a detailed analysis"[21] and also quoted the relevant passages from the *Asclepius*.

The Astrologer-Magician and the Pope

Pope Urban VIII totally believed in astrology and feared for his imminent death due to an astrological prediction made by Orazio Morandi, a Spanish priest. The predicted "death" of the pope was to be during the periods between an eclipse of the moon in January 1628, an eclipse of the sun in December 1628, and finally another eclipse of the sun in June 1630. To offset the influence of these eclipses Urban VIII called on Campanella to help with his "magic." During the whole summer of 1628 Campanella and the pope performed many sessions in a special room in the Castel Gandolfo and probably also later at the Palazzo Barberini, where the artist Andrea Sacchi, as we shall see later, had painted a very telling heavenly or "cosmic" scene, *La Divina Sapienza,* on the ceiling.

The Palazzo Barberini, owned by Urban VIII, had been under construction since 1627. The original architect was Carlo Maderno, but after he died in 1629, the work was taken over by Bernini. It would seem extremely unlikely that Bernini had not met Campanella, who was at the time acting as the personal astrologer to the pope. At any rate, there can be no doubt that the magic performed was based on Marsilio Ficino's talismanic magic, which he obtained from the Hermetica. The room was sealed from the air outside, perfumes were used as well as aromatic woods and herbs, and lamps and candles were lit to represent the planets. Also music was used to bring down the beneficial influences of the positive planets, Jupiter and Venus. There were also stones and plants and "sympathetic colors" decorating the room, as well as the drinking of "astrologically distilled" beverages. These sessions went on for several months until the danger of the eclipses passed.

Campanella, now an old man of fifty-nine, was received by Pope Urban VIII with open arms. The pope immediately asked the old magus to prepare all that was necessary to perform the magic that could counteract the nefarious prediction of the forthcoming eclipse. It is not clear how long the session of magic organized by Campanella for Urban VIII went on, but it may have been several months, perhaps even a few years. The room where Campanella and the pope carried out these sessions of magic can be regarded as a model of the Earth whose ceiling was the sky. Now the ceiling of this particular room, as we indicated earlier, had a fresco painted by the Baroque painter Andrea Sacchi, which supposedly was an allegory of *La Sapienza Divina* [Divine Wisdom], see plate 10. But according to art historian Joseph Lechner the fresco was much more than this: it was a sort of astrological-*cum*-astronomical allegorical representation of the sky showing benevolent conjunctions that took place on August 6, 1623, the day Urban VIII was made pope. Intriguingly, Lechner claimed that Sacchi was influenced by Campanella and, even more intriguing, that this fresco may be the first representation in art of the heliocentric system and, in a roundabout way, an allegory of Campanella's *The City of the Sun*.[22] Interestingly, the very same view is expressed by Professor Frederick Hammond, a specialist of Italian art and music in the seventeenth century at Bard College, who wrote, "Andrea Sacchi's Divine Wisdom, painted under the direct supervision of the Barberini and finished in 1630, appears in fact to represent a heliocentric universe."[23]

Lechner points out that the most detailed and reliable contemporary source that explains the iconography of the fresco is the so-called *Barberini Codex* found in the Vatican Library. Essential the *Barberini Codex* "pinpoints the *Book of Wisdom** as the primary source for Sacchi's imagery."[24]

Lechner, basing himself on this *Codex* and also referencing various passages from the *Book of Wisdom,* associated the various figures in the

---

*The *Book of Wisdom,* or the *Book of the Wisdom of Solomon,* is one of the books of the Bible that are considered deuterocanonical by some churches such as the Roman Catholic Church, and non-canonical by others such as the Protestant Church. It is one of the seven Sapiental or *wisdom books* bound with the Septuagint Bible.

fresco with constellations.[25] As for the goddess seated on a golden throne and flanked by two lions, she is Divine Wisdom, Divina Sapienza, and according to Lechner she is seated on the "throne of Solomon" as described in I Kings 10:18–19 in the Bible. Lechner also notes that on her chest is drawn the sun; thus when combined with the lions of her throne and the relative position of the various constellations and figures around her, Divine Wisdom, concludes Lechner, is to be associated to the sun in Leo, which occurs in late July and early August, and more particularly the "second decan of Leo," that is, the "ten days from July 31 to August 9."[26]

> The reference to these particular days suggests that there is a specific event associated with the fresco of Divine Wisdom. The conclusion is inescapable that it represents the heavens of the day of the eleva-tion to the Papacy of Urban VIII: 6 August 1623.[27]

On the whole we tend to agree with Lechner's analysis on the iconography of the Sacchi fresco. Yet there was another astronomical event in Rome in the month of August that seems to suit much better the iconography and symbolism of Sacchi's fresco and, more particu-larly, the philosophy and magic of Campanella. On or near August 9 would have occurred the so-called heliacal rising of the star Sirius, a well-known event associated with divine rebirth and also with the god-dess Isis. After about seventy days of invisibility the star Sirius would, as if miraculously, rise again at dawn—an event that in ancient Egypt coincided with the annual flooding of the Nile and the divine rebirth of Isis. The ancient Egyptians began their "year" with this astrological event, which also, based on its longer cycle known as the Sothic Cycle, which occurred every 1,460 years, indicated the opening of a new age with the "return of the phoenix."[28]

Oddly, one such new age or Sothic Cycle was due to occur around the year 1600—coinciding with the burning of Giordano Bruno, the crowning of Pope Urban VIII in 1623, and the trial of Galileo in

1630. This Sothic Cycle was mentioned in Tacitus's *Annals* and also by the Roman chronicler Censorinus, and may well have been known to Hermetists such as Bruno and Campanella.[29] Indeed, Campanella was utterly convinced that a new age of great reform would begin in 1600 and that he was duty bound to announce it and usher it in with the building of the City of the Sun.[30]

Returning to the Sacchi fresco, and bearing in mind the possible links with the star of Isis, we also see something else concerning the goddess seated on the throne in the center. She is meant to be, of course, Divina Sapienza. First, the name Divina Sapienza itself would imply Minerva, the Roman Athena, the celestial virgin goddess of divine wisdom, who was extremely well known to all concerned, especially Campanella. But Minerva is nearly always shown in classical art not seated on a throne but standing and holding a shield in much the same manner as her Greek counterpart, Athena. A goddess on a throne flanked by lions was more recognizable as Cybele and, even more so, as the Egyptian goddess Isis.*

If Campanella did influence the painter Sacchi, as Lechner thinks, then the whole iconography is to be seen as Hermetic, which Lechner also clearly recognizes as well. Lechner notes, too, that the wand with the "all seeing eye" held by the enthroned goddess is pointing to Egypt and Italy, both countries illuminated by the sun on the terrestrial globe right below the goddess. This depiction no doubt was meant to symbolize that the wisdom of Egypt is linked to Italy. Campanella, like all Hermetists, was very much aware of the Hermetic tract known as the *Kore Kosmou* [The Virgin of the World], referring to the goddess Isis. He surely was also aware that since 1527 there was much discussion in Rome about the so-called "Isis Table" discovered by Cardinal Bembo, where the goddess Isis is seen seated on a throne over and flanked by two lions.†

---

*Cybele is usually shown on a throne or chariot pulled by two lions. Isis, however, is shown on a throne flanked by two lions, fitting the iconography of Sacchi's fresco much better.
†The Bembo Table, or Isis Table, is today in the Museum of Turin.

Perhaps Lechner was also not aware that a very similar depiction was drawn not much later in 1667 in France for the opera titled *Isis,* performed at Saint-Germain-en-Laye for Louis XIV, whose birth was hailed by Campanella as that of the Sun King who would build the City of the Sun in Paris. Let us note in passing that the depiction of Isis on the throne flanked by two lions appeared in Place de la Bastille in 1792, and thirty-five years later in 1827, a very similar fresco was painted by the artist Edouard Picot on the ceiling of the south wing of the Louvre, clearly showing the goddess Isis seated on a throne flaked by lions. In all those scenes there is "Hermes" flying above the goddess holding a torch in his hand, the idea being that he is illuminating, that is, revealing the mysteries and wisdom of ancient Egypt. (See appendix 1 for a full discussion on Campanella and the Sun King in Paris.) In any case, whether we are to see Minerva or Isis in Sacchi's fresco is purely academic, for both these goddesses were regarded as being the same, with Isis being the dominant or generic entity. The main literary source for Renaissance philosophers was Lucius Apuleius's *The Golden Ass,* where he has Isis stating:

> I am she that is the natural mother of all things, mistress and governess of all the elements, the initial progeny of worlds, chief of powers divine, Queen of Heaven, the principal of the Gods celestial, the light of the goddesses: at my will the planets of the air, the wholesome winds of the seas, and the silences of Hell be disposed; my name, my divinity is adored throughout all the world in divers manners, in variable customs and in many names, for the Phrygians call me the mother of the Gods: the Athenians, Minerva: the Cyprians, Venus: the Candians, Diana: the Sicilians, Proserpina: the Eleusians, Ceres: some Juno, other Bellona, other Hecate: and principally the Ethiopians who dwell in the Orient, and the Egyptians who are excellent in all kind of ancient doctrines, and by their proper ceremonies accustom to worship me, do call me Queen Isis.[31]

Fig. 4.4. Kircher's depiction of Isis-Minerva. (Athanasius Kircher)

We shall see in chapter 5 how the Renaissance Jesuit astronomer Athanasius Kircher, who had tremendous influence at the Vatican, clearly saw Isis and Minerva as being the same entity, that is, Divine Wisdom.[32] But let us now go back to Campanella and Pope Urban VIII and the talismanic astrological magic that was performed in the course of 1627 to 1630 in the Palazzo Barberini.

They sealed a room against the outside air, hung it with white cloths, and burnt certain herbs in it. Two lamps and five torches were lit, representing the planets, and the signs of the zodiac were imitated in the same way "for this is a philosophical procedure, not superstitious as the vulgar think." There was Jovial and Venereal music; stones, plants, colors belonging to the good planets were used, and they drank astrologically distilled liquors.[33]

The upshot of these bizarre magical séances at the Vatican was that Pope Urban VIII was cured from his paranoiac fear and survived the allegedly deadly effect of the eclipse of June 1630. The pope had already fully acquitted Campanella of his heretical crimes and now even asked Campanella to found the Collegio Barberini and become its head. Ironically, even the Dominicans, once Campanella's enemies, conferred on him the title of master of theology.[34]

In an amazing twist of fate Campanella, after enduring nearly three decades of incarceration and torture in the papal dungeons in Naples, now found himself in Rome in a position where he could have immense influence on the pope and Vatican affairs for several years.

Trouble, however, always seemed to lurk around Campanella. In August 1633 a young Dominican monk in Calabria called Tommaso Pignatelli, once a student of Campanella, was accused of being involved in a conspiracy to poison the Spanish viceroy and other officials in Naples. This led the authorities to also suspect Campanella. Now an old man of sixty-six and understandably terrified to fall again into the hands of the Inquisition, Campanella asked one of his new friends, the French ambassador to Rome, to help him escape to France. On the night of October 31, 1634, wearing a disguise, Campanella was smuggled out of Italy in the personal carriage of the ambassador.*

After a short spell in Aix-en-Provence at the home of his friend, the scholar Nicolas-Claude Fabri de Peiresc, Campanella arrived in Paris early in December and found a place to stay at the Dominican convent in the Rue St. Honoré. In February 1635 Cardinal Richelieu received Campanella, "embracing him, complimenting him warmly, and assuring him a pension."[36]

In that same year of 1635, the French King Louis XIII and his

---

*It would appear, however, that Pope Urban VIII was somehow aware of Campanella's departure, because the pope had apparently asked his spies at the French court to prevent Campanella "from revealing anything without special permission from His Holiness as he promised before leaving Rome."[35]

queen, Anne of Austria, had already been married nearly twenty years with no offspring to inherit the throne. Virtually everyone had given up hope that the frail king, who apparently disliked having sex with his wife and instead preferred the favors of his butler, Cinq Mars, would produce a male successor. Ever the astute gambler, Campanella took on the challenge: in the winter of 1637 he prophesied at the French court that not only would the royal couple soon bring forth a son, but also that this son would become le Roi Soleil, the Sun King, who would build the City of the Sun, from which he would rule the whole world.

Sure enough, on September 5, 1638, the future Louis XIV was born: by an amazing synchronicity, this was the day of Campanella's seventieth birthday! The great Italian magus, however, would never know how accurate his prophecy had been regarding the French Sun King, for he himself died on May 21, 1639, when the future Louis XIV* was only a few months old.[37]

It is clear that Campanella had transferred his life mission for the building of the Hermetic City of the Sun from the Vatican in Rome to the Louvre in Paris. Campanella had tried, much like others before him—Pico della Mirandola, Patrizzi, Bruno—to soften the heart of the Roman pope to reform Catholic Christianity with the prisca theologia and natural magic, but to no avail. So Campanella now sought the sponsorship of the more open-minded and far more powerful French monarchy.

Many researchers before us, however, supposed that Campanella's dream remained just that, *a dream.* As far as we know, no one tried to find out if the City of the Sun could have actually been built, let alone in Rome *under the pope's nose.*

Yet this, as strange as it may seem, is exactly what we intend to show . . .

---

*See appendix 1. For more on the possibility that Louis XIV did begin the building of a Hermetic city of the sun in Paris, see Graham Hancock and Robert Bauval, *Talisman: Sacred Cities, Secret Faith,* chapters 17 and 18.

5

URBI ET ORBI: TO THE CITY AND TO THE WORLD

Urbi et orbi (To the city of Rome and to the world)
WORDS SAID BY THE POPES
TO THE CROWD IN ST. PETER'S SQUARE
ON CERTAIN IMPORTANT OCCASIONS

Et benedictio Dei omnipotentis, Patris et Filii et Spiritus Sancti descendat super vos et maneat semper (And may the blessing of Almighty God, the Father, the Son, and the Holy Spirit, descend on you and remain with you always).
THE POPE'S BLESSING OF PILGRIMS
IN ST. PETER'S SQUARE

As it is above, so it is below.
MOTTO OF THE HERMETIC TRADITION

TEAMING UP

As always with this type of historical sleuthing there are strange synchronicities that can happen and that give new impetus and direction to the quest. In this quest for the City of the Sun, the synchronistic event occurred in November 2012 in the hills of the Chianti region in southern Tuscany at a conference organized by my friend Leonardo Lovari from Arezzo. I have briefly recounted aspects of this event in chapter 2, but it merits a few more words in view of the strangeness of how such things happen in life and the consequences that ensue.

A few days before going to the conference I had contacted the Italian author Chiara Dainelli (now Hohenzollern), who lives in Rome. I knew of Chiara's work from my friend Adriano Forgione, the editor of *Fenix Magazine,* who had published an article about Chiara's book, *Il Codice Astronomico di Dante.* Chiara had wanted to attend the conference, so I offered to drive her there. On the morning of November 10, I boarded a flight from Malaga to Rome's Fiumicino Airport, where Chiara and her mother, Adrianna, a professor of Latin and ancient Greek, had arranged to meet me. In the drive to Arezzo I had the opportunity to tell Chiara of my research related to the Hermetic City of the Sun. Chiara was immediately captivated and told me of her own keen interest on the subject. By the time we reached Arezzo, Chiara and I had decided to collaborate together on this book project. As I parked the car in the driveway of the hotel, there was an almighty downpour of rain. We waited in the car for the torrential rain to stop.

Meanwhile I told Chiara my idea for the title of the book: *The Vatican Mystery* (now *The Vatican Heresy*). The pitter-patter of the rain on the windshield almost muffled my words. Suddenly there was a narrow break in the clouds that allowed a thin ray of sunshine to fall on the dark hills in the distance. Taking this a good omen, Chiara and I stepped out of the car and ceremoniously shook hands to seal the deal of our coauthorship. Later that evening, after I had given my talk at the conference, we went to a restaurant for dinner. Sitting alone at one of the tables was a young man. Something compelled us to join him. Again, synchronistic fate played its part, for the young man was Sandro Zicari, a mathematician from Sapienza University of Rome who also happened to have a passion for the astronomy and science of the Renaissance. Sandro was very interested in hearing of our project and agreed to give us a hand with the technical side of the research (see appendices 1 and 2). I believe that certain people are meant to get together, and when they do, a strange synergy takes place that can bring to the surface some new revelation or idea or, perhaps, a long-lost plan.

A somewhat similar synchronistic encounter had occurred in Rome in 1655 that would set into motion the right conditions for the *actual construction* of the City of the Sun. I have had this very strange but unshakable sensation that somehow these two synchronistic encounters, ours in 2012 and the one of 1655, are related, although I admit I cannot explain how or why. Perhaps there is no explanation for synchronicities, at least none that could fit the present paradigm. We are now approaching the end of our investigation. The last few vital pieces of the giant puzzle I have been putting together over the last year will be revealed to complete the overall image. And when this is done, I expect you to see as we do a wonderful Hermetic heliocentric solar city emerging right before your eyes. So let us board an intellectual time machine and go to Rome to meet the protagonists who will put closure to a fantastic plan that was, in more ways than one, hatched in Alexandria long, long ago . . .

IL CAVALIERE BERNINI

In May 1639 Campanella died in Paris. At that time in Rome the great Italian Baroque architect and sculptor Gian Lorenzo Bernini—*il Cavaliere* (the Knight)—was forty-one years old and already world famous as the superintendent of works for the Vatican.

It is very probable that the two men met a few years before at the Vatican when both were working closely with Pope Urban VIII and his family. If so, no written record of such a meeting exists. What is more

Fig. 5.1. Gian Lorenzo Bernini (self-portrait)

certain, however, is that Bernini, like everyone else in high places, knew of Campanella and especially of his utopian vision of the Hermetic *City of the Sun*. And, of course, Campanella knew of Bernini. In that same month of May 1639 Bernini was about to get married to a twenty-two-year-old Roman lady, Caterina Tezio. She was to bear him eleven children. Bernini was definitely not averse to large families since he himself was the sixth of thirteen children of the Neapolitan child-bride Angelica Galante, who had been only twelve when she married Bernini's father, Pietro, the latter a fairly accomplished mannerism artist and sculptor.

Bernini was born in 1598 in Naples. When he was just a boy of eight his father took him to Rome, where the latter had been commissioned by Pope Paul V to do work on the Pauline Chapel. This was a golden opportunity for the young Bernini for it would bring him into direct contact with powerful individuals connected to the Vatican. One such individual was Maffeo Barberini, the future Pope Urban VIII, who was thirty-eight at the time. It is said that when Barberini visited Pietro Bernini's workshop in Rome when Gian Lorenzo was only eight years old, the future pope exclaimed to Pietro, "Take care, signore Bernini, this child will soon surpass you, and will be greater than his master." Barberini, like others who came to Pietro's workshop, had noticed that his son, the young Bernini, was endowed with superior artistic abilities. This soon brought him into the inner circle of artists under the patronage of the powerful and immensely wealthy Cardinal Scipione Borghese, the favorite nephew of Pope Paul V. From there on things moved fast for Bernini: when only twenty-one years old he was nominated a cavaliere (knight) of the church by Pope Gregory XV, and in 1629 Pope Urban VIII appointed Bernini chief architect of the Fabbrica Di San Pietro (effectively chief architect of the Vatican), a position that sealed his reputation as *the* master architect and sculptor in Italy and in all of Europe.

To Urban VIII, Bernini was the "Second Michelangelo," and honor upon honor, flattery upon flattery were bestowed upon him. Such fame and admiration must have gone a little to his head, for there is a letter from his distraught mother—apparently the only letter from her ever found—addressed to Cardinal Francesco Barberini, the nephew of the pope (Urban VIII), in which she laments that her son thinks he has become *padrone del mondo* (master of the world) and is misbehaving in the most appalling manner and needs to be reined in! Bernini's mother was probably referring to a scandal involving a

Fig. 5.2. Pope Urban VIII

beautiful but very promiscuous lady, Costanza Piccolomini, who had an affair with Bernini. She also seduced Bernini's younger brother, Luigi. When Bernini found out he went berserk and chased Luigi with a sword. When he caught up with Luigi, Bernini broke two of his brother's ribs with an iron bar. He then had one of his servants slash Costanza's face with a knife.[1]

Paradoxically art historians describe Bernini as affable and generous but also as conceited and choleric—characteristics typical of high-strung Italian artists of that period. Somewhat self-conscious about his uncouth origins, Bernini pretended to be a Florentine even though everyone in Rome knew he had been born and raised in Naples.*

Florence, of course, was one of the great cultural centers of Europe, the city of Leonardo and Michelangelo and the cradle of the Renaissance with its highly educated and refined Florentine scholars and artists, whereas Naples and Neapolitans were looked upon (unjustly, no doubt) as uncultured and inferior. Indeed, one of Bernini's less tactful biographers referred to Bernini as *un uomo senza lettere* (a man without letters), meaning one who is not well-read at all.[2] But such harsh criticism is probably an exaggeration. Nonetheless, in the inventory of his personal goods made after his death in 1680, there is no mention of a library or books. Be that as it may, no one except perhaps his most bitter rivals—and Bernini had many—could deny that Bernini was the supreme artistic genius of his age.

And what an age! In this latter part of the Italian Renaissance, Rome was the number one place to be. It was the crossroads for painters, poets, writers, architects, sculptors, scholars, and philosophers, and not just from Italy but from France, England, and Germany, and even from as far away as Japan! The 1600s saw intellectuals like the brilliant oddball Queen Christina of Sweden and the German Jesuit

---

*Bernini's father, Pietro, was from Florence but had moved to Naples before Bernini was born.

Fig. 5.3. View of Rome in the Baroque age, ca. 1650.

archaeologist Athanasius Kircher coming to settle in the Eternal City, many of whom were keen to rub shoulders with il Cavaliere, the Knight, as Bernini now enjoyed being called.*

Bernini had even received the highest possible compliment ever handed out in public by a pope. This occurred during the coronation of Maffeo Barberini as Pope Urban VIII in August 1623. Since 1617 Maffeo Barberini had taken a great interest in Bernini, treating him as his own son, and it was no secret that the cardinal was totally smitten with this young artist's genius and talent, so much so that immediately after he was made pope, Urban VIII summoned Bernini and enthusiastically told him, "It is your great good luck, Cavaliere, to see Maffeo Barberini pope. But we are even luckier in that the Cavaliere Bernini lives at the time of our pontificate." But as we shall soon see, it was not so lucky for one of Pope Urban VIII's other old friends, the astronomer Galileo Galilei . . .

---

*In 1898, the three-hundredth anniversary of Bernini's birth, a plaque was placed at his (still existing) house in Via della Mercede, today no. 12, which states, "Popes, Princes, and throngs of people to bow reverently before Bernini, the sovereign of all arts."

Fig. 5.4. Plaque outside Bernini's house in Rome, Via della Mercede. (Sandro Zicari)

THE ART OF DISSIMULATION

Bernini was thirty-five in February 1633, when Galileo, now an old man in his seventieth year, was dragged in front of the Papal Inquisition under the orders of Pope Urban VIII. Accused of supporting and promoting Copernicus's heliocentric theory—that the Earth moved around the sun and not vice versa—and thus going against the Holy Scriptures, Galileo was put under immense pressure to recant.

Galileo, of course, was acutely aware of the fate of Bruno and Campanella and, understandably, reluctantly but wisely took the decision to abjure and recant all that the inquisitors had demanded. Galileo thus avoided the severe punishment for heresy and got away with a life sentence in house arrest, a very "lenient" punishment in those days.

Fig. 5.5. Galileo Galilei

Ironically, Pope Urban VIII, while still a cardinal, had not only been a close friend of Galileo but also had shown interest and support for his work. Even after he became pope, Urban VIII had tolerated discussions on Copernicus's heliocentric theory as long as it remained just that: a *theory.* But Galileo was convinced that he could demonstrate, and thus prove, the theory. He overestimated his friendship with the pope and unwisely did not dissimulate his true opinions and, worse, his intentions to *prove* that Copernicus was right, this by observations with his newly acquired *perspicillum,* or telescope. Such proof, however, was precisely what the pope did not want him—or anyone else—to present. To put the position of the Vatican as simply as possible: heliocentric theory, "yes"; heliocentric *fact,* "no." Although Galileo knew this very well—the pope had actually made it clear to him a few years before—Galileo erroneously assumed that common sense and scientific proof would prevail. He couldn't have been more wrong.

Galileo, to say the very least, was not one for the "art of dissimulation," an essential social tool in those very dangerous times in Italy and, indeed, in other European countries. He could have, for instance, kept the heliocentric theory *a theory,* that is to say, a hypothetical model of the world, and let others later accept or reject the evidence. He could have, but he didn't, for the simple reason that most scientists don't: ego. It was too much for Galileo to let this enormous chance pass him by, namely to go down in history as the man who not only proved the heliocentric theory but, even more so, also got the Vatican to accept and ratify it. And we certainly cannot blame him. On the other hand perhaps he would not have gone down in history had he not been forced by the pope to recant, because most people today remember Galileo for this outrage rather than the scientific discoveries he made. It is his recanting and the way the inquisitors so viciously humiliated this old and tired man that touches the very heart of people to this day.

Galileo's contemporary fame was for his huge improvement of the simple spyglass invented by the Flemish spectacle maker Hans Lippershey in 1608 (which was but an amusing gadget for the rich) into a much more powerful scientific instrument, the telescope. The telescope permitted Galileo to make various discoveries about the motion of celestial bodies, which he published in his book *Sidereus Nuncius* [The Starry Messenger] in 1610. The text accompanying the frontispiece reads:

> **SIDEREAL MESSENGER**, *unfolding great and very wonderful sights and displaying to the gaze of everyone, but especially philosophers and astronomers, the things that were observed by* **GALILEO GALILEI**, *Florentine patrician and public mathematician of the University of Padua, with the help of a spyglass lately devised by him, about the face of the Moon, countless fixed stars, the Milky Way, nebulous stars, but especially about four planets flying around the star of Jupiter at unequal intervals and periods with wonderful swiftness; which, unknown by anyone until this day, the first author detected recently and decided to name* **MEDICEAN STARS** (in honor of Galileo's sponsor and ex-student, the Grand Duke of Florence, Cosimo II de Medici). (bold added)

It is very understandable that courtiers, artists, scientists, and philosophers at the Vatican, Bernini included, were well advised to be extremely cautious not to expose their true feelings and ideas, especially if these were related, or even construed to be related, to issues deemed heretical by the church. No matter how much the pope might have been openly friendly or even privately supportive of such ideas, such dissimulating precautions were highly advisable. Indeed, the art of dissimulation was *actually taught* to those serving powerful and thus potentially dangerous masters or sponsors. This was especially the case for those close to or working directly under Pope Urban VIII, Maffeo Barberini. This pope had a very volatile temper, to say the least. He would often burst into fits of rage at the slightest provocation. The Italian scholar Franco Mormando writes, "Tempestuous fits of irrational anger were to be a disturbingly recurrent feature of Maffeo's behavior even after his election, with no one to restrain the Supreme Pontiff."[3]

In a guidebook titled *Il Segretario* [The Secretary], written by a contemporary of Galileo and Bernini, Battista Guardini, the author gives advice on how to deal with such masters and warns, "Patricians (*I grandi*) are like lions, that can never be so tamed that they forget they are lions . . . the shrewd servant must never abandon his demeanor of subaltern."

Mormando, in his recent biography of Bernini, points out that Bernini, working so closely for the Vatican and also receiving lavish praise and financial benefits from the pope, had become particularly skillful in this lugubrious "art of dissimulation." Mormando explains:

> It is the art of hiding your true self behind a mask of silence or polite evasive answers to potentially troublesome questions. It is one of the defining characteristics of the "Baroque" mentality including Bernini's. . . . It was a habit born out of sheer necessity in that age . . . a mechanism of self-defense in the face of autocratic, and often despotic, government and at times violently enforced religious orthodoxy . . . dissimulation was considered nothing less than an indispensable survival tool, if not an outright virtue.[4]

One of Bernini's closest and dearest of friends in Rome, the highly controversial Queen Christina of Sweden, had once said, "To be unable to dissimulate was to be unable to live." Another of Bernini's close friends, a priest called Francesco Butti, once exclaimed to Bernini, "I beg you to *dissimulate,* as you know how to do when you wish to!"* (italics added).

Indeed, to speak, to write, or to show the wrong thing to a powerful cardinal or, worse, to the pope, could lead you into serious trouble, likely to total disenfranchisement or even to an untimely death. Ficino, Pico della Mirandola, Campanella, and now Galileo had all learned their lessons the hard way and thus wisely backed away when the lion growled too loud. But Francesco Pucci and Giordano Bruno paid dearly with their lives in the most grueling manner for not dissimulating. Bernini, ever the expert dissimulator, largely benefitted from papal sponsorship by clever dissimulation throughout his long career and died in bed at the ripe old age of eighty-two. Let us hold this thought because, as we shall later see, Bernini deliberately undertook, or at the very least was lured to undertake, a daring project at the Vatican that would have been considered the most vilified of heresies had it not been so well dissimulated . . .

Before we go into this, however, there are five special individuals linked, directly and indirectly, to Bernini—two prominent Jesuit scholars, a foreign queen, a pope, and a German astronomer—whom we need to introduce and to take a closer look at. For this most incredible dissimulation that we are about to reveal—the actual construction at the Vatican of the Hermetic City of the Sun, modeled on the heliocentric system—is linked to these five special individuals. But before we meet them, let us set the scene in Rome during those fateful years that will lead to this mind-boggling event.

---

*This was apparently said during an occasion when Bernini was at the risk of offending the all-powerful king of France, Louis XIV. And Marie Mancini, the Italian beauty who was the niece of Cardinal Mazarin and also Louis XIV's first love, once wrote that in Rome "*dissimulation . . . among families reign more supreme than any other court.*"

THE COMING TOGETHER

Rome, 1633: Bernini is now the superintendent of works for the Vatican. He is also Pope Urban VIII's favorite. At about the same time, the pope has just had Galileo tried and convicted of heresy for, inter alia, supporting the Copernican heliocentric theory. Galileo has been condemned to life imprisonment, but it has been reduced to perpetual house arrest. Meanwhile the pope, grateful to Campanella for having saved his life from the threat of the eclipses, had turned against him for allowing the publication of the private magic sessions they performed together in a book, *Astrologicorum Libri.* Although it was two jealous Dominican monks, Niccolò Ridolfi and Niccolò Ricardi, who sent the manuscript to France for publication without Campanella's consent, the latter was, nonetheless, held responsible by the pope. As we have seen in chapter 4, Campanella, sensing the looming danger from this and also from fear of being connected to political events in Calabria, fled to France. There are no records to establish if Bernini met Galileo and Campanella—two staunch advocates of the Copernican heliocentric theory—in those tense times at the Vatican or even whether Bernini held any scientific or religious opinions on this matter. Be that as it may, it is certain, however, that Bernini would have been extremely familiar with the work of these two scholars. Being the papal architect, he would have certainly been keenly interested in Campanella's ambition to have the pope build the City of the Sun. Let us also note in passing that Bernini, too, was at the Vatican when Galileo had come to meet with Urban VIII on several occasions.*

There now enter in our story the five protagonists who will have an enormous influence on Bernini and who we believe planted the intellectual and spiritual seeds in this artist's mind that would lead him to create his lifelong dream: a huge, highly symbolic architectural project right in front of St. Peter's Basilica . . .

---

*Galileo came six times to Rome—in 1587, 1611, 1615, 1624, 1630, 1633—and stayed several months on each occasion. He had many private audiences with Maffeo Barberini before and after the latter became Pope Urban VIII in August 1623.

THE LAST PROTAGONISTS, 1633

Protagonist 1

FABIO CHIGI

In 1633 Cardinal Fabio Chigi (the future Pope Alexander VII) was in Rome. He was soon to be sent as an apostolic delegate to Malta in 1634. It was there that he would meet the encyclopedic Jesuit scholar Athanasius Kircher in 1638, and they remained close friends all of his life. Chigi was also a very close friend of Bernini. When Chigi was crowned as Pope Alexander VII in 1655, Bernini became his personal architect and was conferred many commissions, not least the design of the great Piazza St. Peter's.

Fig. 5.6. Fabio Chigi,
Pope Alexander VII

Protagonist 2

ATHANASIUS KIRCHER

In October 1633 the German Jesuit scholar and Egyptologist Athanasius Kircher, now aged thirty-two, arrived in Rome. He had been recommended to Francesco Barberini, the nephew of Pope Urban VIII, by the French scholar Nicolas-Claude Fabri de Peiresc, who, as we recall from chapter 4, was a personal friend of Campanella. (Campanella had stayed at the de Peiresc home in Aix-en-Provence after escaping from Rome.) Soon after his arrival in Rome, Kircher joined the famous Collegio Romano as a teacher of mathematics, astronomy, and Hebrew. Kircher would become a close friend of Bernini and would collaborate with him on some architectural projects, including a fountain in Piazza Navona involving ancient Egyptian obelisks.

Fig. 5.7. Athanasius Kircher

The Italian scholar Franco Mormando, the most recent biographer of Bernini, explained that he believed that Kircher must have taught Bernini his odd theory that "the ancient Egyptians believed in a kind of cosmic, divine sperm continually raining down upon the earth, traveling on the rays of the sun. As icons of solar rays, obelisks, including that in Piazza Navona, served to attract this life-giving 'solar spermatic power' to the planet."[5] Kircher called this divine sperm "a certain universal seminal power." Bernini and Kircher were brought together by their common friendship with Pope Urban VII and Pope Alexander VII. A curious synchronistic event also linking those two important men is that they both died on the same night of November 27, 1680.

Protagonist 3

QUEEN CHRISTINA OF SWEDEN

In 1633 Christina inherited the throne of Sweden. She was only seven years old. Later, in 1654, she would shock the whole of Protestant Europe by converting to Catholicism, then abdicating and going to Rome to live under the protection of Pope Alexander VII. So close was she to this pope that on the day of her consecration at the Vatican Alexander VII renamed her Alexandra Maria after his own name and that of the Virgin.

Christina would become one of Bernini's closest friends and for many years was the darling of Roman high society. Eccentric and steeped in books, Christina had a good grasp of classical history, philosophy, alchemy, astrology, and the new sciences, and she was a correspondent of and even met some of the great scholars of her epoch, including Athanasius Kircher, the mathematician René Descartes, Blaise Pascal, and the famous astronomer Pierre Gassendi. It is reported that Henry II of Lorraine, the fifth duc de Guise, wrote of her:

> She speaks eight languages but mostly French and that as if she had been born in Paris. She knows more than our [French] Academy and

Fig. 5.8. Queen Christina of Sweden being tutored by Descartes.

the Sorbonne put together, understands paintings as well as anyone, and knows much more about our court intrigues than I do. In fact she is an absolutely extraordinary person.[6]

Christina is among the very few women to be buried in St. Peter's Basilica at the Vatican.

Protagonist 4

NICCOLÒ ZUCCHI

In 1633 the Italian Jesuit astronomer Niccolò Zucchi was aged forty-seven. Zucchi had taught mathematics and astronomy at the Collegio Romano until 1630 and now was head of the Jesuit College in Padua. In 1623 Zucchi had been part of a delegation sent by Pope Urban VIII to the court of the Holy Roman Emperor Ferdinand II in Prague, where he met the famous astronomer Johannes Kepler. Zucchi would also befriend Bernini and collaborate with him on the publication of certain scientific works.

Fig. 5.9. The Jesuit astronomer Niccolò Zucchi

Zucchi's study of light and vision, the Optica philosophica . . . was
in fact directly relevant to Bernini's art. In creating his works of
art, sculptural or architectural, Bernini was always exceptionally
aware of the crucial importance of light—specifically, the proper
manipulation of its source, its angle, and its intensity—for the
final successful effect of the work in question. This is especially
true in his chapel designs, noteworthy for their cleverly staged
theatrical lighting.[7]

It seems that Bernini got the idea from Zucchi of using a lens in the
Cornaro Chapel positioned in such a way as to cast a ray of light on
the October 15 Feast of St. Teresa of Avila, so that "Teresa's statue
(*Saint Teresa in Ecstasy* by Bernini, in Cornaro Chapel) is flooded with
golden light." It also is highly likely, as we shall see in this chapter, that
Zucchi might have influenced and even perhaps assisted Bernini in the
elliptical astronomical design of Piazza St. Peter's in 1656.

Protagonist 5

JOHANNES KEPLER

This fifth protagonist, although central to our historical puzzle, has
never been to Rome and has only met one of the other four we have just
introduced. Yet, as we shall soon see, Kepler, or rather his discoveries,
is the key to the mystery we are about to unravel. Let us quickly note
that it was the Jesuit astronomer Niccolò Zucchi (protagonist 4) who
had met Kepler and also had maintained with him a regular correspondence. Also Athanasius Kircher (protagonist 2), although he never actually met Kepler, by a curious twist of fate was asked by the Holy Roman
Emperor Ferdinand II in 1631 to replace Kepler as his court astrologer
in Prague. Let us also note that Galileo, too, although he never met
Kepler in person, nonetheless had maintained a correspondence with
him from as early as 1597. In one of his early letters, dated August 4,
1597, Galileo had written to Kepler:

Many years ago I became a convert to the opinions of Copernicus, and by that theory I have succeeded in fully explaining many phenomena . . . I have not dared to publish, fearful of meeting the same fate as our master Copernicus.[8]

Johannes Kepler started his scientific career as assistant to the famous Polish astronomer Tycho Brahe at the court of the Holy Roman Emperor Rudolf II in Prague. After Brahe's death in 1601, Kepler became personal astronomer to the emperor and also to his successors, Mathias I and Ferdinand II, until his death in 1630. Although Kepler's primary function was to provide astrological advice to the emperor, his own personal interest was scientific astronomy. Kepler was a staunch supporter of Copernicus's heliocentric theory but with one important difference: using the data collated by his mentor, Tycho Brahe, Kepler's calculations showed that the planets did not orbit the sun in *circular* paths as Copernicus (and Galileo too) maintained, but rather in elliptical paths with the sun occu-

Fig. 5.10.
Johannes Kepler

pying one of the two foci of each planet's ellipse. In the religiously tinged rhetoric of his epoch, Kepler discovered the truth behind the manner and shape in which God made the world and set it into perpetual motion. Less than a century later Isaac Newton, using Kepler's theories, would complete the picture by discovering the law of gravity and other laws that governed celestial mechanics. Today Kepler's discovery is known as *Kepler's first law of planetary motion.*

In 1609 Kepler published *Astronomia Nova* [The New Astronomy], in which he expounded his ellipse-based system, only dealing with the planet Mars. It was followed in 1615 with the publication of *Epitome astronomiae Copernicanae* [Epitome of Copernican Astronomy],* in which he presented the elliptical orbits of all known planets in the solar system as well as his second and third laws of planetary motion. The book soon gained popularity and was read by scientists throughout Europe. By the end of the seventeenth century these scientific truths would become universally accepted. The older idea that philosophers, artists, architects, and theologians had that the circle was a reflection of God's perfection gradually gave way to its elongated counterpart: the ellipse. And even though the heliocentric theory (circular orbits by Copernicus and elliptical orbits by Kepler) was still refuted by the Vatican, it began to creep into art, literature, and architecture like a thief in the night . . .

ROME: FAST-FORWARD TO 1656

By the early 1650s it had become clear—unless you were a biased and close-minded scholar—that Kepler's theories of planetary motion, especially the first law regarding the elliptical orbits of the planets, were correct.[9] Kepler's ice-cold logic and meticulous calculations, when coupled with the telescopic observation of Galileo, made it an undeniable fact

---

*This work appeared in three volumes: volume 1 (books I–III) in 1615, volume 2 (book IV) in 1620, and volume 3 (books V–VII) in 1621.

not only that the Earth and the other planets revolve around the sun instead of vice versa but also that the orbits in which they moved were elliptical.

The Three Laws of Planetary Motion

First Law: The orbit of every planet is an ellipse with the sun occupying one of its two foci.

Second Law: A line joining a planet and the sun sweeps the same area in equal time intervals.

Third Law: The square of the orbital period of a planet is directly proportional to the cube of half of the main axis of its elliptical orbit.

Everyone should have acknowledged this were it not for one huge obstacle: the Vatican still insisted that heliocentrism was a heresy to be detested because it was contradictory to the teachings in the Holy Scriptures.

Pope Alexander VII, in spite of being highly educated and liberal in his attitude toward scholars and artists, nonetheless was to have the

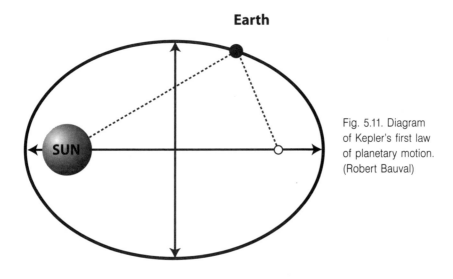

Earth

Fig. 5.11. Diagram of Kepler's first law of planetary motion. (Robert Bauval)

new index of forbidden books (*Index Librorum Prohibitorum*), which banned all books that supported heliocentrism, published in 1664–1667. Still it is possible, as we shall see, that although Alexander VII officially opposed heliocentrism, as indeed was expected of him, he did so because he was perhaps obliged to stick to the stance that his predecessor Urban VIII had taken. There are clues, however, that Alexander VII may have privately embraced the heliocentric truth or, at the very least, turned a blind eye toward those who did. Let us see why . . .

FAILING INFALLIBILITY

Galileo died in 1647 while still under house arrest. By the 1650s, however, he was fast becoming a symbol of the intractable and narrow-minded position of the Catholic Church. The obstinate stance taken by the Vatican lords over this important issue, especially when undeniable scientific proof was laid before their very nose, was becoming an embarrassing contradiction for the church. To many enlightened minds it was more than that; it was an untenable situation. There was, too, the question of *ex cathedra,* or papal infallibility, which irked the situation. Although papal infallibility was made dogma in 1870 by Pope Pius IX, it had long before been practiced as ex cathedra. The dogma of papal infallible was first proposed in the thirteenth century by the French Franciscan priest Pierre Olivi because it was obvious that popes were not merely asking people to believe in the dogmas of the church, they were *demanding* it under the threat of severe punishment. But by the mid-1500s most of these dogmas were in contradiction to empirical science, to logic, and to basic common sense. This was especially the case regarding the heliocentric issue, yet the Vatican got its own way for more than a century and a half after Galileo, and it was not until 1757 that Pope Benedict XIV issued a papal bull removing the ban on the heliocentric theory, and still not until 1822 that books supporting heliocentrism were allowed to be printed in Rome. Legend has it that even when Galileo had set up a telescope for the cardinals to see with their own eyes some of the evidence that supported heliocentrism, the cardinals refused to look for fear of shaking the foundation of their faith in the church and, also, perhaps more so, because the Vatican had shown its brutality toward those suspected of embracing heliocentrism. It is unfortunately in the nature of weak or cowardly men to turn away from evidence that may make them fall out with the powers that be. Pope Alexander VII himself typified this mental conflict. He was definitely not a simpleton; in fact, he was highly educated and thus quite capable of understanding the scientific arguments supporting heliocentrism.

Fabio Chigi was born in 1599 in the city of Siena. As a child he had suffered from severe apoplexy, resulting in a weak physical disposition throughout his adult life. But such a physical impediment did not fore-stall his extremely bright mind and sensitive nature. One of his big passions was poetry; he also earned several doctorates in philosophy, law, and theology from the University of Siena. Chigi was also well traveled. He served for many years as a papal apostolic delegate in Malta (1635–1639) and also as a *nuncio* (papal representative) in Germany (1639–1651). In 1651 he was summoned back to Rome and made secretary of state by Pope Innocent X. He was made a cardinal the following year. At the death of Innocent X the conclave voted Fabio Chigi pope in May 1655. He took the name Alexander VII, apparently in honor of his hero, Alexander the Great. Alexander VII disliked the administration of the state.

> [Instead] he delighted in the company of scholars and writers, enriched Rome university, the Sapienza, bequeathing to it his own library, and the Vatican library, which he helped to acquire the rich collection of the Dukes of Urbino, and was a splendid patron of art, above all of architecture.[10]

We are justified to wonder, therefore, whether an educated scholar such as Alexander VII was not also victim of that common intellectual ailment of the epoch: conflict of conscience between scientific truth and religious truth, that is, between facing facts and facing faith. Indeed, what could really have gone on inside the mind of such a cultured person when confronted with this kind of dichotomy? As a matter of fact, what could have gone on in the mind of any scholar, especially a Jesuit scientist-priest of the Collegio Romano?

We now turn to protagonist 2 . . .

KIRCHER'S OBELISKS

A very close friend of Pope Alexander VII was the Jesuit mathematician-astronomer Athanasius Kircher. They had met in 1637 in Malta when Alexander VII was still simply Fabio Chigi, and there the two scholarly clerics had begun a friendship that lasted until the pope's death thirty years later. Kircher had an almost obsessive interest in ancient Egypt and its mysteries. Indeed, he had been brought to teach at the Collegio Romano by Pope Urban VIII a few years before with the mandate to focus his scholarly efforts on deciphering the hieroglyphs on the Egyptian obelisks and the other Egyptian monuments that were strewn all over Rome since the time of the empire. Professor Joscelyn Godwin of Colgate University, an acclaimed authority on Athanasius Kircher, gives a very concise but accurate curriculum vitae of Athanasius Kircher: "A Christian Hermeticist in the mold of Marsilio Ficino and Pico della Mirandola, his work also examined alchemy, the Kabbalah, and the Egyptian Mystery tradition exemplified by Hermes Trismegistus."[11]

Kircher's passion for Egyptian mysteries was something that was shared by Pope Alexander VII. Indeed, Professor Eugenio Lo Sardo, also an acclaimed authority on Kircher, pointed out, "Many common interests linked them [Kircher and Alexander VII], principally among them being the passion for the Egyptian mysteries and the Hermetic tradition."[12]

In 1631 Kircher, being a Jesuit priest and a staunch Roman Catholic, had to flee Germany when a Protestant army was about to attack the Jesuit monastery in Würzburg where he was teaching and researching. Kircher managed to make his way into France and eventually to Avignon, where he stayed until late 1633. His sponsor and mentor in France was the scholar Nicolas-Claude Fabri de Peiresc, who encouraged Kircher to pursue his studies in Egyptian hieroglyphs. Kircher also befriended the great French astronomer-priest Pierre Gassendi in Aix-en-Provence, the latter also a protégé of de Peiresc. It was de Peiresc who recommended Kircher to the papal legate in Avignon, Cardinal Francesco Barberini, the nephew of Pope Urban VIII, for a post at the Collegio Romano in Rome to teach mathematics and astronomy. Francesco Barberini had studied at Pisa under Galileo and was also the sponsor of the architect Bernini. Francesco Barberini was more interested in Kircher's Egyptian studies, and he made it clear to the dean of the Collegio Romano that Kircher was to devote himself principally to the deciphering of the Egyptian hieroglyphs. Kircher was utterly convinced that the Egyptian hieroglyphs were magical signs and believed they would reveal the prisca theologia, the original divine wisdom that had been imparted to Hermes Trismegistus. However, being a Jesuit and a devout Catholic, Kircher maintained the same argument as Ficino and Pico della Mirandola, namely that the prisca theologia was to be seen as prophecy for the coming of Christianity. In other words, Kircher was a Christian Hermetist, and his work must be understood as such. From the day he was appointed head of the Collegio Romano in 1636, Kircher spent the rest of his life in Rome studying and writing, mostly about his own interpretation of Egyptian hieroglyphs and symbols, and also collecting natural specimens and antiquities that would become part of a museum, the first of its kind in Europe: the Musaeum Kircherianum, inaugurated in 1651. As a star of the Collegio Romano and director of the Musaeum Kircherianum, Kircher's fame extended across the whole of the scholarly world. A meeting with Kircher became a must for the rich and famous, such that the German Jesuit scholar became a sort of intellectual tourist attraction. According to one of Kircher's best-known biographers, the American scholar Ingrid D. Rowland:

> Visitors to seventeenth-century Rome often hoped to see a living monument among the city's attractions of art and architecture. That living monument was Father Athanasius Kircher. . . . His position ranked among the most prestigious in the Jesuit world.[13]

In the same year of 1651 when the construction of the Musaeum Kircherianum was being completed, Kircher was also much implicated in the construction of another famous landmark of Rome: the Fountain of the Four Rivers in Piazza Navona. This project was a very extravagant sculpture by Bernini that served as a base for an Egyptian obelisk, which Kircher assumed (wrongly) was from Heliopolis, the City of the Sun in Egypt. The obelisk, in actual fact, was quarried in Syene (modern Aswan) in Upper Egypt by orders of Emperor Domitian (51–96 CE), who brought it to Rome and placed it in the Campus Martius in front of a temple dedicated to Isis and Serapis. But this was not known to Kircher who, erroneously, believed it had been brought to Rome from Heliopolis by the Emperor Caracalla (188–217 CE). Kircher and Bernini had collaborated closely for several years in order to have the fountain ready as part of the massive embellishment scheme for Rome for the mid-century jubilee of 1550—sort of cultural Counter-Reformation propaganda—to impress the populace. Kircher was to produce for the occasion a guidebook, *Obeliscus Pamphilius,* which he, of course, intended to dedicate to Pope Innocent X, Giovanni Pamphilii, hence the title.

A newcomer to Rome who was following this *Obeliscus Pamphilius* project with curious interest was Fabio Chigi, soon to become a cardinal (1652) and later Pope Alexander VII (1655). Being Kircher's friend since 1637 and also an adept of Egyptian mysteries, it must have been

Fig. 5.12. The
frontispiece of Kircher's
Obeliscus Pamphilius.
(Athanasius Kircher)

obvious to Chigi, and to other scholars, that the placing of this ancient
Egyptian solar symbol in the center of a circular or oval-shaped piazza
was very suggestive of Copernican heliocentrism. True, Chigi, as well as
all scientifically minded Jesuit scholars, such as Kircher, could not *officially* support this theory as it was still deemed to be a heresy to do so.
But according to Ingrid D. Rowland, "In 1633, Kircher had admitted
to friends in Avignon that several of the most prominent Jesuit astronomers . . . actually believed in a Sun-centered, Copernican universe;
the tone of Kircher's remarks suggest that he must have shared these
Copernican convictions as well."[14]

John Milton and the Italian Scholars

In 1638, a few years after the scandalous trial of Galileo, the English poet John Milton visited Rome. He met many of the city's learned men, although he did not name them. In those days most learned men in Rome were Jesuits or scholars attached to the Vatican. Milton described the mood of these Italian learned men in his great oration on the freedom of the press in 1644.

> When I had sat among their learned men, for that honor I had, and been counted happy to be born in [England] such a place of philosophic freedom, as they supposed England was, while themselves did nothing but bemoan the servile conditions into which learning amongst them was brought. [15]*

---

*The Galileo condemnation sent prominent members of the Barberini court who supported the scientist and the new scientific speculation fleeing, literally or metaphorically, for safety. Papal favorite Bernini did not have to flee in any sense, but the lesson was not lost on him: don't rock the boat.

One such prominent Jesuit astronomer was probably the Jesuit scholar Niccolò Zucchi, whose involvement with Bernini will be discussed later on in this chapter. It must be noted that there existed the so-called Jesuit Curriculum, which bound all Jesuit scholars to rigorously stick to the Aristotelian theories and the Ptolemaic Earth-centered model, that is to say, the geocentric model that the church insisted conformed to the Holy Scriptures. The penalty for deviating from this, let alone supporting the heliocentric theory openly, was extremely severe and, if taken to its limit by the Inquisition, could lead to imprisonment and even execution. The fairly recent trial of Galileo in 1633 and the burning of Giordano Bruno in 1600 were constant, grim reminders of how the Vatican would react to such a violation. Just talking openly with friends about the heliocentric theory, let alone supporting it openly, was, quite literally, playing with fire. Knowing this,

Kircher had understandably openly expressed his objections to Galileo's theories, but based on a book that he wrote later, we are led to believe that these objections were not at all genuine, but rather were a form of dissimulation to protect himself. [16]

Yet in spite of such a cautious stance over this very dangerous controversy, in 1656—a most crucial year in Rome, as we shall soon see—Kircher felt emboldened to finally express his views on this matter, albeit vaguely and dressed in a fictional dialogue. This was in a book titled *Itinerarium Extaticum Coeleste* [Ecstatic Celestial Journey], which he, interestingly, dedicated to Queen Christina of Sweden. So before we review this strange but most revealing book by Kircher, we now need to turn to protagonist 3 . . .

ISIS REBORN

In November 1632 the king of Sweden, Gustav II Adolfo, the fiercest opponent of the Catholics and the Vatican, was killed at the Battle of Lützen in Germany. Dubbed "The Lion of the North," Gustav II, with his well-trained army, had turned Sweden into a military power to be reckoned with, and with his many victories over the Catholics, he managed to tilt the balance of power in favor of Protestantism in Europe. His death was a huge blow to the Lutherans and other Protestants, but only politically.

His only surviving legitimate child, Christina, was six years old. Christina's mother, Maria Eleonora of Brandenburg, was from the noble House of Hohenzollern of Prussia. (By a strange twist of fate my present coauthor's husband, Kenneth-Wilhelm Hohenzollern, is from the same noble "House.") Christina was declared queen of Sweden the following year. However, in June 1654, when she was only twenty-eight years old, Queen Christina abdicated and, to the horror of Protestants all over Europe, declared her intention to convert to Catholicism. Because she was the daughter of the late Gustav II Adolfo, who had been the most ferocious and dangerous opponent of the pope, such shocking news spread like wildfire across Europe. Needless to say, Christina's conversion pleased the Vatican immensely. It pleased even more Cardinal Fabio Chigi, who was soon to be made pope. Chigi's closest friend, Kircher, was already in correspondence with Queen Christina, and what he heard of her was most encouraging, at least in Kircher's way of seeing things. It had been Jesuit infiltrators at the Swedish court, after all, who had successfully persuaded Christina to convert to Catholicism, and this stunning coup provided the opportunity to put into action one of the most amazing public relations stunts in the history of the Vatican.*

The daughter of the most feared Protestant general, a queen no less, throwing away her Lutheran and Protestant mantle and embracing Roman Catholicism! Clearly she must be brought to Rome in triumphal pomp and circumstance worthy of Queen Cleopatra of Egypt! This was an event that cardinal Fabio Chigi dreamed to put into action if and when he became pope. So, when Innocent X died in April 1655 and Chigi became Pope Alexander VII in May 1655, the first thing he did was to invite Christina to come settle in Rome.

This most unusual young and very virginal queen was, to say the very least, a most moody and eccentric individual. Almost masculine (some even believed she was a hermaphrodite) in her physical aspect and quirky behavior, her main interests were music, the theater, and, above all else, reading. Christina was extremely fond of all things Baroque and dabbling in ancient books and manuscripts such as the Hermetica, books on alchemy, Kabbalah, magic, astronomy, astrology, and, especially, the new sciences. She fancied herself a "Semiramis" or "Minerva" of the North, and more especially a "reborn Isis." As an aside, it is also thought that C. S. Lewis modeled the Snow Queen of his famous The Chronicles of Narnia series on Queen Christina of Sweden. Unquestionably, Christina was the quintessential dilettante and "New Ager" of the late Renaissance.

---

*The Jesuit priest-scholars who most influenced Queen Christina to convert to Catholicism were two Italians: Paolo Casati, a mathematician from the Collegio Romano, and Francesco Malines, a theologian from Turin; there was also a Spaniard, the Jesuit Antonio Macedo.

"I love my books with passion!" Christina would often exclaim.* And when she departed from Sweden in 1654, making her way to Rome with an entourage of 250 servants, bodyguards, friends, and almost as many horses, her most precious cargo was her vast library of books and manuscripts.[17]

Without exaggeration, Christina was a living encyclopedia and, to occult-minded scholars such as Kircher, an incarnation of Divina Sapienza! It is no wonder that Kircher referred to this most erudite virgin queen as the reborn Minerva and Isis! At any rate, Christina received much attention and respect from the great scholars of her age, not least the Jesuit-educated René Descartes, who in 1649 accepted a post in Sweden to teach her astronomy and mathematics. Unfortunately Christina insisted that lessons begin at five in the morning, and being winter and bitterly cold, Descartes eventually caught pneumonia and died in her castle on February 11, 1650.

One of Christina's interests—perhaps even her main interest—was astronomy. She had studied astronomy under Lubenitz and later, in 1667 and 1668, had her own private observatory built in Rome in Palazzo Riario (now Palazzo Corsini) and manned by two live-in Jesuit astronomers. Christina maintained a regular correspondence with many eminent astronomers and philosophers, including Pierre Gassendi, a friend of Kircher, who also founded the Paris Observatory for the Sun King, Louis XIV. Gassendi, like many astronomers of his time, was at first a geocentrist but by the 1650s almost certainly accepted the Copernican and probably even the Keplerian models, even though he discretely kept such thoughts to himself. In 1631, using a Galilean telescope, Gassendi observed the transit of Mercury as predicted by Kepler a few years before. As his official statement on Copernican heliocentrism, Gassendi maintained that it depended on probabilities and was not yet proven, yet he also strongly refuted all objections against it. Like all scientists whose intense Catholic religious conscience did not permit them to

---

*After Christina's death in 1689 the Vatican bought her vast library.

embrace the heliocentric system, Gassendi compromised by adhering to the so-called Tychonian system, namely that all planets revolved around the sun but that the sun itself revolved around the Earth, a compromise acceptable to the Vatican since it retained the idea that the Earth was the fixed focus of the universe. Ironically, Gassendi died in October 1655, about the same time that Queen Christina was on her way to Rome. In 1656 the famous Italian astronomer Giovanni Cassini, who was to replace Gassendi in Paris, dedicated one of his most important publications to Queen Christina. Cassini, like Gassendi before him, was at first a believer in the geocentric system but later accepted a version of the Copernican heliocentric system. Also like Gassendi, Cassini went to France and worked for the Sun King, Louis XIV, at the Paris Observatory.

Christina's glorious entry into the Eternal City in late December 1655 was, as far as pomp and pageantry go, akin to the Egyptian Queen Cleopatra's entry into Rome in 44 BCE. She, too, was seen as the reincarnated or reborn Isis. One of Queen Christina's biographers was not off the mark when he wrote of Christina that she "is undoubtedly the most discussed of all queens in history, second only to Cleopatra."[18]

A few days after her arrival in Rome Kircher gave Christina a gift of a model Egyptian obelisk on which he had inscribed, "Great Christina, Isis Reborn, erects, delivers and consecrates this obelisk on which the secret marks of Egypt are inscribed."[19] As we mentioned on page 184, Kircher also dedicated to Christina his latest book, *Itinerarium Extaticum Coeleste.* In this book Kircher seems to be revealing, albeit in a blurry manner, the heliocentric truth of the world as seen through the eyes of a fictitious character, an angel called Cosmiel. Interestingly, also to commemorate Christina's arrival in Rome, Kircher gave a similar model obelisk to Pope Alexander VI, calling him Osiris Reborn, thus suggesting some sort of mystical union between the "virgin" Christina and the pope.[20]

Kircher knew, of course, that Cleopatra's famous Roman lovers, Julius Caesar and Mark Antony, had been seen as the New Osiris, and that Cleopatra herself was the New Isis, claiming Alexander the Great as her "divine ancestor." Kircher, who, like Bernini, often had flattered Pope Alexander VII as being the "new Alexander [the Great]," couldn't have been more enthralled to welcome to Rome this New Isis from the North, Queen Christian of Sweden. It was the architect Bernini who designed the imposing archway at Piazza del Popolo through which Queen Christina made her famous entry into the Eternal City with all her retinue. She, in return, would soon be totally enthralled by Bernini.

Soon after her arrival in Rome, Christina visited the Collegio Romano, where Kircher was the director. Christina's favorite specialist and also very intimate friend, however, was to be Bernini, whom she adored from the outset. Of Bernini she once said, "Whoever does not esteem Bernini is not worthy of esteem himself!" Bernini was to remain very close to Queen Christina until his death in 1680; indeed, he would ask for her to come to his deathbed to pray for his soul.

On Christmas Day 1655 Pope Alexander VII consecrated Christina into Catholicism at the Vatican and rebaptized her Alexandra Maria—implying, to say the least, a union between himself and the Virgin. Many years later, when Christina passed away in 1689, the Roman Curia would honor her by having her buried in the vaults of the Vatican, an honor that very few women in history were given.

But let us return to Kircher's book *Itinerarium Extaticum Coeleste,* which was dedicated to Queen Christina. According Rowland, the encouragement Kircher got to write this rather illuminating book came from his ex-student and one-time personal assistant at the Collegio Romano, Kaspar Schott. Like Kircher, and indeed most mathematicians and astronomers in those days, Schott publically accepted the Tychonian system, but also seemed to have much respect for Kepler.[21] There is little doubt, however, that Kircher was also—and probably mostly—emboldened by seeing in May 1655 his old friend Fabio Chigi become Pope Alexander VII. According to Ingrid D. Rowland, "[Fabio Chigi] was an intellectual figure of international prominence . . . whose ties, like Kircher's, extended from freethinking Protestants to conservative Catholics."[22]

Christina and Bernini

Queen Christina of Sweden was not just a very close and intimate friend of Bernini, but actually came to his rescue and that of his family on several occasions. In 1670 Luigi, Bernini's brother, raped and sodomized a young lad. And not anywhere, mind you, but behind the equestrian statue *The Vision of Constantine* in the Vatican that Bernini had recently sculpted! A huge scandal ensued, and Luigi had to escape out of Rome. Bernini went to Queen Christina for help, and it was thanks to her personal intervention with the pope and the cardinals that Luigi was eventually pardoned. In 1673 the Bernini family had its reputation in tatters due to Luigi's insane indiscretion and other matters that had infuriated Romans and brought out Bernini's enemies in droves. To counter this very negative situation Bernini commissioned a well-known author to write a biography of him, which presented him in the most glorious, pious, and benevolent manner—much being either highly exaggerated or simply made up!

Amazingly, Queen Christina was happy to endorse the book and even claimed to have herself commissioned it. All this goes to show that Christina had a very special liking for Bernini and probably had much influence on him as well. Let us note in passing that of all the pious people in high places that Bernini knew in Rome—cardinals and high-ranking Jesuits—it was Christina that he asked for when he was dying because, according to Bernini, she knew a special language to communicate directly with God.

At any rate, Kircher's *Itinerarium Extaticum Coeleste* is presented as a dialogue between an angel called Cosmiel and a scholar called Theodidactus (Taught by God), the latter clearly meant to be Kircher himself. The discussion between them is, inter alia, about how the heavens are made. Even though Kircher does not state it outright, it is obvious from the discussion that he favors heliocentrism or, at the very least, the Tychonian system. Rowland, who reviewed Kircher's book, pointed out that he uses the angel Cosmiel as a mouthpiece to explain that *each individual star in the firmament behaves exactly like the sun, shedding heat and light, and is surrounded by planets of its own*—this being as close as one could get, albeit using vague language, to describing not only heliocentrism but also Giordano Bruno's vision of "many worlds."[23]

Kircher, like all astronomers at that time, was very familiar with the works of Copernicus and Kepler, probably before they were put in the *Index of Forbidden Books* of the Vatican in 1621. Kircher, who was a man convinced that the ancient Egyptians possessed divine knowledge, would have been pleased with Kepler's introduction of book V of his *Harmonices Mundi*.

> I am stealing the golden vessels of the Egyptians to build a tabernacle to my God from them, far, far away from the boundaries of Egypt. If you forgive me, I shall rejoice; if you are enraged with me, I shall bear it. See, I cast the die, and I write the book. Whether it is to be read by the people of the present or of the future makes no difference: let it await its reader for a hundred years, if God himself has stood ready for six thousand years for one to study him.[24]

Did Kircher, like so many of his contemporaries, privately recognize the Keplerian heliocentric model as very likely to be true? But then, being a staunch Jesuit, did he have the usual problem of conscience to even admit it to himself, let alone to others? Yet perhaps when his friend Fabio Chigi became pope, did Kircher feel he could at least hint at his private thoughts by means of fictionalizing them in a dialogue, as indeed Galileo and Kepler had also done before him?

Professor Georg Schuppener of the University of Leipzig, an authority on this particular topic, pointed out, "It is well known that the Order of the Jesuits was the most important and the most active

Catholic Order in the field of science during the seventeenth and eighteenth centuries."[25] Schuppener also showed that Kepler, even though he was a staunch Lutheran, maintained a very special relationship with the Jesuit Order, especially those Jesuits who were mathematicians and astronomers. Two such Jesuit scholars were Paul Guldin and Niccolò Zucchi, prominent mathematician-astronomers like Kepler and at one time senior teachers at the Collegio Romano, where Kircher would be the director from 1636 to the end of his life. But we are getting ahead of our story. More on Guldin and especially Zucchi shortly.

Meanwhile, returning to Athanasius Kircher, we feel it is important to emphasize again that he was not just a prominent mathematician-astronomer but also a natural philosopher with an obvious penchant for all things Egyptian, that is to say, all things Hermetic. Perhaps less known, however, is Kircher's belief in something he termed *panspermia,* a seminal power of things or universal sperm that he believed was stored in the sun and constantly came down to affect all things on Earth.[26]

Kircher believed that living and inanimate objects could receive this panspermia and be energized or animated with this subtle but powerful solar force. Kircher also believed that the ancient Egyptians were the first to have harnessed panspermia and embed it into statues and obelisks. This is precisely the type of talismanic magic found in the *Asclepius* and developed by Marsilio Ficino. Kircher must have thought that an authentic obelisk from Heliopolis was ideal for such a magical purpose. Professor Anna M. Partini, vice president of the Accademia Tiberina di Roma, in her book *Roma Egizia: culti, temple e divinità Egizie nella Roma Imperiale,* which she coauthored with Boris de Rachewiltz, asserted that this was precisely what Kircher had in mind.

> The obelisks were for Kircher the supreme expression of Egyptian wisdom, solar symbols par excellence through which the divine Light manifests and descends into men and matter.[27]

In the *Obeliscus Pamphilius,* which he dedicated to Pope Innocent X, Kircher incorporated a diagram bearing the caption "Obeliscus Heliopolitanus"[28] and made a connection between the crux ansata (the Egyptian ankh) inscribed on this obelisk and the Christian cross placed on the top of the Vatican obelisk by Pope Sixtus V in 1586. According to Frances A. Yates:

> Kircher [stated] that Hermes Trismegistus invented the Egyptian form of the cross, the *crux ansata,* which he calls the "crux Hermetica." The Egyptian or Hermetic cross, says Kircher, was a "most potent amulet" . . . and Marsilio Ficino has described its power. Kircher thus is in agreement with Ficino about the power of the Egyptian cross . . . the hieroglyphs on the obelisk of Heliopolis [the Piazza Navona obelisk], which include several representations of what Kircher calls the Egyptian cross, are explained as having the meaning of the obelisk shown in the center [of the diagram], on which there is a Christian cross and sun.[29]

Even more startling, Kircher goes on to propose that the texts in Latin to be put on the obelisk of the Piazza Navona should contain a reference to Heliopolis *and* the Hermetica (Athanasii Kircheri, Obeliscus Pamphilius, Roma MDCL, ed. Ludovici Grignani, sheet 32–34). Although the texts are shown in his book, they were eventually not used on the obelisk itself.

TEXT (SOUTH FACE)

HERMETICUM OBELISCUS, A SOTHI REGE HELIOPOLI ERECTUM AB IMPERATORE CARACALLA ROMANO DELATUM INTER CIRCI CAST-RENSIS RUDERA IACENTEM FRACTUMQVE INNOCENTI X P.M.: AD ORNANDUM ERUDITIS AEGYPTIORUM MYSTERIIS AQUA VIRGINIS FONTEM TRANSTULIT, INSTAURAVIT, EREXIT.

(The Hermetic Obelisk erected by Savior King in Heliopolis / transported to Rome by the Emperor Caracalla / [found] lying broken in pieces among the ruins of the circus castrense / by Innocent X P.M. / to decorate the water fountain virgin by scholars of the mysteries of the Egyptians / who moved, restored and raised it.)

TEXT (WEST FACE)

INNOCENTIUS X P.M. AMANEAM SALUBRITATEM CUM MAGNIFICA ERUDIZIONE CONIUNGENS LITERATUM HERMETICIS AENIGMATIS LAPIDEM AQUAE VIRGINIS FONTI IMPOSUIT AD SEDAMDAM COR-PORUM ET ACUENDAM INGENORIUM SITIM

(Innocent X P.M. / The pleasant well with the noble teaching / combining stone with engraved letters of the enigmatic Hermetic texts / at the water source of a virgin / raised to quench the thirst of the body and insatiable desire of the minds)

The frontispiece of Kircher's book *Obeliscus Pamphilius* shows the ancient obelisk still fallen while Mercurio-Hermes hovers above the ground holding a scroll with the words "Obeliscus Pamphilius." We are meant to understand that Mercurio-Hermes is the author of the mysterious inscriptions and that Kircher knows their secrets. This allegorical message is directed to a female angel looking up in gratitude at Mercurio-Hermes, indicating that the wisdom inscribed on the obelisk is now being revealed by Kircher. Next to the angel is a small child with a finger in his mouth and with one foot on a crocodile, a well-known depiction of Horus-Hapocrates, the son of Isis and Osiris. The reader will recall from chapter 3 that much of the same symbolism was used by Edmund Spenser for Elizabeth I as Britomart when she is transformed into the goddess Isis and copulates with the crocodile to produce a lion-king. At any rate, it is not known what Pope Innocent X made of such blatant Hermetic symbolism alongside his name on the obelisk. But

Fig. 5.13. The Fountain of the Four Rivers with the ancient Egyptian obelisk. (Robert Bauval)

whatever the pope might have thought, he seemed quite happy to allow Kircher's book with all its Hermetic implications to be printed and be widely circulated in Rome.

The Controversy of the Piazza Navona Obelisk

Pope Innocent X was not well viewed because of this and other projects. Huge funds were used for the bicentennial jubilee (1650) to embellish Rome, mainly as a form of propaganda for the Counter-Reformation. People accused the pope of squandering money when much of the population of Rome suffered from malnutrition. Another problem with Innocent X was that he was much influenced by his sister-in-law, Olimpia Maidalchini. It was even rumored that she was his mistress. She was called "La Papessa" (the She-Pope) behind her back.

Regarding the Piazza Navona obelisk, the text proposed by Kircher was not used. Yet in a letter dated November 16, 1650, written to Kircher by a Jesuit called Judok Kedd, the author jocularly commented, "Pope Innocent X read Kircher's *Obeliscus Pamphili* in his private room!" Kircher was a prolific letter writer. He corresponded with more than 760 notorieties, including popes, monarchs, princes, cardinals, scientists, Jesuit colleagues, and friends from all over Europe and beyond. Most of his correspondence is archived at the Pontifical Gregorian University in Rome.

Fabio Chigi, Kircher's old friend whom he had met fifteen years before in Malta and who was as keen as he was in Egyptian mysteries, had just arrived in Rome. Chigi, who was soon to become Pope Alexander VII, would even surpass all his predecessors in expenditures on massive embellishment projects for the Eternal City involving ancient Egyptian obelisks. Let us also not forget Bernini in this Piazza Navona affair, for it was he who designed the fountain on which the obelisk was placed. We may safely assume that having worked closely with Kircher on this project for several months, they would have discussed the symbolism of the inscriptions, perhaps even Kircher's ideas of panspermia and his own private views on the heliocentric controversy. If they did, there is, however, no record of such conversations. Yet even if Kircher had not discussed the heliocentric controversy with Bernini, there probably was another Jesuit priest-astronomer with whom he almost certainly did.

We now turn to our fourth protagonist . . .

THE CONFESSOR OF
THE CONCLAVE

When Kircher joined the Collegio Romano in 1633, he was replacing another Jesuit astronomer-priest who had been director of the Collegio but now was the rector of the new Jesuit College in Padua. His name was Niccolò Zucchi. Ten years earlier, in 1623, Zucchi had been part of a high-powered delegation sent to Prague by Pope Urban VIII to the court of Ferdinand II, the Holy Roman Emperor. There Zucchi had met the great German astronomer Johannes Kepler, and the two men struck up a close friendship. Zucchi had tried to convert Kepler to Catholicism but to no avail. Nonetheless, Zucchi had shown amazing kindness toward Kepler by gifting him with a telescope he had brought from Rome, a very precious and rare object in those days. Kepler was never to forget this generous and kind act by Zucchi. A few years later, in 1630, Kepler brought it up in his last work, *Kepler's Somnium* (Kepler's Dream).[30] This was in the dedication of the book, in the form of a letter addressed to the Swiss Jesuit priest-mathematician Paul Guldin, a Lutheran who had converted to Catholicism, and a close friend of Zucchi. Guldin, like Zucchi, had also taught at the Collegio Romano, and it was he who apparently had urged Zucchi to give the telescope to Kepler on behalf of the Society of Jesus, that is, the Jesuit Order. This is what Kepler wrote about Guldin and Zucchi in the dedication:

> To the very reverend Father Paul Guldin, priest of the Society of Jesus, venerable and learned man, beloved patron. There is hardly anyone at this time with whom I would rather discuss matters of astronomy than with you. Father Zucchi could not have entrusted this most remarkable gift—I speak of the telescope— to anyone whose efforts in this connection please me more than yours.[31]

The mere fact that Kepler dedicated the book to Guldin and Zucchi, both of whom were not only senior members of the Jesuit Order but also eminent mathematician-astronomers linked to the Collegio Romano, should tell us plenty. Are we to read between the lines of Kepler's dedication that now, at the end of his life (Kepler died that same year of 1630) he wanted to solicit the support of these open-minded Jesuits to do something about the impasse caused by the obstinate stance taken by the Vatican regarding the heliocentric truth? Was this the real intention of the *Somnium*?

At any rate, when Zucchi returned to Rome he maintained a correspondence with Kepler. Zucchi, in fact, was a highly accomplished astronomer in his own right. He is accredited for inventing the reflecting telescope in 1616 and also for discovering the belts of Jupiter in 1630. It is even believed that his *Optica philosophia experimentalis et ratione a fundamentis constituta* probably inspired Newton to refine the reflecting telescope.* Did Zucchi privately support Kepler's theories? We shall consider this question later in this chapter.

Zucchi, of course, knew Kircher. For example, both were together during the famous "water column vacuum experiment"† conducted by the mathematician Gasparo Berti in Rome circa 1641. Zucchi was also a very close friend of Bernini and had a special relationship with Fabio Chigi. In April 1655, after the death of Innocent X and while the papal conclave of cardinals was about to make Fabio Chigi pope, Zucchi was appointed as confessor to the conclave.[32] And when elected, Pope Alexander VII nominated Zucchi as his apostolic preacher, a very

---

*The Zucchi moon crater is named after this underestimated Jesuit. Interestingly, another moon crater is named after Athanasius Kircher. There are some thirty-five moon craters named after Jesuit scientists.

†Gasparo Berti attached a forty-foot lead pipe to the side of his house, filled it with water, sealed the top, and opened a cock at the bottom, which stood in a large vessel of water. Ten feet of the water flowed out, leaving a column suspended some thirty feet high and a space above it that posed a difficult puzzle, since the reigning Aristotelian physics held the vacuum to be an impossibility (Heilbron, *Oxford Companion to the History of Modern Science*, p. 80).

Fig. 5.14. Frontispiece of Zucchi's *Optica philosophia experimentalis et ratione a fundamentis constituta.* (Gian Lorenzo Bernini)

privileged position that would bring the two men extremely close to each other. Bernini was a great admirer of Zucchi and openly complimented the Jesuit astronomer-priest for "being the best preacher he ever heard."[33] Zucchi and Bernini clearly developed a very close friendship that lasted until their old age, as can be ascertained from the warm and intimate tone in the numerous letters of their correspondence.*

More importantly, Bernini and Zucchi had collaborated together in 1631 on a project that seem to be supportive of the heliocentric theory.[35] As often was the case, the frontispiece design was intended to be a powerful and important message, but veiled in allegorical language. In Zucchi's frontispiece, which was designed for him by Bernini, an eagle is shown flying from the Earth toward the sun. Irving Lavin, Ph.D., an art professor at Pennsylvania State University, carried out a detailed study of the frontispiece and concluded that it may be a depiction of the heliocentric system.

---

*In 1664, when Bernini was in Paris, he corresponded with Zucchi on very personal matters.[34]

[Bernini] portrays what can only be described as a real cosmic event involving a magnificent interplanetary eagle and two celestial bodies in dynamic relationship to each other . . . it can scarcely be a coincidence that a significant step in this direction had been taken twenty years earlier in a monumental composition with which Bernini was intimately familiar, involving the sun, an eagle, and a spherical earth in a similar cosmic design. . . . The design focuses mainly on the sun and earth, and their eccentric relationship has been interpreted as an allusion to the heliocentric system.[36]

The monumental composition with which Bernini was intimately familiar is the fresco *La Divina Sapienza* done by Andrea Sacchi for the Palazzo Barberini, which we discussed in chapter 4. Although Zucchi is often cited by historians as being an opponent of Galileo, his relationship with Kepler would suggest otherwise, and the frontispiece of his book, made by Bernini, is, like Sacchi's fresco, an allegory of the heliocentric system or, at the very least, an attempt to reconcile the conflict of "faith versus fact" imposed by the Vatican on the Jesuit scientists. The year that Sacchi painted the fresco—1629 to 1630—was the same year that Pope Urban VII appointed Bernini architect for the Vatican and also when Campanella was at the Palazzo Barberini doing magical rituals with the pope to ward off the "death threat" of the forthcoming eclipses.

Coming now to the fateful year of 1656, when Zucchi and Bernini were closely working together and when Queen Christina of Sweden was enjoying the new friendship with Bernini as well as the flattering attention and consideration of Pope Alexander VII and the full courtesy of Athanasius Kircher, we can see how this congregation of luminaries—an astronomer, an architect and artist, a Hermetic Kabbalist, an erudite and highly strung virgin queen, and a poet-pope at the helm of Roman Catholicism—could create quite an explosive concoction of ideas. Few could have been closer to Alexander VII at this precise moment than these four highly influential individuals. Zucchi and

Kircher were Jesuit priests as well as astronomers; Bernini, the greatest living architect of his time; and Christina, the "Reborn Isis" and incarnation of divine wisdom who charmed them all.

An amazingly daring yet highly inspiring plan was about to be hatched: the actual building of the long-awaited City of the Sun.

But let us pause and take another excursion back in time . . .

EXCURSION SEVEN, PIAZZA ST. PETER'S, 1608

A DELIBERATE ERROR

After the papal architect Fontana had raised the obelisk in front of the new St. Peter's Basilica in 1586, there was a run of five popes in a twenty-two-year period. Four of them died shortly after becoming pope—Urban VII, Gregory XIV, Innocent IX, and Leo XI—and the fifth, Clement VIII, ruled for twelve years. We are now, in 1608, three years into the pontificate of Pope Paul V.

The work on the new St. Peter's Basilica was nearly over. However, most of the popes who had been involved with this project since work had began in 1506 had been unhappy with the so-called Greek cross design by Bramante and wanted instead to modify the plan so as to create a more elongated Latin cross. This would entail making the nave much longer. After the death of Michelangelo in 1564, the project to extend the nave was given to the architect Carlo Maderno. He was also commissioned to design a new facade for the basilica. Work began in February 1608. While these works were still in progress, a series of seemingly unrelated events occurring in various parts of Europe were about to cause one of the greatest controversies in history.

Event 1, Holland: A spectacle maker called Hans Lippershey had just invented a tube-like instrument with an optical lens at both ends that allows distant objects to appear closer.

Event 2, Italy: The astronomer Galileo Galilei, after seeing a description of Lippershey's invention, made some major improvements to it by increasing the magnifying power manifold. On a clear night he pointed the instrument toward the sky. What he saw supported the heliocentric theory of Copernicus. A few months later, Galileo completed his book, *Sidereus Nuncius,* in which he presented the evidence he had observed with the tubelike instrument, which was now called a telescope.

Event 3, Prague: The mathematician and astronomer Johannes Kepler was finishing his book *Astronomia Nova,* which presented his first and second laws of planetary motion. This not only strongly supported the Copernican heliocentric theory but also improved on it by showing that the orbits of planets were elliptical (and not circular as Copernicus and Galileo had thought).

Hell was about to break loose, or rather a "revolution" that would badly shake the foundations of the Vatican. And it was at this point in time, around 1608, that the architect Carlo Maderno decided to make a radical and controversial decision regarding the astronomical alignment of the new St. Peter's Basilica . . .

TWO DEGREES TO THE NORTH

We can perhaps imagine Maderno gazing attentively at the Egyptian obelisk that stood like a lithic sentinel in front of the new basilica. He was quick to notice that something was wrong in its relationship with the alignment of the new building being finished (see plates 3 and 4). Maderno needed to make a quick and bold decision to "make good" this apparent mistake.

Let us point out that Maderno was the nephew of Domenico Fontana, the engineer who just a few years earlier had brought the ancient Egyptian obelisk from the Circus Nero to the Vatican and raised it. In fact Maderno was in Rome in 1586 when this event took place and probably had assisted his uncle in some of the preparations. But now, twenty-two years later, Maderno realized that his uncle had placed the obelisk a little off-center to the alignment of the new basilica! So to rectify this discrepancy, Maderno decided to turn the new facade a little toward the north, that is, a little counterclockwise, so that it would align with the obelisk. Maderno achieved this by simply making the south wall of the facade slightly longer than its north wall.[37]

There is much disagreement, however, with historians of architecture over why Fontana had "misplaced" the obelisk and why Maderno opted to twist the new facade of the basilica. For example, some specialists believe that "the nave [that Maderno extended] shifts orientation imperceptibly to align with the Vatican Obelisk, which Fontana had *accidentally* set off-center: Maderno considered it easier to turn the nave than to move the Egyptian needle"[38] (italics added).

However, others, such as Professor Terry Kirk, a lecturer in architectural history at the American University in Rome, see things somewhat differently.

> Fontana placed this obelisk off axis in relation to the orientation of the church construction. This can be easily verified by noting in any view of the exterior of St. Peter's today the lack of alignment of the obelisk's tip to reference points behind it. It never aligns to both the façade's pediment and the central window of the dome's drum. The new church, continuing under Michelangelo's plans, was in Fontana's day still a work in progress; its nave and facade had not yet been conceived, and parts of the old church still stood in the midst of the work site. *But it is unlikely that a discrepancy of the obelisk's alignment was the engineer's oversight.* By this specific placement of the obelisk approximately thirteen feet (four meters) to the left while looking out from the church's front door, the imagined visual axis extending away from the complex was shifted a few degrees to the north. It would have run down the center of the spina block, as can be seen on accurate maps like the plan by Giovanni Battista Nolli. Thus, a long, westward axial approach could have been realized economically by simply extracting the spina.[39]

Finally there is Federica Goffi, a Ph.D. in architecture and design research, who referred to the Italian architect and archaeologist Pierluigi

Silvan, who studied plans of the new St. Peter's Basilica by the artist Tiberio Alfarano (1526–1596). Apparently Alfarano had been present during part of the construction period from 1564 to 1596 and made sketches and drawings of the new basilica layout, but Goffi notes, "Silvan pointed out that Alfarano did not take into consideration the fact that the old Basilica and the new have slightly diverging orientations. *The main east/west axis of the old Basilica is rotated 2 degrees counterclockwise in respect to the axis of the new one*"[40] (italics added).

Let us look at this enigma more closely.

BECOMING FLESH

When Bramante had started the construction work in 1506 and as the project progressed, he was obliged to knock down much of the old basilica of Constantine. Not everyone was happy with this demolishing. The old basilica, after all, had stood there since 326 CE and thus was deemed to be imbued with twelve centuries of Christian history. Many saw it as a sacred building, not to be tampered with in this disrespectful manner. When Fontana brought the obelisk from the Circus Nero to raise it in front of the basilica, much of the frontage of the old Constantine basilica was still there, and behind this was the nearly completed new basilica. Fontana thus had two alignments to choose from: that of the new basilica and that of the old basilica. The difference between both alignments was 2°, such that the axis of the old basilica ran to the left, that is, counterclockwise to the axis of the new basilica.

Fontana was one of the most respected engineers and architects in Rome. He was known to be very meticulous and precise. In consideration of the huge prestige and importance of this project, it would seem odd, indeed improbable, that such an accomplished engineer would make an error of 2° when placing the obelisk in front of the new basilica. We must, therefore, take it that it was not an error but rather a deliberate choice. At any rate, because of this choice, the obelisk is now about 1.5 meters to the left of the extended axis of the new basilica.

This misalignment is very noticeable today if you try to sight the cross on top of the obelisk with the cross on top of the cupola.

So why did Fontana make this choice in placing the obelisk? And why, indeed, did Maderno follow suit with the new facade?

We recall from chapter 3 that when Fontana moved the obelisk, Pope Gregory XIII had reformed the old Julian calendar just four years earlier with the help of the Jesuit astronomer Christopher Clavius of the Collegio Romano. It is not generally appreciated by modern historians that the principal reasons—indeed probably the main reason—for the reformation of the calendar were not practical but religious. The most important feast in Roman Catholicism was, and still is, the Annunciation, also known as the Incarnation. This is when the Archangel Gabriel announced to Mary that she would be made pregnant (the Annunciation) and, consequently, the Holy Spirit would be incarnated in the womb of Mary, that is, would become flesh. This is really the very point when Christianity truly begins. To put it very simply, without the Incarnation, Christianity would not have happened. Let us look at the facts and also the context of the situation.

Fontana was in Rome in 1581 to 1582, when the matter of the reformation of the calendar was being hotly debated at the Vatican and the Collegio Romano. He was doing work on the villa of Cardinal Felice Peretti, the future Pope Sixtus V. When Peretti became pope in 1585 he appointed Fontana as the Vatican architect and commissioned him to bring the Egyptian obelisk from the Circus Nero and raise it in front of St. Peter's Basilica. At that time the last stages of the construction work for the new basilica were being implemented, but as we already pointed out, parts of the *old* basilica's facade were still in place.

The first thing to note here is that the new Gregorian calendar brought back the date of the true astronomical vernal equinox to March 21 (in the Gregorian calendar), which was the true astronomical vernal equinox when Constantine *built* the old basilica, circa 330 CE. But the alignment of this old basilica was not toward the sunrise at the true astronomical vernal equinox but some 2° to the north of that. It is also clear that Fontana used the alignment of the old basilica to place the obelisk. So what sunrise date was the old basilica aligned to? Why this 2° to the north?

Sir Norman Lockyer, the renowned British astronomer who is regarded as the "Father of Archaeo-astronomy," wrote:

> In regard to *old* St. Peter's in Rome, we read that "so exactly due east and west was the basilica, that on the vernal equinox the great doors of the porch of the quadriporticus were thrown open at sunrise, and also the eastern doors of the church itself, and as the sun rose, its rays passed through the outer doors, then through the inner doors, and penetrating straight through the nave, illuminated the High Altar." [41] (italics added)

But is Lockyer right in saying this? Lockyer is actually quoting from an article he saw in *The Builder* magazine of 1892. In 1967 the same statement was repeated by the British architectural historian James Lee-Milne, who wrote, "In fact at the vernal equinox the great doors of the porch and those of the church were thrown open at dawn to allow the first beams to illuminate the Apostle's shrine, while the choir and congregation burst into a paean of thanksgiving."[42]

I have learned through experience, however, that when it comes to such matters of alignments of important buildings, the only way to be absolutely sure of the true orientation is, quite literally, to measure it oneself and, if possible, have the result confirmed independently by a qualified surveyor-astronomer. To this end I asked Sandro Zicari, my colleague in Rome, to do an initial survey.

Sandro is a Ph.D. in applied mathematics and statistics, and is very meticulous in all things to do with measurements. His initial survey confirmed that there was a difference of some 2° between the alignment of new basilica and that of the obelisk. In astronomical jargon, the azimuth of the obelisk, as sighted from the center of the facade of the new basilica is azimuth 88°. From the latitude of Rome this means that this alignment is toward sunrise on March 25. This date is, of course, the Feast of the Incarnation. Fontana did not make a mistake after all, but simply maintained the original alignment of the old basilica of Constantine, which was set to celebrate the most important feast in Christendom: the Incarnation.

The "New Rome" and the "Second" Basilica

In 330 CE, at about the time that the first St. Peter's Basilica was being completed at the Vatican in Rome by Constantine the Great, he also decided to found a second capital for the new Roman Empire. He chose a site in Byzantium (modern Turkey) at the entrance of the Bosporus. From a strategic viewpoint this was an ideal location, being at the juncture between the eastern and western parts of the Empire. Thus was founded Konstantinopolis, "The City of Constantine"—a "New Rome" symbolically linked to the "Old Rome" in Italy. There may be, however, an astronomical and astrological reason for choosing this location. For the basilica in Constantinople the architects selected a site that was in direct alignment to the Vatican. The basilica was given the name Holy Wisdom—in Italian, Divina Sapienza, or Hagia Sophia. Nadine Schibille, a professor of art history who studied the astronomical design of the Hagia Sophia, showed that it was originally aligned to the winter solstice.[43] It is also known that the Hagia Sophia was consecrated on December 25, 360 CE, and that its main axis runs close to azimuth 123.5°, marking very closely the winter solstice. The same azimuth would also work optically for December 25, that is, marking the birth of the Jesus—the birth of the Incarnation. December 25 is, of course, nine months after March 25, which is the orientation of the old St. Peter's Basilica in Rome. The connection between the two basilicas is thus the calendric cycle of the two most important events in Christendom, namely the conception and birth of the Christ.

Fig. 5.16. Emperor Constantine offering to Hagia Sofia/Sapienza Divina/Divine Wisdom the Virgin the twin basilicas of St. Peter's in Rome (right) and St. Sophia in Constantinople (now Istanbul) (left). Mosaic in the Hagia Sofia basilica, now converted into a mosque.

THE MADERNO FOUNTAIN

When Maderno completed the facade of the new basilica in 1612 he was asked by Pope Paul V to design a fountain to replace an older one that had been there since 1490. This fountain was located some sixty meters to the north of the obelisk.* The Maderno Fountain (see p. 208), as it is called today, was completed in 1613. This schematic arrangement of the single fountain and obelisk in the then open space that would later become the Piazza St. Peter's remained the status quo until the advent of Pope Alexander VII in 1655.

---

*The water supply for this fountain would come from an ancient aqueduct from the times of Trajan, the Acqua Traiana, which was restored by Paul V and thus renamed the Acqua Paola.

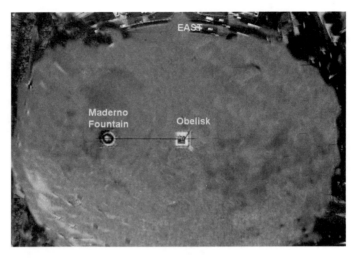

Fig. 5.17 This is how the open space (the future Piazza St. Peter's) looked when Maderno completed his work, and before Bernini built the colonnade. (Robert Bauval)

FLASH FORWARD TO MAY 1655

The coronation of Alexander VII on the throne of St. Peter in May 1655 blew a breath of fresh air into the stuffy corridors of the Vatican and also into scholarly establishments in Italy and the rest of Europe, for this new pope was known to be an affable, sensitive, educated, and well-read man, and, above all, he had a keen interested in topics such as Hermetism and the Egyptian mysteries, probably fueled by his Jesuit friend Athanasius Kircher. After attending to all the matters of administration and finances that required his immediate attention—the budget of the Vatican was in shambles—Alexander VII turned to his more engaging interest: the embellishment of the Eternal City with monumental projects to restore it to its former imperial glory of the golden age of Rome.

But first things first . . .

In December 1655 Pope Alexander VII organized a lavish reception for Queen Christina of Sweden, who arrived in Rome with her huge courtly retinue. The celebration in her honor started early in the day and went on throughout the night with displays of fireworks and pageantry. As

Fig. 5.18. A drawing of the St. Peter's Basilica and the Bernini Colonnade ca. 1670.
Note the single fountain of Maderno north of the obelisk, which served as
the focal point of Bernini's ellipse.

we have seen earlier, on Christmas Day 1655 the pope made Christina a Catholic and renamed her Alexandra Maria. In the following weeks, the pope devoted most of his attention to Christina. Then hardly a few weeks into the New Year, in February 1656 to be precise, Alexander VII called on his favorite artist, Bernini, to tell him about a great project he had in mind. Now a mature man and enormously famous throughout Europe, Bernini was granted the architectural commission he had long dreamed of: the design of a huge piazza in front of St. Peter's Basilica.

After various discussions on the choice of design and costs, Bernini was formally awarded the commission for the project on July 31, 1656.*

---

*Bernini was to receive a bonus of sixty escudi per month for five years—the estimated duration of the work—on top of his regular monthly salary of two hundred escudi. The project actually took eleven years, but Bernini got the sixty escudi bonus for only five years.

We have to imagine this extraordinary situation. Bernini was in his fifty-ninth year, an old man as far as seventeenth-century reckoning went. He was, however, in top physical and mental health.* A contemporary biographer of Bernini, Filippo Baldinucci, reported that when Bernini was just a boy he found himself in the company of the great artist Annibale Carracci and other masters as they were walking and chatting outside St. Peter's Basilica. Carracci apparently turned to the young Bernini and said, "Believe me, the day will come, but when no one knows, that a prodigious genius will make two great monuments in the middle and at the end of this temple on a scale keeping with the vastness of the building."[44]

Such words were more than enough to make Bernini dream of being that prodigious genius. He apparently beamed and replied to Carracci, "Oh, if only I could be the one."

And now finally here he was, about to design one of the greatest projects of Christendom! It must have seemed as if God himself, in his infinite wisdom, had kept Bernini in good health and high spirits to tackle this mother of all projects, perhaps like Imhotep, the Egyptian Ascelpius, must have felt when asked by pharaoh to design the very first great pyramid complex. And here it was, the design of a great piazza for the Vatican handed to him on a silver platter.

Such benevolent, divine attention, however, had definitely not been forthcoming for Bernini's good friend and patron, Pope Alexander VII. The pontiff was now suffering terribly from gallstones and had also lost all his teeth, forcing him to eat only soft food, like a newborn. Indeed, so worried was the pope of dying soon that he commissioned Bernini to make for him a coffin and a marble skull, which he then kept in his bedchamber just in case. The pope was also much troubled by political problems he had with the powerful Sun King, Louis XIV of France, as well as serious financial problems that plagued the Vatican coffers. Not unexpectedly, the gargantuan costs for the embellishment proj-

---

*Actually, the year before this Bernini had nearly died from a bad fever caused by malaria, but by the end 1655 he had fully recovered.

ects, especially the Piazza St. Peter's, which he just had commissioned from Bernini—estimated to cost as much as half the annual budget for the city—brought on much criticism, not just from the population but also from some outspoken cardinals. To put it mildly, the pope was not being reasonable with such a massive expenditure. But in spite of his bad health and the growing opposition to his exorbitant financial excesses, Alexander VII nonetheless forged ahead with the Piazza St. Peter's project.

The Sun King and the Solar Pope

By the mid-1600s, to say that relations between Rome and Paris were somewhat strained would be a gross understatement. When Cardinal Fabio Chigi was elected as Pope Alexander VII in 1655, the political situation between the French and the Vatican state had deteriorated to its lowest point. It was no secret that the young King Louis XIV, then only seventeen in 1655, was being regarded, and, more to the point, regarded himself, as a miracle from God and a sort of sun king in the fashion of the ancient pharaohs or some mythical Apollo or a reincarnated Alexander the Great. His parents, Louis XIII and Anne of Austria, had remained childless for nearly twenty years into their marriage. Queen Anne had produced several stillborn offspring, and by 1637 the court and the whole country were convinced, what with rumors that Louis XIII was a homosexual, that the royal couple would remain childless. But then the Dominican Hermetic magician-astrologer Tommaso Campanella made his famous prediction that Queen Anne would soon give birth to an heir, a son of the sun who would one day rule the world as the most "Christian King." To everyone's surprise and delight, on September 5, 1638 (which happened, by strange fate, to also be Campanella's birthday), was born the future Louis XIV. His birth was seen as a miracle, and he soon acquired the epithet Dieudonné (God Given). And pretty soon he was called Roi Soleil, the Sun King.

On the death of the young Sun King's frail and homosexual father in May 1643, Queen Anne handed power to her trusted advisor Cardinal Mazarin, an Italian who despised the Vatican. Historians have suspected that Mazarin and Queen Anne were lovers, and there was even a rumor that he was the real father of Louis XIV, although it was never proven. It was Mazarin who negotiated and sealed the famous Peace Treaty of Westphalia between the Protestants and the Catholics, which ended the terrible Thirty Years' War, but which also exposed the Vatican as weak and fast losing its authority over Christendom. On the other hand, France under Louis XIV became the superpower in Europe. By 1655, at the point when Pope Alexander VII was toying with the idea of commissioning Bernini to design the Piazza St. Peter's in Rome, it was common knowledge that the young Louis XIV of France saw himself not only as the Sun King and Roi Trés Chretién (Most Christian King), but that he also had shown his serious ambitions to rule all of Europe, if not the whole world. It must have seemed to those in the know as if Campanella's dream of a solar monarch to rule a Catholic world from a city of the sun was becoming a reality (see appendix 1). Could all this have spurred Pope Alexander VII to commission Bernini to design his own city of the sun for the Vatican in Rome, even against the huge public opposition to this project?

THE NEW MICHELANGELO AND THE MODEL OF THE UNIVERSE

When Bernini took possession of the site, the open area in front of the basilica was bordered by old buildings, especially on the south side with the Rione di Borgo, an ancient district that had once been an independent city known as Civitas Leonina (the Lion City). In 1586, however, Pope Sixtus V had annexed it to the Vatican, the same year that Fontana raised the Egyptian obelisk in front of the basilica.

We can well imagine the aged Bernini walking calmly around the Egyptian obelisk, looking all around him; to the north of the obelisk was the Maderno Fountain, and to the south the old Borgo, and to the east a straight avenue called the Spina, flanked by houses and villas. At the far end of the Spina, Bernini could just about see the south side of Castel Sant'Angelo, the imposing papal fortress that also served as a prison. This was where Giordano Bruno had been incarcerated sixty years before.

Since childhood Bernini had dreamed of becoming the "Michelangelo of his age." And now here was the opportunity to surpass even the great Michelangelo by adding an architectural masterpiece to the Vatican, the epicenter of Christendom. We would not be far off the mark to say that Bernini and probably also Pope Alexander VII felt the hand of divine providence in this. And perhaps, too, so did Athanasius Kircher and Queen Christina, who were also major players in that eventful year of 1656 in Rome. The critics and opponents to the project could very well rant, but this was a project for the glory of Rome and Catholicism that would bring many back to the church. No expenses or efforts would be spared. Indeed, in a passionate pronouncement Bernini made against the critics of the pope and this project, he declared:

> In view of his merits, Cardinal Fabio Chigi seemed destined above all others to occupy the throne of Peter when indeed in the year 1655 the unceasing prayers of the Church and the acclamation of the people gave birth to an Alexander [the Great] . . . he thus decided to undertake the building of this great structure [the Piazza St. Peter's]. . . . For since the Church of Saint Peter's is, as it were, the Mother of all others, it must have a portico that expresses the fact that she, with maternally open arms, receives Catholics to confirm them in their faith, heretics to reunite them with the Church, and infidels to illuminate them into the true faith.[45]

Fig. 5.19. The alleged symbolism of the colonnade of the Piazza St. Peter's: the open arms of Mother Church to receive the people.

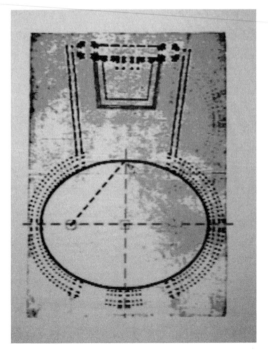

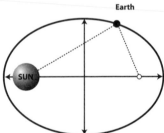

Fig. 5.20. The schematic design showing Bernini's final scheme. Bernini used the obelisk as the center point of the ellipse and the Maderno Fountain as one of the foci. This, whether by deliberation or by fluke, is precisely the same as a diagram of Kepler's first law of planetary motion. (George L. Hersey)

Michelangelo had immortalized his name at the Vatican with the designs of the cupola for the new basilica, the *Pietà,* and, more dramatically still, the paintings on the ceiling and walls of the Sistine Chapel. Bernini was about to do the same, indeed, perhaps even better. He would turn the empty space with the lone obelisk in front of the basilica into a universe and make the seat of St. Peter and his successors the epicenter of the world, like the Copernican sun or, better still, the Keplerian sun.

Bernini's concept was not merely an artistic allegory, like the *La Divina Sapienza* fresco at the Palazzo Barberini, but a true representation of the geometrical perfection of the world that he, Bernini, would cast in stone. In 1656 much talk was heard behind closed doors that the true shape of a planet's orbit was not circular but elliptical. It would indeed seem very odd if his very close astronomer friends, the Jesuits Niccolò Zucchi and Athanasius Kircher, did not discuss such matters with Bernini, albeit in private since such ideas were still held heretical by the Vatican. There was, too, Christina of Sweden, who gravitated around these men, herself a keen amateur astronomer who had studied under Descartes and held correspondence with the astronomers Gassendi and Cassini, both of whom had accepted the heliocentric system in the latter part of their careers. With all these scientific luminaries around him, *it would seem very strange if Bernini did not realize that his architectural plan for Piazza St. Peter's mirrored Kepler's first law of planetary motion.* And even if by some quirky reason he did not, then surely one of the astronomers around him at least should have. Be that as it may, Bernini selected to design the piazza as a giant ellipse. He even used the Maderno Fountain as one of the foci of the ellipse. An ellipse with only one of the two foci showing is precisely the diagrammatical expression of Kepler's first law of planetary motion.

Is the uncanny resemblance of the Piazza St. Peter's to Kepler's first law nothing more than a strange fluke? Are we looking at some coincidence—albeit a very weird one—but nonetheless a coincidence?

Let us take a closer look . . .

Some of Bernini's Other Related Projects

In 1643, under the pontificate of Urban VIII, Bernini was commissioned to design a small chapel dedicated to the Magi. While he was producing the plans and starting the work, Urban VIII died and was succeeded by Innocent X. The latter handed the project to Bernini's rival, Francesco Borromini. By that time the heliocentric theories of Copernicus and Kepler were well known. It should not surprise us that Bernini had designed the floor plan of the chapel in the shape of an ellipse. This shows that Kepler's heliocentric model was already in Bernini's mind as early as 1643.[46] In 1666, while the Piazza St. Peter's was nearing completion, Pope Alexander VII commissioned Bernini and Kircher to build a monument in the Piazza della Minerva, where an obelisk had once stood in front of a temple dedicated to the Egyptian goddess Isis. Bernini sculpted an elephant, on the back of which was placed the obelisk. Ironically, the elephant's rear is directed toward the convent of the Dominicans, where the trial of Galileo took place in 1633. Eight years after the death of Pope Alexander VII, in 1675, Bernini designed the second fountain for the south side of the Vatican obelisk.

THE PLAN

Bernini would have been acutely aware that the Vatican obelisk in the center of his elliptical plan was an Egyptian solar symbol from Heliopolis, the City of the Sun. We recall his involvement with Kircher a few years before with the obelisk of the Piazza Navona. Kircher had also called this obelisk "Hermeticum Obeliscus" and also had linked it to the Vatican obelisk, which he called "Obeliscus Heliopolitanus" (Obelisk of the City of the Sun).

It is clear that Kircher was also associating these obelisks with Campanella's vision of the utopian City of the Sun, as noted by Frances A. Yates: "Kircher's passion for Egypt leads him into elaborate geo-

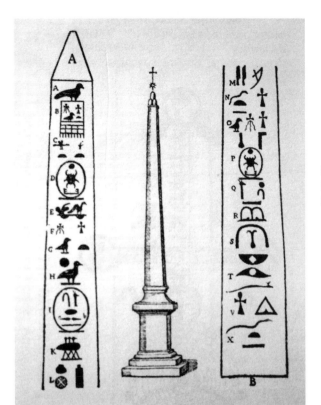

Fig. 5.21. The "Obeliscus Heliopolitanus." (Athanasius Kircher)

graphical research, in the course of which he comes to the Egyptian city called Heliopolis, or *Civitas Solis,* the City of the Sun" [47] (italics added).

Civitas Solis was, of course, the title in Latin of Campanella's book *The City of the Sun.* We also recall from chapter 4 how Campanella had imagined this solar city being like the Copernican heliocentric diagram with a central sun temple surrounded by seven concentric circles representing the "seven planets." We also recall how Campanella had influenced Andrea Sacchi, who painted the *La Divina Sapienza* fresco as an allegory of the heliocentric system and the City of the Sun. We recall how Bernini had worked closely with Niccolò Zucchi and had designed the frontispiece of Zucchi's *Optica philosophica experimentalis et ratione a fundamentis constituta* as an allegory of the heliocentric system. We recall how Zucchi had actually met Kepler in 1623 in Prague and kept a correspondence with him. Finally we recall how Marsilio Ficino, the initiator of the Hermetic tradition in the Renaissance, had called for the making of a talisman in the "image of the universe" to benefit mankind with the benevolent influences of heaven and how Campanella had used such a talismanic magic in the rituals performed with Pope Urban VIII in the room at the Palazzo Barberini containing the *La Divina Sapienza* fresco.

We do not here propose to go through all the usual architectural design stages for the Piazza St. Peter's, but only the final design, which is an oval-elliptical plan flanked by a covered colonnade. Although Bernini always insisted that the choice of an oval-elliptical plan was actually the pope's idea, he clearly had a hand in the decision.[48]

There are hundreds of architectural studies on Bernini's design of the Piazza St. Peter's. Much has been said about whether the layout plan is an ellipse, an oval, or a "pseudoellipse," that is, two circles lined with curved lines. Basically, an ellipse is nothing more than an elongated circle that has one center point and two foci on each side of this point along the main axis. George L. Hersey, an emeritus professor of art history at Yale University and a renowned authority on Italian Renaissance architecture, explained, "In Kepler's ellipse, as in all ellipses, the sum of the distances from any point on its perimeter to the two foci . . . is always equal to the major axis total length."[49]

The main axis of the ellipse for the Piazza St. Peter's is 240 meters (787 feet), and it is clear that Bernini made its center the existing obelisk and Maderno Fountain one of the foci. This can be very easily verified mathematically, as was indeed done by Hersey.*

The natural center for such a piazza—the crossing of its major and minor axes—was (or became) the obelisk that Domenico Fontana had set up there in 1585 to 1586. The ellipse's two foci were marked with fountains—one on the left as you face St. Peter's of 1613 by Carlo Maderno, and the other, its twin—dating from 1677 [by Bernini] . . . as far as I know Bernini's colonnade became the first true monumental ellipse of the Baroque era.[50]

---

*See appendix 2.

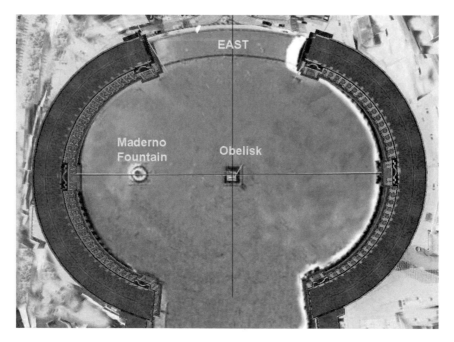

Fig. 5.22. The simple elliptical geometry of the Piazza St. Peter's, conforming to Kepler's first law of planetary motion. Although two fountains are seen today, there was only one fountain, that of Maderno, when Bernini designed the piazza in 1656. The second fountain (that on the south of the obelisk) was only added in 1667 and inaugurated in 1675. (Robert Bauval)

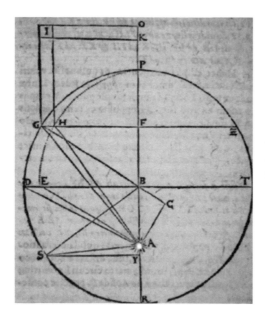

Fig. 5.23. Some of Kepler's diagrams of the first law of planetary motion from his own book, *Astronomia Nova,* published in 1609. (Johannes Kepler)

Making the "natural center" of the ellipse the Egyptian obelisk was an obvious choice. But the main axis of the ellipse did not have to be the line passing through the obelisk *and* the Maderno Fountain. The fact that Bernini did make this main axis pass through the Maderno Fountain as well as make the latter one of the foci of the ellipse strongly suggests, if not proves, that Bernini had in mind Kepler's diagram for his first law of planetary motion. There can be no question that an ellipse with only one of the foci—in this case only one fountain (the second fountain was built much later)—immediately evokes Kepler's first law of planetary motion, which is exactly that: *an ellipse with only one focus.*

It seems impossible that with so many astronomers, professionals or very keen amateurs, directly involved with Bernini at the time—Zucchi, Kircher, Christina of Sweden, not to mention others at the Collegio Romano—none noticed such a blatant correlation between Bernini's design and Kepler's diagram! Indeed, all mathematicians, physicists, astronomers, and philosophers at the Collegio Romano and elsewhere would and *should* have noticed! The question, therefore, is why did no one point it out?

One reason, of course, was that Kepler's books were listed on the *Index of Forbidden Books* since 1620. To support Kepler's theory, let alone build a giant piazza to represent it smack in front the Vatican, was tantamount to an act of heresy of monumental proportion. Today, of course, the threat of heresy does not exist, and it is thus not at all surprising that the uncanny similarity between Bernini's ellipse for the Piazza St. Peter's and Kepler's diagram has been noticed and mentioned by many architects, historians, and other researchers. However, to the best of our knowledge, all have assumed it to be a coincidence. For example, Isabelle Hyman, a professor emerita at New York University Department of Art History, and her colleague, Marvin Trachtenberg, a renowned professor of Renaissance architecture, remarked:

> It is not irrelevant that in 1609 one of the many remarkable dis-
> coveries of the century was made—Kepler's first law of planetary

motion—proving the shape of each planet's orbit to be an ellipse, with the sun at one focus. That the piazza should be given an elliptical form while the Church vigorously opposed the astronomer's threat to the traditional picture of a fixed universe is one of the ironies of the history of this period.[51]

Dozens if not hundreds of modern researchers have made similar comments. So if it is so obvious today, why was it not so obvious then, in 1656 when Bernini designed the project? Why did none of the Jesuit scholars at the time, not one, point out this heresy?

THE OPEN ARMS OF MOTHER CHURCH

Our colleague Sandro Zicari has a Ph.D. in applied mathematics and statistics from Sapienza University of Rome. Understandably, he was initially very skeptical about this strange conundrum. But after reviewing the draft manuscript of this book, he has become convinced that we are not dealing with a coincidence here. The statistics, affirms Sandro, are stacked against this eventuality. But he, too, is perplexed why no one mentioned this obvious correlation until recently in modern times. Because in spite of Kepler's books being banned by the Vatican, you would expect some mention of this obvious correlation, even in a critical or condemning manner. So was there another reason for this peculiar silence that needs to be considered? Indeed there is: simple human nature.

If someone powerful and in a high place, who wields full authority and demands total respect, makes a statement and repeats it often enough, then that statement may be accepted by most, perhaps even everyone, as the truth, even though it may not be the whole truth. We are not suggesting, of course, that Pope Alexander VII or Bernini lied about their motives and intentions regarding the design of the piazza. What we are suggesting, however, is that Bernini offered only one layer of the truth as his explanation for the elliptical plan, which was easy to understand and also totally acceptable to all, but omitted revealing the other, deeper layers. In the Renaissance, this manner of expressing a truth was known as dissimulation. It allowed someone, with hand on heart and a clear conscience, to make a statement that avoided exposure to further scrutiny and dangers. It is not lying per se but simply withholding other aspects of the truth. Indeed, people in government do this all the time, except today we call it *politics*.

Like all educated artists and scholars of his time, Bernini was a child of the Renaissance. He was, quite literally, a Renaissance man. Being extremely involved with the affairs of the Vatican, Bernini was obliged to acquire a good mastery of the art of dissimulation for self-protection. This must not be mistaken for deceit or lying, but merely revealing one thin layer of a multilayered truth. As an accomplished and talented artist, allegory and symbolism were the obvious tools for a master dissimulator such as Bernini.

All religious architecture is intensely symbolic. But we must bear in mind that the symbolism is multilayered. Think of the new tower for the World Trade Center in New York. There will almost always be one symbolic layer, perhaps the most important, that the designer or the commissioner of the edifice will prefer not to reveal. When it comes to such an important project as the Piazza St. Peter's, the whole edifice is not to be seen as a mere building but as a talisman, a sort of permanent theatrical stage to service the highest religious rituals. As University of Cambridge scholar Alex Dougherty said, "[It] transformed into rhetorical stages for the Christian drama of Incarnation and Salvation."[52]

When Bernini designed the piazza he naturally took into consideration that this was where the people would gather to receive the blessings of the pope on important religious feasts and events. The most important occasion was the *Urbi et Orbi,* when a new pope announced the start of his pontificate to "Rome and to the World." On such occasions the pope faces the piazza and opens his arms in a gesture to embrace the crowd and, symbolically, the city of Rome and the world. There are freehand sketches attributed to Bernini that show a man, probably meant to be St. Peter, superimposed on the piazza with his two arms over the two semicircular colonnades flanking the ellipse.[53]

According to most architecture and art historians, this proves that Bernini's choice of the ellipse was to symbolize the "motherly arms of the church" and that the basilica together with the piazza "actually represents, though in a cursory way, the dome as the head, the facade as the body, and the colonnade as the arms of a man."[54]

The sketch is indeed cursory, almost childish, with the human figure awkwardly drawn and the "arms" obscenely warped and distorted to fit the otherwise perfect geometrical contour of the colonnade. It is difficult to imagine that a perfectionist such as Bernini, hailed for his talent and genius to draw, paint, or sculpt the human body with flawless accuracy, would make an amateurish sketch such as this one to explain the meaning of the piazza. True, apparently, "Bernini was fond of comparing . . . the colonnade with the arms of a man,"[55] as Rudolf Wittkower, the eminent professor of the History of Art at the Warburg Institute in London, also pointed out, and Bernini did write the following explanation for the elliptical piazza that matches the sketch.

Essendo la Chiesa di S. Pietro quasi matrice di tutte le altre doveva haver'un Portico che per l'appunto dimonstrasse di riceverre a bracia aperte maternamente i Cattolici per confirmarli nella credenza, gl'Heretici per reunirli alla Chiesa, e gl'Infideli per illuminarli alla vera fede.

(For since the Church of St. Peter's is, as it were, the Mother of all others, it must have a portico that expresses the fact that she, with maternally open arms, receives Catholics to confirm them in their faith, heretics to reunite them with the church, and infidels to illuminate them into the true faith.)

Wittkower, however, did add, "In order to justify his architectural design he [Bernini] connects human proportions and features to it."[56] Be that as it may, Bernini's affirmation that the elliptical piazza represents the motherly arms of the church has been repeated ad nauseam by all historians of Baroque architecture and art. It is so ingrained in the minds of students of Baroque architecture that none question its validity. The possibility that it may be a dissimulation has not been raised, let alone seriously considered. This is not a question of what is taught but rather of what can be seen. As the comedian Groucho Marx once asked his audience, "Do you believe what I say or what you see with your own eyes?"

THE WOMB OF THE CELESTIAL VIRGIN OF THE WORLD

It is an odd fact that although St. Peter's Basilica is aligned precisely due east, the elliptical piazza is not. Careful observation will show that its main axis, which runs north-south, is slightly tilted counterclockwise. This gives an orientation of about 2° toward the north (azimuth 88°). This matches the orientation of the facade built by Maderno in 1608 and provides a solar alignment for March 25, the Feast of the Annunciation or Incarnation. This is when, according to Catholic tradition, the Theotokos (Mother of God, Queen of Heaven, the Virgin of the World) was made pregnant. The Incarnation, literally, "becoming flesh," is the defining moment of Catholic Christianity, when the Holy Spirit entered the womb of the Virgin to become flesh. Everything for Christianity begins from this moment. The Incarnation is the alpha of the Christian era. Exactly nine months after, December 25, is the "birthday" of the Christ. Bearing this in mind, when Bernini described the elliptical design of the Piazza St. Peter's he used the word *matrice,* which, in Italian, means "womb." Indeed, the "womb of the church" or the "womb of the Virgin" would be a perfect allegory for the elliptical shape of the piazza, with the phallic obelisk acting as a sundial to define the nine-month cycle of human gestation, from spring equinox to winter solstice.

The two colonnades stop short on the elongated sides of the ellipse to create a wide entrance to the piazza in the east and an entrance to the basilica in the west. These openings or entrances when viewed from the obelisk direct the observer to points on the horizon that mark the sunrise and sunset at the two solstices. The piazza, then, becomes a sort of open-air astronomical observatory or, to make use of other terminology, a stage or theater that represents the world or, to be even more precise, the heliocentric Keplerian model of the solar system. Dougherty further explains:

> Bernini was famously fond of the *theatrum mundi* notion. In this design [of Piazza St. Peter's] we have the fullest architectural expression of the Christian world. The oval plan was completed with the *pope's sanction* in the last months of 1656. . . . At the *caput mundi* [capital of the world] architecture takes on a paradigmatic significance as a mirror of the universe. Its oval geometry mediates between the heavenly curve and the terrestrial straight line, as in Kepler's understanding of the significance of the ellipse. The piazza becomes an image of the perfectly harmonious universe.[57] (italics added)

Dougherty's statement comes closest to what we believe Bernini had in mind when designing the piazza. But Bernini could not have decided on this design on his own. He must have had the full approval of Pope Alexander VII. So, did the pope know that the final design represented the Keplerian diagram? Also, in consideration of the precise astronomical alignments required, Bernini would have needed the assistance of a proficient astronomer to help him set out the layout of the piazza on the ground. Was it the Jesuit astronomer Zucchi, or Kircher, or both? And did Queen Christina, herself a very keen amateur and philosopher, also get into the act?

Pope Alexander VII died on May 22, 1667. Three years later, on May 21, 1670, Zucchi died. And on November 28, 1680, Bernini and Kircher died on the same day.

The answers to these questions were taken, quite literally, to the grave.

FINAL EXCURSION, TO ROME, 1675

ANOTHER "PLAN" FOR PIAZZA ST. PETER'S

In 1675 Bernini and Carlo Fontana (no relations to Domenico Fontana who raised the Vatican obelisk in 1586) built a second fountain in the north side of the Piazza St. Peter's. It was designed to match and counterbalance the existing Maderno Fountain and to mark the position of the second focus of the ellipse. Also in 1675, while this fountain was being constructed, a Dutch engineer and amateur astronomer by the name of Cornelius Meyer was at the piazza examining the ground around the obelisk. Meyer had in his hands a drawing pad, seemingly checking the shadow cast by the obelisk. Like Queen Christina, Meyer was a Lutheran Protestant who had converted to Catholicism. He had come to Rome to propose a series of projects to the pope, one of which involved the Egyptian obelisks that graced the many piazzas of the city: Piazza Navona, Piazza del Popolo, and, of course, Piazza St. Peter's.[58]

Meyer submitted his project to Pope Clement X in 1676. Unfortunately the pope died that same year, and the new pope, Innocent XI, refused to pay Meyer for his work. To recover some of his money, Meyer published a book titled *L'Arte di restituire à Roma la tralasciata navigatione del suo tevere* [The Way to Restore to Rome the Navigation of the Tiber, Which Was Neglected]. In this book Meyer explains, with a wonderful diagram, the project he had proposed for the Piazza St. Peter's.[59]

The Square of St. Peter's would represent the entire world, and also the universe, via eight planispheres symmetrically placed around

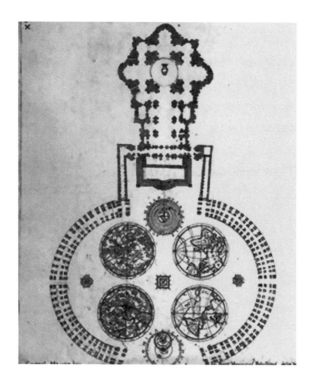

Fig. 5.24. Meyer's plan for the Piazza St. Peter's. (Cornelius Meyer)

the great obelisk moved there in 1585-6 by Pope Sixtus V. Two planispheres would present our globe, one for the old, the other for the new world; two more would bear the projections of the northern and southern stars and constellations; and the remaining four would display the structure of the universe according to the four systems then entertained: the Ptolemaic, Copernican, Tychonic, and Cartesian.[60]

What Cornelius Meyer was proposing would have been seen immediately by Marsilio Ficino, Giordano Bruno, and, more especially, Tommaso Campanella as pure, undiluted Hermetic talismanic magic. Indeed, if this project had been implemented, it would have completed the very precise architectural-*cum*-astronomical expression of a "talisman of the world," which, in a more vague artistic allegory, had been already done for Pope Urban VIII with the *La Divina Sapienza* fresco: the Hermetic City of the Sun.

Meyer was very well known in Rome, and his presence definitely did not escape Bernini's attention. Meyer was a member of the Accademia Fisio-Matematica, the most illustrious scientific academy in Rome. He also was the designer and chief engineer on a major hydraulic project on the Tiber commissioned by the Vatican. Carlo Fontana, who was involved with Bernini on the second fountain at the Piazza St. Peter's, had a huge personal feud with Meyer over this project.

ROLE-PLAYING THE HERMETICA?

Paula Findlen, a professor of the history of science at Stanford University, reviewed the fateful encounter between Queen Christina of Sweden and Athanasius Kircher. She made this most intriguing comment:

> Like Alexander VII and Kircher, Christina came to Rome to fulfill the destiny portended in the historical ruins of the papal city. She was the new Isis, consort of Osiris, whom Kircher identified to Alexander VII, and patron of Hermes (Trismegistus), Kircher's chosen persona. No doubt Kircher saw her as the living embodiment of the statues of Minerva and Isis.[61]

Findlen is not mincing her words. She is clearly implying that some curious role-playing was going on, with these three protagonists implicated with the papacy at the highest of levels. Findlen may indeed be very near the truth. In fact we see a fourth player in this live theatrical setting: Bernini, the architect *supremo*. It truly must have seemed to these protagonists that divine providence brought them together to fulfill Campanella's plan of the City of the Sun.

A pope, a virgin queen, a Hermetic astronomer, and an architect
Alexander, Christina, Kircher, and Bernini
Osiris, Isis, Hermes Trismegistus, and Asclepius

In the Hermetic sense, Asclepius was, of course, the great Egyptian architect Imhotep, who designed the very first religious architectural project of the world. We will close, therefore, with that haunting forecast found in the *Asclepius,* where Hermes Trismegistus predicts that in some future time the magical religion of Egypt will be restored and, "The gods who exercised their dominion over the earth will be restored one day and installed in a city, which will be founded toward the setting sun, and into which will hasten, by land and sea, the whole race of mortal men."

> *Things are not always what they seem; the first appearance deceives many.*
>
> PHAEDRUS (15 BCE–50 CE)

> *Truth is stranger than fiction, but it is because fiction is obliged to stick to possibilities; Truth isn't.*
>
> MARK TWAIN

> *You do solemnly state that the testimony you may give in the cause now pending before this court shall be the truth, the whole truth, and nothing but the truth, so help you God. (italics added)*
>
> OATH TAKEN IN COURT,
> STATE OF CALIFORNIA

THE JESUIT POPE

As we were closing the last chapter of this book, the Vatican was put into turmoil with the sudden announcement of the resignation of Pope Benedict XVI (Joseph Ratzinger) on February 11, 2013. He had become pope in April 2005, and now, taking everyone by surprise, even the Curia apparently, he felt he had become too old and too tired to cope with the demands of his post. This was the first time since the sixteenth century that a pope had actually resigned. For a few days the Vatican was at a loss. The pope officially stepped down on February 28, 2013. Within days the conclave to vote a new pope began, and on March 13, the white smoke from the Vatican chimney indicated that the cardinals had finally reached a decision. Again, to the surprise of everyone, it was announced that Cardinal Jose Mario Bergoglio of Buenos Aires had been chosen as the new pope. To everyone's delight, the new pope chose the name Francis I, apparently inspired by St. Francis of Assisi. It was the first time that a pope had chosen this name. The international media just loved it, comparing the humble demeanor of Pope Francis I and his compassion for the poor with that of the eponymous saint. It then occurred to everyone that Pope Francis I was the "first" in many other things. He was first pope from the Americas, first Jesuit pope, and first pope to use a totally new appellation since the tenth-century Pope Landus.

The fact that Pope Francis I was the first ever Jesuit to sit on the throne of St. Peter's certainly grabbed our attention. In this present book we had written much on the Jesuit Order and, more specifically, had concluded that it was Jesuits who had influenced the main protagonists of our thesis—Bernini, Queen Christina of Sweden, and Pope Alexander VII—in that fatal year of 1656 when the design of the Piazza St. Peter's was determined. We considered, therefore, the possibility that the name of Francis chosen by the new pope might not, in fact, be that of St. Francis of Assisi but of St. Francis Xavier (one of the founding fathers of the Jesuit Order in 1542). St. Francis Xavier is particularly venerated among Jesuits around the world, especially in Goa, India, where he carried out his missionary work and converted the whole region into Christianity. But this possibility of the new pope having chosen the eponymous Jesuit saint as his archetype was soon denied by various cardinals and, eventually, by Pope Francis I himself. We were not so convinced, however.

Another odd coincidence was the date of the first day of the election, March 12, which, by a fluke, happened to be the same day that St. Francis Xavier was canonized in 1622 by Pope Gregory XV. Cardinal Bergoglio was voted in as pope the next day. On March 18, five days into his pontificate, Pope Francis I chose his coat of arms. Not surprisingly, at least not to us, he elected to have incorporated the logo of the Jesuit Order at the center of the heraldic device. This logo, very familiar to all Jesuits, is a glowing sun with thirty-two rays, at the center of which are the letters IHS, standing for the Holy Name of Jesus or, more precisely, the first three letters in capital of the name of Jesus as written in Greek: IHSOUS. This logo, quite obviously, is intensely solar or, alternatively, implies that Christ was "solar." Next to this Jesuit logo was placed a five-pointed star, a symbol of the Virgin Mary, to whom Pope Francis I is particularly devoted. His first official Mass as pope was at the Church of Santa Maria Maggiore on March 14, 2013. The coat of arms of Pope Francis I also has, of course, the traditional papal miter with the triple crown. This crown had been slightly modified in 1963 by having the three crowns now linked by a vertical bar. It is well known among historians of religion that the origin of this miter is from the Zoroastrian solar cult of Mithras, once very popular and widespread in the Roman Empire until well into the fourth century CE. Mithras, like Jesus Christ, was said to be born on December 25 (the general sun festival in ancient Rome) and, also like Christ, was often depicted as Sol Invictus, the Unconquered Sun.

We should all be acutely aware that the pope is the head of over one billion Catholics today and that everything he does or says will have a very powerful meaning. This would be particularly true for a pope who is trained as a Jesuit priest and scholar. It was the Jesuits who founded the Collegio Romano in 1551, which we have written much about in this book. The Collegio Romano is now the Pontifical Gregorian University, effectively the University of the Vatican. Its present rector, not unexpectedly, is called Francis-Xavier Dumortier. The protagonists in our present book who were Jesuit priests, among them Athanasius Kircher, Niccolò Zucchi, and Paul Guldin, were all leading professors at the Collegio Romano.

Suspected—rightly or wrongly—of intrigue and manipulation in high quarters, the Jesuit Order was suppressed in France, Spain, and Portugal in 1767 and, later, in 1773, also by the Vatican. It was reinstated gradually in many countries, starting around the early 1800s, with the last country to lift the ban being Switzerland in 1973. The Jesuit Order is today the largest single Catholic order in the world.

We predict that Pope Francis I will use his simple but very effective marketing skills to put into action a massive public relations campaign to restore trust in the Vatican and even expand its popularity worldwide, especially in those Catholic countries where poverty is rampant. Whether this is a good or bad thing depends from which perspective you view it. As for us, we cannot help wondering what the seventeenth-century utopianist Tommaso Campanella would have said if he had been informed that his solar logo—the very same one that he had put on the cover of his book *The City of the Sun*—would adorn the coat of arms of a Jesuit pope born in the New World . . .

BREAKING NEWS: FIVE TO EIGHT

It was announced on March 18, 2013, that Pope Francis I had chosen his coat of arms on which was an obvious solar symbol in the center and also a five-pointed star. The five-pointed star is well known to principally be of ancient Egyptian origin used to symbolize the "Star of Isis" (i.e., Sirius). It is also used extensively as the "pentagram" in occult tradition as well as in many military institutions.

The goddess Isis along with the Infant Horus on her lap has often been compared to the Madonna with the Infant Jesus on her lap. It was, therefore, rather telling that when Cardinal Federico Lombardi, the spokesman for the Vatican, presented the coat of arms of Francis I to the media, he very specifically associated the five-pointed star to the Madonna. Displaying the coat of arms to the press, Cardinal Lombardi stated that "there is a star that symbolizes Mary, his (Pope Francis's) Marian devotion . . ."[1]

Yet amazing as it may seem, a little more than a week later, on March 27, 2013, the Vatican suddenly announced that it had decided

Fig. P.1. Cardinal Federico Lombardi showing the coat of arms of Pope Francis I to the media, March 18, 2013. Note the five-pointed star.

Fig. P.2. The original coat of arms of Pope Francis I (left) of March 18, 2013, and the "adjusted" coat of arms (right) of March 27, 2013.

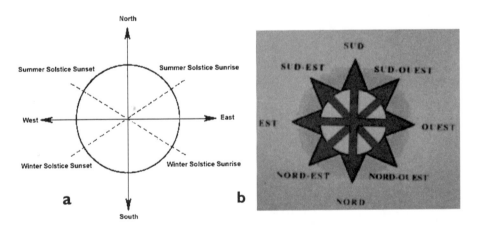

Fig. P.3. (a) The circular "horizon" showing the eight "stations" of the sun, the four points marking the rising and setting of the solstices, the rising and setting of the equinoxes, and the south and north cardinal directions of the meridian. (b) The eight-pointed star marking the solar solstice stations and cardinal directions.

to "adjust" the symbol of the five-pointed star with a new eight-pointed star. According to Cardinal Andrea Cordero Lanza di Montezemolo, apparently an expert on heraldry, the five-pointed star had "military significance," whereas the eight-pointed star "has always symbolized Mary" in Catholic Church tradition.[2] The question arises, of course, as to why a five-pointed was chosen in the first place for Pope Francis I's coat of arms only to be hastily changed a few days later into an eight-pointed star?

Be that as it may, the new eight-pointed star raises a very interesting issue that links up with our thesis regarding the design of the piazza of the Vatican and the "City of the Sun." This is because the eight-pointed star is well known to have been used in many ancient traditions to represent the "eight festivals" of the year linked to the sun, as well as the four cardinal and four solstice directions (at rising and setting) of the sun during the year. At the summer solstice the sun rises in the northeast and sets in the northwest. At the equinoxes the sun rises in due east and sets due west. At the winter solstice it rises in the southeast and sets in the southwest. An X can thus be traced between the northeast and

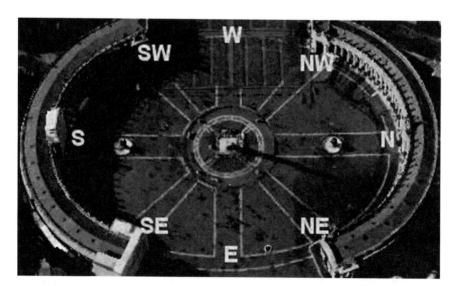

Fig. P.4. The eight-pointed "star" pattern on the Piazza St. Peter's of the Vatican. This is clearly part of the City of the Sun notion and brings it into direct relation to the current Pope Francis I with his "new" eight-pointed star on his coat of arms.

Fig. P.5. An eight-pointed "star" or "solar" symbol with obvious celestial connotation in a six-century Basilica of San Vitale in Ravenna, Italy.

Fig. P.6. (Left) The Chi-Rho symbol of early Christianity, the celestial sign said to have been seen by Constantine the Great, the founder of Roman Catholicism in 313 CE, may have been a "solar" symbol as Constantine was a devotee of the solar cult of Sol Invictus (below) before adopting Christianity.

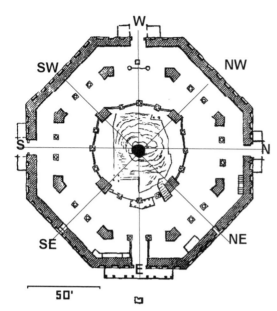

Fig. P.7. The eight-pointed "star" defined by the plan of the Dome of the Rock in Jerusalem on Temple Mount. The octagonal pattern was once believed to be the plan of Solomon's Temple in medieval times and used in Templar churches in Europe.

the southwest, and the southeast and the northwest. If another cross is then superimposed along the east/west and north/south axes, then the circle joining the eight points marks the main station of the sun, and the star thus becomes intensely "solar."

Considering the intense "solar" symbolism of Pope Francis I's coat of arms, and also considering that it was Jesuit astronomers such as Niccolò Zucchi and Athanasius Kircher who played a major role with Pope Alexander VII and Bernini in 1656 in the design of the Piazza St. Peter's, we are justified to wonder if the first ever Jesuit Pope may not be harboring the same ideologies as his Renaissance predecessors as he sat on the "Throne of St. Peter" in March 2013 . . .

CAMPANELLA, THE ROSICRUCIANS, AND THE MIRACULOUS BIRTH OF THE SUN KING

Campanella's "Citta del Sole" was ultimately Egyptian in origin.

FRANCES A. YATES,
GIORDANO BRUNO AND THE HERMETIC TRADITION

The following information is adapted from *Talisman: Sacred Cities, Secret Faith* by Graham Hancock and Robert Bauval.

THE INFANTA AND THE KING OF FRANCE

The last of the Valois kings, Henry III, died in 1589, murdered by one of his own citizens, and the throne passed to Henry III of Navarre, now crowned Henry IV of France. Henry IV belonged to the powerful Bourbon family. He was a Protestant but had converted to Catholicism in 1593 in order to neutralize those who opposed his coronation as king of France. Not everyone was convinced of Henry's sincerity. Among those who most doubted this were the Jesuits, whom the king himself had, in fact, much distrusted all his life. "They will kill me one day," he is reported to have confided to a close friend. "I can see that they are putting all their resources into my death."[1] Sure enough on May 14, 1610, Henry IV was assassinated by a religious fanatic, Francois Ravaillac, and many, especially the Protestant Huguenots, believed that he had been put up to it by the Jesuits. Ravaillac suffered the traditional penalty for regicide: first he was tortured with red-hot pincers, then was seethed in hot oil, and finally, still alive, was ripped apart by four farm horses tethered to his arms and legs.

Henry IV's eldest son, Louis—the future Louis XIII—was only nine years old when his father was assassinated, and his domineering mother, Marie de Medici, a staunch Catholic with a taste for astrology and magic, became his co-regent. Louis XIII was crowned in 1614 when he reached the required age of thirteen, and only began to assert his kingly authority over his ambitious mother in 1631, when he was thirty years old. Louis XIII had been married to the Spanish *infanta,* Anne of Austria, daughter of Philip III of Spain and Portugal, when they were both only fourteen years old. The marriage, however, had remained unconsummated for many years. Of a very curious nature and disposition, Louis XIII was more interested in his hobbies of repairing locks and making jams than in having sex with his wife. In this respect he was totally unlike his father, Henry IV, who had seduced so many women during his short reign that it had earned him the nickname of Le Vert Galant, seventeenth-century French slang for "playboy." To make things worse, Louis XIII at first did not much like his Spanish wife, even though she was beautiful, intelligent, openly affectionate to him, and perhaps even loved him. Things in that department were so bad that on one cold night in January 1619 Louis had to be dragged out of his own bed by leading courtiers and taken forcibly to the queen's chamber in order finally to consummate the marriage. Two years later the queen—no one knows how—was found to be pregnant, but the joy at the court quickly dissipated after she miscarried. The king's reaction, oddly, was not sympathy for her but fury, and he became even more reluctant to do his marital duties. By 1634 a solemn mood had fallen over the royal couple, as everyone at the court had given up on seeing a male heir for the Bourbon dynasty. This was the time that the Dominican monk-*cum*-magician Tommaso Campanella arrived in Paris after fleeing from Rome for fear of being reincarcerated in the papal dungeons, and he was well received at the court of Louis XIII. Things were about to radically change . . .

The Rosicrucian Furor in Paris

In 1623, nine years into the reign of Louis XIII and eleven years before Campanella would arrive in Paris, a secret organization made itself known in Paris. Clandestinely, they placed placards on public buildings of the city announcing:

> We, being deputies of the principal College of the Brothers of the Rose Cross, are making a visible and invisible stay in this city through the Grace of the Most High, toward whom turn the hearts of the Just. We show and teach without books or marks how to speak all languages of the countries where we wish to be, and to draw men from error and death.

Another poster contained a variant of the message with more specifically religious overtones.

> We deputies of the College of the Rose Cross, give notice to all those who wish to enter our Society and Congregation, that we will teach them the most perfect knowledge of the Most High, in the name of whom we are today holding an assembly, and we will make them from visible, invisible, and from invisible, visible.

Not unexpectedly, this poster campaign caused a huge furor in Paris. It has never been known for sure who it was that started this strange propaganda effort. But historians, among them Frances A. Yates, have suspected the so-called Rosicrucians, who had recently been appearing invisibly in Germany. Interestingly, one of their main suspect members was Tobias Adami, the man who had visited Campanella in his dungeon in Naples in 1613 and to whom Campanella had given the manuscript of *The City of the Sun* for publication.

The name Rosicrucian is from Christian Rosenkreutz (Christian Rose Cross or Rosycross), the knightly hero of two booklets that were published in Germany around 1615, the same year Campanella's *The City of the Sun* was published in Germany by Adami. The title of the first booklet is *Fama Fraternis, Or a Discovery of the Fraternity of the Most Noble Order of the Rosy Cross*. Scholars refer to it simply as *The Fama*. The second is titled *Confessio Fraternitatis, Or the Confession of the Laudible Fraternity of the Most Honourable Order of the Rosy Cross, Written to All the Learned of Europe*. Scholars refer to it as *The Confessio*.

These two booklets amount to about twenty-five pages and are known as the Rosicrucian Manifestos. For more on this topic see Graham Hancock and Robert Bauval, *Talisman: Sacred Cities, Secret Faith*.

A HERMETIC MAGUS IN THE COURT OF THE FUTURE SUN KING

When Campanella arrived at the French court, twenty years had elapsed without Louis XIII and his queen, Anne of Austria, producing a child, and the prospects for the continuation of the Bourbon dynasty looked very dim indeed. All sorts of rumors began to circulate that Louis XIII was either impotent or not interested in women or, even, preferred the amorous company of men. The frustrated queen, hearing of how Campanella had performed magic to save the life of Pope Urban VIII (see chapter 4), asked that the priestly magician be brought to her. Campanella had been highly recommended to the queen by Cardinal Richelieu, and now she wanted to hear his prophetic opinion on the matter of the succession to the throne of France. The queen and Richelieu, like most people in those times, believed in astrological predictions, something that Campanella, as we also have seen in chapter 4, was reputed to be an adept in. Indeed, through intermediaries, Richelieu had already consulted Campanella on many occasions while the latter was still in Rome. The two men were to become close friends, and Campanella dedicated the new edition of his *The City of the Sun* to the powerful cardinal, hoping that he might be induced to have it built in Paris.[2]

At any rate, the meeting with the French queen went very well and was followed by Campanella predicting—with an amazing faith in his own prophetic powers, it must be said—that within a year the French royal couple would be blessed with an heir, a male child who would, like the very sun itself, illumine the world and usher in a glorious and golden era for humanity.

> Everyone will acknowledge a single Father and a single God and love will unite them all. . . . Kings and nations . . . will gather in a city, which will be named *Heliaca,* The City of the Sun, which will be built by this illustrious hero [the future "solar" king of France].[3] (italics added)

Campanella modeled his prophecy on Virgil's *Fourth Eclogue* (prophesying the golden age of Augustus Caesar) as also had done the poet Edmund Spenser in *The Faerie Queen* for the Virgin Queen Elizabeth I of England (see chapter 3). A flash thunderstorm over the city of Paris on a cold December night was to play in Campanella's favor. Louis XIII at that time slept in a residence at Versailles, while the queen lived at the Louvre Palace. On this particular night the king had been on a visit at the convent of St. Marie in Paris when a terrible storm broke out. One of his musketeers, who was very devoted to the queen, advised the king that it would be safer for him to spend the night at the Louvre Palace rather than return to Versailles. This he did, and, miraculously, nine months later, the queen gave birth to a baby boy, on September 5, 1638, which was also by some amazing coincidence Campanella's seventieth birthday. Campanella paid at least two visits to the queen's private chamber after the birth. He was allowed in there when she breastfed the infant and was even given the immense honor of holding the future king in his arms. In the eclogue that he wrote for this occasion (printed in January 1639), Campanella's now expanded prophecy leaves no doubt about what he expected from the forthcoming reign of Louis XIV. The Hermetic magus had cleverly transferred his dream of the City of the Sun to the French monarchy, to be built by the future Sun King, Louis XIV. As Frances A. Yates noted:

> In September 1638 a son was born to the French Monarch, and was saluted by Campanella in an eclogue modeled on the Messianic Virgilian *Fourth Eclogue* . . . all kings and peoples will assemble in a city, which they will call Heliaca, the city of the Sun, which will be built by the illustrious hero [Louis XIV, the Sun King]. . . . In this prophecy, the return of an imperial golden age is combined with the Egyptian strain of the City of the Sun . . . as foretold in the *Asclepius* . . . Campanella is prophesying at court that the infant Louis XIV will build the Egyptian City of the Sun.[4]

Was Louis XIV influenced by Campanella's prophecy to carry his plan to its logical conclusion and leave an Egyptian city of the sun in the architecture of Paris? It is either an extraordinary coincidence or something else that the development of the central axis of Paris, the so-called Historical Axis running from the Louvre to the new modern development of La Defence, when seen from the air, bears an uncanny resemblance to the quintessential solar city of ancient Egypt, Thebes (the modern Luxor).*

---

*See Graham Hancock and Robert Bauval, *Talisman: Sacred Cities, Secret Faith* for a full discussion on this issue.

We must recall (see chapter 4) that Campanella was in Rome at the service of Pope Urban VIII from 1626 to 1634. At the Vatican was also Bernini, who was forty-eight years old at the time. Bernini was at the apex of his career as the papal architect. He was extremely close to the pope, and it would be most unlikely that he did not meet

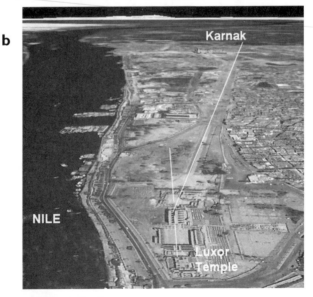

Figs. A1.1a and A1.1b. Aerial views of (a) Paris and (b) Luxor. Note the similarity in the deviation of the alignments/axes, and the relative positions of the Seine and Nile Rivers to the "temples."

Campanella. Campanella's book, *The City of the Sun,* was extremely popular, and Bernini surely was not ignorant of Campanella's hope to have the pope build such a solar city in Rome. In 1632 the new St. Peter's Basilica was now completed, and in front of it had stood, since 1586, the Egyptian obelisk from Heliopolis, the Egyptian original and archetypal City of the Sun. When Campanella left for France in 1634, the possibility that he would transpose the plan for a city of the sun to Paris must surely have crossed the minds of Bernini and others at the Vatican. When, some three decades later, Bernini went to Paris at the court of Louis XIV to design the new facade for the Louvre, the work on the Piazza St. Peter's in Rome was well underway. Did Bernini also know that the French architects at the court of Louis XIV had also begun the development of the Historical Axis—the Champs Élysées—which would be set out, by design or by coincidence, to resemble the other Egyptian City of the Sun, Thebes (modern Luxor)?* Was Bernini secretly snickering to himself that at precisely that same time in Rome a fantastic city of the sun modeled on the true Keplerian design was on the verge of being completed in front of the Vatican, at the center of which was already standing a genuine Egyptian sun, the obelisk from Heliopolis?

We shall probably never know for sure . . .

---

*Luxor, which comes from the Arabic word *El Aksar,* that is, "the palace," would have implied "light," that is, *lux,* in Latin. It is an odd coincidence, if a coincidence it is, that not only was Louis XIV called the "Sun King" but also that the new Paris that he built was referred to as La Cité Lumière (the City of Light).

THE ELLIPSE OF ST. PETER'S SQUARE

Sandro Zicari, Ph.D. in applied mathematics, Sapienza University of Rome

The objective of this appendix is to explain mathematically what is an ellipse and to verify whether St. Peter's Square is elliptical.

WHEN IS AN OVAL AN ELLIPSE?

The terms *oval* and *ellipse* are sometimes taken as being the same thing. According to the mathematician P. L. Rosin:

> Compared to ellipses, triangles, rectangles, etc. the definition of ovals is rather vague. The term oval covers different degrees of elongation, asymmetric tapering, squareness, etc. A more recent means of generating ovals is to generalize the concept of the ellipse.[1]

In other words, an ellipse can be called an oval but only *some* ovals can be called ellipses.

Let us first give the mathematical properties of an ellipse. An ellipse is generally defined as having "the set of all points in a plane such that the sum of the distances from two fixed points (foci) is constant." It simply means that an ellipse is defined by two points, each called a focus ($F1$, $F2$). If you take any X point on the ellipse, the sum of the distances to the focus points is constant, and it is equal to the main axis. In a Cartesian diagram, an ellipse with the center at the origin $(0,0)$ is the graph of:

with $a > b > 0$. The length of the major axis is $2a$, and the length

$$\frac{x^2}{a^2} + \frac{y^2}{b^2} = 1$$

of the minor axis is $2b$. The two foci are at $(\pm c, 0)$, where $c = \sqrt{a^2 - b^2}$.

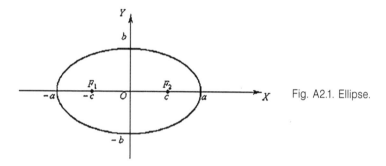

Fig. A2.1. Ellipse.

HOW TO DRAW AN ELLIPSE:
THE TRAMMEL OF ARCHIMEDES

A method for drawing an ellipse, defined as the Trammel of Archimedes, consists of a line of fixed length whose ends slide along two perpendicular axes and on which a fixed point is used to trace the shape. It can be realized physically as a sliding ladder or as a sliding door moving with its ends on two perpendicular tracks. During the motion, the fixed point on the segment traces an ellipse with one-quarter of the ellipse in each quadrant.

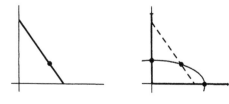

Fig. A2.2. The Trammel of Archimedes.

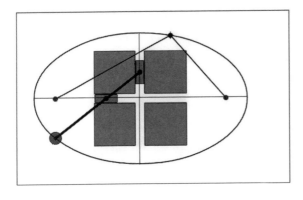

Fig. A2.3. Drawing of an ellipse using the Trammel of Archimedes method.

This particular ellipsograph, the Trammel of Archimedes, was known to ancient Greek geometers, although it is not known who actually invented it.[2]

THE ELLIPSE AND ASTRONOMY

Johannes Kepler (1571–1630) determined three laws of planetary motion. These laws are of great significance, not least because they later provided the basis for Newton's discoveries on planetary interaction and the law of gravity. Kepler's first law published in 1609 in his book *Astronomia Nova* states that the path of each planet around the sun is an ellipse with the sun at one of the two foci.

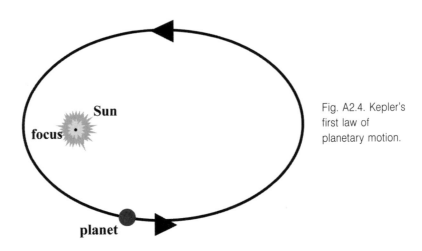

Fig. A2.4. Kepler's first law of planetary motion.

ST. PETER'S SQUARE

St. Peter's Square—a misnomer since it is not square but ovoid—is located immediately east of Vatican City, in front of St. Peter's Basilica. Its open-space dimensions are impressive: 240 meters (787 feet) long and 200 meters (656 feet) wide, forming an area capable of containing some 400,000 people. It is surrounded by 284 columns set out in curved rows of four, and 88 pilasters. Circa 1670 Bernini's students sculpted 140 statues of saints, each about 3.2 meters high, that were placed along the balustrades over the colonnades. On either side of the ancient Egyptian obelisk, which marks the center of the piazza, there are two fountains, the first one designed by Maderno in 1614, and much later another by Bernini, in 1675. At the west side of the piazza, near the staircase in front of the basilica, the statues of St. Peter and St. Paul seem to guard the entrance to the basilica.

The best way to verify whether St. Peter's Square is a real ellipse is to compare actual measurements taken on the ground with the mathematical formula for the ellipse given above. Measurements were taken

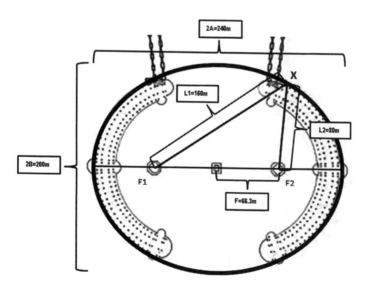

Fig. A2.5. Hypothesis testing on the shape of St. Peter's Square. (Sandro Zicari, 2012)

from digital orthographic photographs (scale 1:10,000) supplied by the Regione Lazio that conform to the national mapping accuracy standards for spatial assessment. The St. Peter's Square shape measurements are as follows: major axis, 240 meters ($2A$); minor axis, 200 meters ($2B$); distance between obelisk and each focus, 66.3 meters (F).

If this area is a true ellipse, the formula $F = \sqrt{A^2 - B^2}$ must be true. Using the distance between the obelisk and each focus (F), as well as the values of half the major axis (A) and half the minor axis (B), we get:

$$\sqrt{(120 \text{ m})^2 + (100 \text{ m})^2} =$$

$$= \sqrt{14{,}400 \text{ m}^2 - 10{,}000 \text{ m}^2} =$$

$$= \sqrt{4{,}400 \text{ m}^2} = 66.33\text{m}$$

The result gives the distance between the obelisk and each focus. Once it is verified that the shape of the square is an ellipse, it is possible to write the formula as follows:

$$\frac{x^2}{120\text{m}^2} + \frac{y^2}{100\text{m}^2} = 1$$

It remains to check the identity of ellipse's definition.

dist(Point, Focus1) + dist(Point, Focus2) = major axis of Ellipse

In figure A2.5 a point X is taken on the external colonnade. The distances from Bernini's and Maderno's Fountains measure, respectively, 160 and 80 meters. Adding these two values, the result is equal exactly to 240 meters, the length of the major axis of the square. This confirms that St. Peter's Square is an ellipse.

NOTES

CHAPTER 1. THE TRUE RELIGION OF THE WORLD

1. Yates, *Giordano Bruno and the Hermetic Tradition,* 4.
2. Ibid., 452.
3. Durrell, *Clea.*
4. Fowden, *Egyptian Hermes,* 161.
5. Scott, *Hermetica,* 15–22.
6. Hancock and Bauval, *Talisman,* 204–9.
7. Magli and Ferro, "Astronomical Orientation," 381–89.
8. Magli and Ferro, "The Astronomical Orientation of the Urban Plan of Alexandria," in *Oxford Journal of Archaeology,* volume 32.2, May 2013.
9. Copenhaver, *Hermetica,* xv.
10. Gardiner, "Notes on Egyptian Magic," 263. See also Bauval, *Secret Chamber,* 47.
11. Boylan, *Thoth,* 124.
12. Jacq, *Magic and Mystery in Ancient Egypt,* 19.
13. Ibid., 15.
14. Yates, *Giordano Bruno and the Hermetic Tradition,* 60.
15. Kamil, *Coptic Egypt,* 15.
16. Copenhaver, *Hermetica,* xxiii.
17. Severinus, *Life of the Apostle and Evangelist Mark.*
18. Dando-Collins, *Great Fire of Rome,* 118.
19. Ibid., 108–120.
20. Tacitus, *Annals,* 44.
21. Baring and Cashford, *Myth of the Goddess,* 550–1.
22. Roullet, *Egyptian and Egyptianizing Monuments,* 2.

23. Giles, *Hebrew and Christian Records,* 86.

24. Voss, *Marsilio Ficino,* 15–16. See also Yates, *Giordano Bruno and the Hermetic Tradition,* 6–8.

25. Copenhaver, *Hermetica,* xxiv.

26. Kamil, *Coptic Egypt,* 7–15.

27. Fowden, *Egyptian Hermes,* 30.

28. Ibid.

29. Socrates, *Ecclesiastical History.*

30. Ibid.

31. Various modern translations of *The Lament of Hermes Trismegistus* into English can be found. See Copenhaver, *Hermetica,* 81–83; Scott, *Hermetica,* 341–43.

32. *Lament of Hermes Trismegistus.*

33. Fowden, *Egyptian Hermes,* 33.

34. Copenhaver, *Hermetica,* 1.

CHAPTER 2. THE HERMETIC MOVEMENT, PART I

1. Corpus Hermeticum, "Egyptian Reflection of the Universe in the Mind."

2. Copenhaver, *Hermetica,* lviii.

3. Hibbert, *House of Medici,* 63.

4. Hankins, *Plato in the Italian Renaissance,* 260.

5. Ibid., 277.

6. Allen and Rees, *Marsilio Ficino,* 8.

7. Hankins, *Plato in the Italian Renaissance,* 273.

8. Voss, *Marsilio Ficino,* 15–16.

9. Plato, *Timaeus,* 21–23.

10. Yates, *Giordano Bruno and the Hermetic Tradition,* 12.

11. Ibid., 13.

12. Copenhaver, *Hermetica,* xlviii.

13. Ibid., xliii.

CHAPTER 3. THE HERMETIC MOVEMENT, PART II

1. Voss, "Natural Magic of Marsilio Ficino," 25–30.

2. Yates, *Giordano Bruno and the Hermetic Tradition,* 60.

3. Voss, "Natural Magic of Marsilio Ficino," 29.

4. Yates, *Giordano Bruno and the Hermetic Tradition,* 69.

5. Ibid., 83.

6. Ibid., 73.

7. Ibid.

8. Ibid., 73–74.

9. Ibid., 74.

10. Voss, *Marsilio Ficino,* x.

11. Yates, *Giordano Bruno and the Hermetic Tradition,* 171–72; see also Mahé in Broek and Heertum, *From Poimadres to Jacob Bohme,* 372.

12. Hanegraaff, *Chymists and Chymistry,* chap. 9.

13. Lazzarelli, in Broek and Heertum, *From Poimadres to Jacob Bohme,* 373.

14. See Slavenburg, *Hermetic Link,* chap. 18.

15. Broek and Heertum, *From Poimadres to Jacob Bohme,* 372.

16. Hanegraaff, *Chymists and Chymistry,* 104.

17. Ibid.

18. Augustine, St. *City of God,* bk. XVIII, 19.

19. Lazzarelli, in Broek and Heertum, *From Poimadres to Jacob Bohme,* 377.

20. Yates, *Giordano Bruno and the Hermetic Tradition,* 43.

21. Scott, *Hermetica,* 32–40.

22. Ibid.

23. Ibid.

24. Yates, *Giordano Bruno and the Hermetic Tradition,* 84.

25. Kreis, "Pico della Mirandola, *Oration on the Dignity of Man.*"

26. Drees, *Late Medieval Age,* 400.

27. Mirandola, *New Essays,* 38–39, n. 13. See also Dorez and Thuasne, *Pic de la Mirandole,* 127–37.

28. For more on Mirandola's life, see More, *Life of John Picus,* in *English Works of Sir Thomas More,* vol. I, 349–62.

29. Iversen, *Myth of Egypt and its Hieroglyphs,* 62–63.

30. Yates, *Giordano Bruno and the Hermetic Tradition,* 75.

31. Baltrusaitis, *La Quete D'Isis,* 133.

32. Yates, *Giordano Bruno and the Hermetic Tradition,* 214.

33. Mormando, *Bernini,* 246.

34. Yates, *Giordano Bruno and the Hermetic Tradition,* 204.

35. Calendar of State Papers, Foreign, January–June 1583, 214.

36. Yates, *Astraea*, 29.

37. Ibid., 30.

38. Virgil, *Fourth Eclogue.*

39. Kamm, *Julius Caesar,* 136.

40. Yates, *Astraea*, 31.

41. Stocker, *Spenser Encyclopedia,* 72.

42. Murdock, *Christ in Egypt,* 157–58. See also Higgins, *Anacalypsis,* 314.

43. King, "Queen Elizabeth I," 63.

44. Lewis, *Studies in Medieval and Renaissance Literature,* 157.

45. Forrest, *Isis Magic,* 204.

46. Bruno, *La cena de le ceneri,* dial. 4.

47. Yates, *Giordano Bruno and the Hermetic Tradition,* 223.

48. Ibid., 215.

49. Spamanato, *Documenti della via di Giordano Bruno,* 44; see also Yates, *Giordano Bruno and the Hermetic Tradition,* 233.

50. Inscription (in Latin) on the east and west sides of the pedestal of the Vatican Obelisk.

51. Hibbert, *Rome,* 355; see also Partini and Rachewiltz, *Roma Egizia,* 105-6.

52. Yates, *Giordano Bruno and the Hermetic Tradition,* 351–52.

53. Ibid., 420.

54. Singer, *Giordano Bruno,* chap. 7.

55. White, *Pope and the Heretic,* 181.

56. Bruno, *De Monade Numero e Figura.*

CHAPTER 4. THE CITY OF THE SUN

1. Yates, *Giordano Bruno and the Hermetic Tradition,* 366.

2. Ibid., 360.

3. Ibid.

4. Ibid., 372, 419.

5. Ibid. 69.

6. Yates, *Giordano Bruno and the Hermetic Tradition,* 233.

7. Ernst, *Tommaso Campanella,* 22.

8. Headley, *Tommaso Campanella.* See also Ernst, *Tommaso Campanella.*

9. Headley, *Tommaso Campanella,* 30–40.

10. Zalta, "Tommaso Campanella."

11. Carpi et al., *Scholarly Knowledge,* 249–51.

12. Yates, *Giordano Bruno and the Hermetic Tradition,* 394.

13. Ibid., 391.

14. Claeys, *Cambridge Companion to Utopian Literature,* 58.

15. Yates, *Giordano Bruno and the Hermetic Tradition,* 369.

16. Ibid., 371.

17. Ibid., 372.

18. Ibid., 371–72.

19. Ibid., 413.

20. Yates, *Rosicrucian Enlightenment,* 137–38, 144–45. See also Hancock and Bauval, *Talisman,* 265-67.

21. Yates, *Giordano Bruno and the Hermetic Tradition,* 374.

22. Lechner, "Tommaso Campanella and Andrea Sacchi's Fresco," 97–108.

23. Coelho, "Music and Science in the Age of Galileo," 78.

24. Lechner, "Tommaso Campanella and Andrea Sacchi's Fresco," 97.

25. Ibid., 101.

26. Ibid.

27. Ibid.

28. Bauval, *Egypt Code,* chap. 2.

29. Ibid.

30. Yates, *Giordano Bruno and the Hermetic Tradition,* 364.

31. Apuleius, *Golden Ass,* book 11, chap. 47.

32. Findlen, *Athanasius Kircher,* 335–36.

33. Yates, *Giordano Bruno and the Hermetic Tradition,* 375.

34. Roush, *Selected Philosophical Poems of Tommaso Campanella,* 10.

35. Haskell, *Patrons and Painters,* 40, fn. 3.

36. Roush, *Selected Philosophical Poems of Tommaso Campanella,* 11.

37. Hancock and Bauval, *Master Game,* 290–92.

CHAPTER 5. *URBI ET ORBI:* TO THE CITY AND TO THE WORLD

1. Carter, "Woman Who Drove Bernini Mad."

2. Mormando, *Bernini.*

3. Ibid., 68.

4. Ibid., 36.

5. Mormando, *Bernini*, 240.

6. Masson, *Queen Christina*.

7. Mormando, *Bernini*, 249.

8. Allen-Olney, *Private Life of Galileo*, 25–26.

9. Russell, "Kepler's Laws of Planetary Motion," 1–24.

10. Kelly, "Alexander VII," 283–88.

11. Godwin, *Athanasius Kircher's Theatre of the World*.

12. Prof. Eugenio Lo Sardo quoted in Findlen, *Athanasius Kircher*, 53–54.

13. Rowland, "Athanasius Kircher and The Musaeum Kircherianum," mmxi.

14. Rowland, "Athanasius Kircher, Giordano Bruno, and the Panspermia of the Infinite Universe," 191–96.

15. Mormando, *Bernini*, 139–40.

16. Fletcher, "Astronomy in the Life and Correspondence of Athanasius Kircher," 52–67.

17. Egherman, "Don't Forget My Books!"

18. Ibid.

19. Findlen, *Possessing Nature*, 389.

20. Fletcher, *Study of the Life and Works of Athanasius Kircher*, 47.

21. Knobloch, "Kaspar Schott's 'Encyclopedia of All Mathematical Sciences,'" 225–47.

22. Rowland in *Athanasius Kircher*, 187–88.

23. Ibid., 187–88.

24. Kepler, *Harmonices Mundi*, intro. to book V, 391.

25. Schuppener, "Kepler's Relation with the Jesuits," 236–44.

26. Findlen, *Athanasius Kircher*, 191–96.

27. Partini and Rachewiltz, *Roma Egizia*, 203.

28. Kircher, *Obeliscus Pamphilius*, 371, 420.

29. Yates, *Giordano Bruno and the Hermetic Tradition*, 420.

30. Kepler, *Kepler's Somnium*, 9.

31. Kepler quoted in Trimble, *Biographical Encyclopedia of Astronomers*, 1268.

32. Padre Bartoli. *Della La Vita del Padre Niccolò Zucchi*, 73.

33. Ibid., 50–51.

34. This is reported in Chantelou, *Journal du voyage du cavalier Bernin en France*, 158.

35. Zucchi, *Optica philosophia experimentalis*, 2 vols.

36. Lavin, *Gianlorenzo Bernini*; Lavin, "Bernini's Cosmic Eagle."

37. Miller, *St. Peter's,* 22.

38. Fazio et al., *World History of Architecture,* figs. 12.5–12.7.

39. Kirk, "Framing St. Peter's," 756–76.

40. Goffi, "Sempiternal Nature of Architectural Conservation," 39, fn. 76. See also Silvan, "Le Origini de la pianta di Tiberio Alfrarano," 3–25.

41. Lockyer, *Dawn of Astronomy,* 96–98. Lockyer also quotes from *The Builder: An Illustrated Magazine for the Architect* 95 (January 2, 1892).

42. Lee-Milne, *Saint Peter's.*

43. Schibille, "Astronomical and Optical Principles," 27–46.

44. Mircea, "Bernini's 'Idea del tempio.'"

45. Tronzo, *St. Peter's in the Vatican,* 111.

46. Mormando, *Bernini,* chap. 4.

47. Yates, *Giordano Bruno and the Hermetic Tradition,* 418.

48. Lavin, *Bernini at St. Peter's,* 111.

49. Hersey, *Architecture and Geometry,* 142.

50. Ibid., 143.

51. Trachtenberg and Hyman, *Architecture,* chap. 9.

52. Dougherty, "Theatre and the City."

53. Miller, *St. Peter's,* 4.

54. Wittkower, "Counter-Project," 103.

55. Ibid.

56. Ibid.

57. Emden et al., *Cultural History and Literary Imagination;* article by Dougherty, "Theatre and the City," 126.

58. Berkel, "'Cornelius Meijer inventor et fecit,'" 278–95.

59. Meyer, *L'Arte di restituire à Roma.*

60. Heilbron, "Copernican Cosmology."

61. Findlen, "Scientific Spectacle in Baroque Rome," 233.

POSTSCRIPT: THE JESUIT POPE

1. Cardinal Federico Lombardi, REPUBLICA TV, March 13, 2013.

2. Glatz, "Symbols Adjusted on Papal Coat of Arms," *Catholic Herald,* March 28, 2013.

APPENDIX 1. CAMPANELLA, THE ROSICRUCIANS, AND THE MIRACULOUS BIRTH OF THE SUN KING

1. Duche, *L'Histoire de France Racontee a Juliette,* 66.

2. Yates, *Giordano Bruno and the Hermetic Tradition,* 390.

3. Yates, "Considerations de Bruno et de Campanella sur la Monarchy Francaise," 12.

4. Yates, *Giordano Bruno and the Hermetic Tradition,* 390–91, 447.

APPENDIX 2. THE ELLIPSE OF ST. PETER'S SQUARE

1. Rosin, "On Serlio's Construction of Ovals," 58–69.

2. Apostol and Mnatsakanian, "New Look," 115–33.

BIBLIOGRAPHY

Allen, Michael J. B., and Valerie Rees, eds. *Marsilio Ficino: His Philosophy, His Theology, His Legacy.* Leiden, the Netherlands: Brill, 1951.

Allen-Olney, Mary. *The Private Life of Galileo.* Boston: Nichols & Noyes, 1870.

Apostol, Tom M., and Mamikon A. Mnatsakanian. "A New Look at the So-Called Trammel of Archimedes." *The American Mathematical Monthly* 116, no. 2 (February 2009): 115–33.

Apuleius, Lucius. *The Golden Ass.* Translated by Sarah Ruden. New Haven, Conn., and London: Yale University Press, 2011.

Augustine, St. *City of God.* New York: Image, 1958.

Baltrusaitis, Jurgis. *La Quete D'Isis.* Paris: Flammarion, 1985.

Baring, Anne, and Jules Cashford. *The Myth of the Goddess.* London: Penguin Books, 1993.

Bartoli, Padre Danielo. *Della La Vita del Padre Niccolò Zucchi della Compagnes di Gesè.* Rome: Presso il Varese, 1682.

Bauval, Robert. *The Egypt Code.* London: Century Books, 2006.

———. *Secret Chamber: The Quest for the Hall of Records.* London: Arrow Books, 1999.

Berkel, Klaas van. "'Cornelius Meijer inventor et fecit': On the Representation of Science in Late Seventeenth-Century Rome." In *Merchants and Marvels: Commerce, Science, and Art in Early Modern Europe.* Edited by Pamela H. Smith and Paula Findlen. New York: Routledge, 2002.

Boylan, Patrick. *Thoth: The Hermes of Egypt.* Oxford: Oxford University Press, 1922.

Broek, Roelof van den, and Cis van Heertum, eds. *From Poimadres to Jacob Bohme.* Amsterdam: In de Pelikaan Press, 2000.

Bruno, Giordano. *La cena de le ceneri.* London: John Charlwood, 1584.

———. *De Monade Numero e Figura.* Frankfurt, Germany, 1591.

Builder, An Illustrated Magazine for the Architect 95 (January 2, 1892).

Calendar of State Papers, Foreign. January–June 1583.

Carpi, Emidio, Simone De Angelis, Anja-Silvia Goeing, and Anthony Grafton. *Scholarly Knowledge: Textbooks in Early Modern Europe.* Geneva, Switzerland: Libraire Droz, 2008.

Carter, Maxwell. "The Woman Who Drove Bernini Mad." *New York Times,* July 13, 2012.

Chantelou, Paul Fréart de. *Journal du voyage du cavalier Bernin en France.* Edited by Ludovic Lannane. Paris: Gazette de Beaux-Arts, 1885.

Claeys, Gregory, ed. *The Cambridge Companion to Utopian Literature.* Cambridge: Cambridge University Press, 2010.

Coelho, Victor, ed. "Music and Science in the Age of Galileo." *The Artistic Patronage of the Barberini and the Galileo Affair.* Dordrecht, the Netherlands: Hammond, Kluwer Academic Publishers, 1992.

Copenhaver, Brian P. *Hermetica.* Cambridge: Cambridge University Press, 1995.

Corpus Hermeticum, Book XI.

Dando-Collins, Stephen. *The Great Fire of Rome: The Fall of Emperor Nero and His City.* Cambridge, Mass.: Da Capo Press, 2010.

Dorez, Leon, and Louis Thuasne. *Pic de la Mirandole en France (1485–1488).* Geneva: Slatkine Reprints, 1976.

Dougherty, Alex. "Theatre and the City in the Baroque Imagination." Presented at "Imagining the City," the Research Group Cultural History and Literary Imagination 2nd International Conference, Cambridge: St. John's College, Cambridge University, 2001.

Drees, Clayton J., ed. *The Late Medieval Age of Crisis and Renewal, 1300–1500.* Westport, Conn.: Greenwood Press, 2001.

Duche, Jean. *L'Histoire de France Racontee a Juliette.* Paris: Presse Pocket, 1954.

Durrell, Lawrence. *Clea.* Vol. 4, *The Alexandria Quartet.* New York: Penguin, 1960.

Egherman, Mara M. J. "Don't Forget My Books! Queen Cristina of Sweden." Presented at the 33rd European Studies Conference, Omaha: University of Nebraska, October 2, 2008.

Emden, Christian, Catherine Keen, and David Midgley, eds. *Cultural History and Literary Imagination.* Vol. 8, *Imagining the City,* Volume 2.

Bern, Switzerland: Peter Lang A. G., 2006. www.peterlang.com/index. cfm?event=cmp.ccc.seitenstruktur.detailseiten&seitentyp=series&pk=428 &concordeid=CHLI.

Ernst, Germana. *Tommaso Campanella*: *The Book and the Body of Nature*. New York: Springer 2010.

Fazio, Michael, Marian Moffett, and Lawrence Wodehouse. *A World History of Architecture*. London: Laurence King Publishing, 2003.

Feingold, Mordechai, ed. *Jesuit Science and the Republic of Letters*. Cambridge, Mass.: The MIT Press, 2003.

Findlen, Paula, ed. *Athanasius Kircher: The Last Man Who Knew Everything*. New York: Routledge, 2004.

———. *Possessing Nature: Museums, Collecting, and Scientific Culture in Early Modern Italy*. Berkeley: University of California Press, 1996.

———. "Scientific Spectacle in Baroque Rome: Athanasius Kircher and the Roman College Museum." In *Jesuit Science and the Republic of Letters*. Edited by Mordechai Feingold. Cambridge, Mass.: The MIT Press, 2003.

Fletcher, John E. "Astronomy in the Life and Correspondence of Athanasius Kircher." *Isis* 61, no. 1 (Spring 1970): 52–67.

———. *A Study of the Life and Works of Athanasius Kircher, "Germanus Incredibilis."* Amsterdam: Brill, 2011.

Forshaw, Peter J. "Astrology, Ritual, and Revolution in the Works of Tommaso Campanella (1568–1639)." Academia.edu. www.Academia.edu/1189982/ Astrology_Ritual_and_Revolution (accessed July 15, 2013).

Forrest, M. Isidora. *Isis Magic: Cultivating a Relationship with the Goddess of 10,000 Names*. Woodbury, Minn.: Llewellyn Publishing, 2004.

Fowden, Garth. *The Egyptian Hermes*. Cambridge: Cambridge University Press, 1986.

Gardiner, Alan H. "Notes on Egyptian Magic." In *Encyclopedia of Religion and Ethics*. Edited by James Hastings. Edinburgh: T & T Clark, 1973.

Giles, John Allen. *Hebrew and Christian Records*. vol. ii. London: Trübner and Co., 1877.

Glatz, Carol. "Symbols Adjusted on Papal Coat of Arms." *Catholic Herald,* March 28, 2013.

Godwin, Joscelyn. *Athanasius Kircher's Theatre of the World*. Rochester, Vt.: Inner Traditions, 2009.

Goffi, Federica. "The Sempiternal Nature of Architectural Conservation and the Unfinished Building and Drawing." Dissertation for doctorate degree in architecture and design research. Virginia State University, Ettrick, Va., October 19, 2010.

Hamilton, Albert C., ed. *The Spenser Encyclopedia.* Toronto: University of Toronto Press, 1997.

Hammond, Frederick. "The Artistic Patronage of the Barberini and the Galileo Affair." In *Music and Science in the Age of Galileo.* Edited by Victor Coelho. Dordrecht, the Netherlands: Hammond, Kluwer Academic Publishers, 1992.

Hancock, Graham, and Robert Bauval. *The Master Game: Unmasking the Secret Rulers of the World.* New York: Disinformation, 2011.

———. *Talisman: Sacred Cities, Secret Faith.* London: Penguin, 2004.

Hanegraaff, Wouter. *Chymists and Chymistry: Studies in the History of Alchemy and Early Modern Chemistry.* Edited by Lawrence M. Principe. Sagamore Beach, Mass.: Watson Publishing International LLC, 2007.

Hankins, James. *Plato in the Italian Renaissance.* vol. 1. New York: Columbia University, 1990.

Haskell, Francis. *Patrons and Painters.* New Haven, Conn., and London: Yale University Press, 1998.

Hastings, James. *Encyclopedia of Religion and Ethics.* Edinburgh: T & T Clark, 1973.

Headley, John M. *Tommaso Campanella and the Transformation of the World.* Princeton, N.J.: Princeton University Press, 1997.

Heilbron, John L. "Copernican Cosmology in Catholic Countries around 1700." Gobierno de Canarias: Un Solo Peublo. www.gobiernodecanarias.org (accessed July 31, 2013).

———. ed. *The Oxford Companion to the History of Modern Science.* New York: Oxford University Press, 2003.

Hersey, George L. *Architecture and Geometry in the Age of the Baroque.* Chicago: The University of Chicago Press, 2000.

Hibbert, Christopher. *The House of Medici: Its Rise and Fall.* New York: Morrow Quill, 1980.

———. *Rome: The Biography of a City.* London: Penguin Books, 1985.

Higgins, Godfrey. *Anacalypsis,* vol. 1. London: Longman, 1836.

Iversen, Erik. *The Myth of Egypt and Its Hieroglyphs in European Tradition.* Copenhagen: GEC GAD Publishers, 1961.

Jacq, Christian. *Magic and Mystery in Ancient Egypt*. London: Souvenir Press, 1998.

Kamil, Jill. *Coptic Egypt*. Cairo: American University Press in Cairo, 1993.

Kamm, Antony. *Julius Caesar: A Life*. London: Routledge, 2006.

Kelly, J. N. D. "Alexander VII." In *Oxford Dictionary of Popes*. Oxford: Oxford University Press, 1996.

Kepler, Johannes. *Harmonices Mundi* (The Harmony of the World). Translated by Eric John Aiton, Alistair Mattheson Duncan, and Judith Veronica Field. Philadelphia: American Philosophical Society, 1997.

———. *Kepler's Somnium: The Dream, or Posthumous Work on Lunar Astronomy*. Edited and translated by Edward Rosen. Mineola, N.Y.: Dover Publications, 2003.

King, John N. "Queen Elizabeth I: Representations of the Virgin Queen." *Renaissance Quarterly* 43, no. 1 (Spring 1990): 30–74.

Kircher, Athanasius. *Obeliscus Pamphilius*. Rome: Typis Ludouicin Grignani, 1650.

Kirk, Terry. "Framing St. Peter's: Urban Planning in Fascist Rome." *The Art Bulletin* 88, no. 4 (December 1, 2006): 756–76.

Knobloch, Eberhard. "Kaspar Schott's 'Encyclopedia of All Mathematical Sciences.'" *Poiesis Prax* 7, no. 4 (June 2011): 225–47.

Kreis, Steven. "Pico della Mirandola, *Oration on the Dignity of Man*." The History Guide: Lectures on Modern European Intellectual History. www.historyguide.org/intellect/pico.html (accessed August 23, 2013).

Lavin, Irving. *Bernini at St. Peter's*. Cambridge: Cambridge University Press, 2005.

———. "Bernini's Cosmic Eagle." *In Visible Spirit, the Art of Gian Lorenzo Bernini*, Pindar Press (2007): 509–23.

———. *Gianlorenzo Bernini, New Aspects of His Art and Thoughts: A Commemorative Volume*. Happy Valley, Penn.: Pennsylvania State University Press, 1985.

Lechner, George S. "Tommaso Campanella and Andrea Sacchi's Fresco of Divina Sapienza in the Palazzo Barberini." *The Art Bulletin* 58, no. 1 (March 1976): 97–108.

Lee-Milne, James. *Saint Peter's*. London: Hamish Hamilton, 1967.

Lewis, C. S. *Studies in Medieval and Renaissance Literature*. Cambridge: Cambridge University Press, 1998.

Lockyer, Norman. *The Dawn of Astronomy*. London: Cassell and Co., Ltd., 1894.

Magli, Giulio, and Luisa Ferro. "The Astronomical Orientation of the Urban

Plan of Alexandria." *Oxford Journal of Archaeology* 31, no. 4 (November 2012): 381–89.

———. *Oxford Journal of Archaeology* 32, no. 2 (May 2013).

Masson, Georgina. *Queen Christina*. London: Secker and Warburg, 1968.

Meyer, Cornelius. *L'Arte di restituire à Roma la tralasciata navigatione del suo tevere*. Fig. XV, *Dell' ornamento, che si potrebbe fare attorno la Guglia della Piazza di S. Pietro in Vaticano* (On the Ornaments That Could Surround the Obelisk in the Piazza di St. Peter's in the Vatican), 169.

Miller, Keith. *St. Peter's*. London: Profile Books, Ltd., 2007.

Mirandola, Pico della. *New Essays*. Edited by M. V. Dougherty. Cambridge: Cambridge University Press, 2008.

Mircea, Iliescu. "Bernini's 'Idea del tempio'" in *Docto Peregrino: Roman Studies in Honour of Torgil Magnuson*. Stockholm: Almqvist and Wiksell, 1992.

More, Sir Thomas. *The Life of John Picus, Earl of Mirandula*. Modernized and edited by W. E. Campbell in *The English Works of Sir Thomas More*, vol. I. New York: The Dial Press, 1931.

Mormando, Franco. *Bernini: His Life and His Rome*. Chicago and London: The University of Chicago Press, Ltd., 2011.

Murdock, D. M. *Christ in Egypt: The Horus-Jesus Connection*. Seattle, Wash.: Stellar House Publishing, 2009.

Partini, Anna M., and Boris de Rachewiltz. *Roma Egizia: culti, temple e divinita Egizie nella Roma Imperiale*. Rome: Edizione Mediterranee, 1999.

Plato, *Timaeus*.

Rosin, P. L. "On Serlio's Construction of Ovals." *Mathematical Intelligencer* 23, no. 1 (2001): 58–69.

Roullet, Anne. *The Egyptian and Egyptianizing Monuments of Imperial Rome*. Leiden, the Netherlands: E. J. Brill, 1972.

Roush, Sherry. *Selected Philosophical Poems of Tommaso Campanella*. Chicago: The University of Chicago Press, 2010.

Rowland, Ingrid. D. "Athanasius Kircher and the Musaeum Kircherianum." *Humanist Art Review* 1, no. mmxi, Rome 2000.

———. "Athanasius Kircher, Giordano Bruno, and the Panspermia of the Infinite Universe." In *Athanasius Kircher: The Last Man Who Knew Everything*. Edited by Paula Findlen. New York: Routledge, 2004.

Russell, J. L. "Kepler's Laws of Planetary Motion: 1609–1666." *The British Journal of the History of Science* 2, no. 1 (June 1964): 1–24.

Schibille, Nadine. "Astronomical and Optical Principles in the Architecture of Hagia Sophia in Constantinople." *Science in Context* 22 (2009), 27–46.

Schuppener, Georg. "Kepler's Relation with the Jesuits: A Study of His Correspondence with Paul Guldin." *NTM International Journal of History & Ethics of Natural Sciences, Technology, and Medicine* 5, no. 1 (December 1997): 236–44.

Scott, Walter. *Hermetica: The Ancient Greek and Latin Writings.* Boston: Shambhala Publications, Inc., 1993.

Severus, Bishop of Al-Ushmunain (ca. AD 955–987). *Life of the Apostle and Evangelist Mark.* Translated from the Arabic by B. Evetts in *Patrologia Orientalis,* 1st series. The St. Pachomius Library, 1996.

Silvan, Pierluigi. "Le Origini de la pianta di Tiberio Alfrarano." In *Atti della Pontifica Romana Academia di Archeologia.* Rome: Rendiconti, 1989–1990, 1992.

Singer, Dorothea Waley. *Giordano Bruno: His Life and Thoughts.* New York: Henry Schuman, 1950.

Slavenburg, Jacob. *The Hermetic Link: From Secret Tradition to Modern Thought.* Lake Worth, Fla.: Ibis Press, 2012.

Socrates Scholasticus. *Ecclesiastical History,* ca. 439.

Spamanato, Vincenzo. *Documenti della via di Giordano Bruno.* Messina, Italy: G. Principato, 1921.

Stocker, Margarita C., ed. *The Spenser Encyclopedia.* Toronto: University of Toronto Press, 1997.

Tacitus. *Annals.* Book XV.

Trachtenberg, Marvin, and Isabelle Hyman. *Architecture: From Prehistory to Postmodernism,* 2nd ed. New York: Prentice Hall, 2003.

Trimble, Virginia, ed. *Biographical Encyclopedia of Astronomers.* New York: Springer, 2007.

Tronzo, William. *St. Peter's in the Vatican.* Cambridge: Cambridge University Press, 2005.

Virgil. *Fourth Eclogue.*

Voss, Angela. *Marsilio Ficino.* Berkeley: North Atlantic Books, 2006.

———. "The Natural Magic of Marsilio Ficino." *Historical Dance* 3, no. 1 (1992): 25–30.

White, Michael. *The Pope and the Heretic: The True Story of Giordano Bruno, the Man Who Dared to Defy the Roman Inquisition.* New York: Harper Collins, 2003.

Wittkower, Rudolf. "A Counter-Project to Bernini's Piazza di S. Pietro." *Journal of the Warburg and Courtauld Institutes* 3, no. ½ (October 1939–January 1940): 103.

Yates, Frances A. *Astraea: The Imperial Theme in the Sixteenth Century.* London: Peregrine Books, 1977.

———. "Considerations de Bruno et de Campanella sur la Monarchy Francaise." *Actes du Congres Leonardo de Vinci, Etudes d'Art,* nos. 8–10. Paris: Alger, 1954.

———. *Giordano Bruno and the Hermetic Tradition.* Chicago: The University of Chicago Press, 1991.

———. *The Rosicrucian Enlightenment.* London: Ark, 1986.

Zalta, Edward N., ed. *Stanford Encyclopedia of Philosophy.* "Tommaso Campanella." Metaphysics Research Lab, CSLI, Stanford University, http://plato.stanford.edu/entries/campanella (accessed August 22, 2013).

Zucchi, Niccolò. *Optica philosophia experimentalis et ratione a fudamentis constituta.* 2 vols. Lyon, France: Guillaume Barbier, 1656.

INDEX

Page numbers in *italics* refer to illustrations.

BOOKS OF RELATED INTEREST

Black Genesis
The Prehistoric Origins of Ancient Egypt
by Robert Bauval and Thomas Brophy, Ph.D.

Breaking the Mirror of Heaven
The Conspiracy to Suppress the Voice of Ancient Egypt
by Robert Bauval and Ahmed Osman

Secret Chamber Revisited
The Quest for the Lost Knowledge of Ancient Egypt
by Robert Bauval

The Lost City of the Exodus
The Archaeological Evidence behind the Journey Out of Egypt
by Ahmed Osman

Gobekli Tepe: Genesis of the Gods
The Temple of the Watchers and the Discovery of Eden
by Andrew Collins

Forgotten Civilization
The Role of Solar Outbursts in Our Past and Future
by Robert M. Schoch, Ph.D.

Forbidden History
Prehistoric Technologies, Extraterrestrial Intervention,
and the Suppressed Origins of Civilization
Edited by J. Douglas Kenyon

Lost Knowledge of the Ancients
A Graham Hancock Reader
Edited by Glenn Kreisberg

INNER TRADITIONS • BEAR & COMPANY
P.O. Box 388
Rochester, VT 05767
1-800-246-8648
www.InnerTraditions.com

Or contact your local bookseller